HOUSING CULTURE

HOUSING CULTURE

Traditional architecture in an English landscape

Matthew Johnson

UCL PRESS

First published in 1993 by UCL Press

UCL Press Limited
University College London
Gower Street
London WC1E 6BT

ISBN:
1-85728-111-X HB

British Library Cataloguing-in-Publication Data
A catalogue record for this book
is available from the British Library.

The jacket illustration features
Corner Farm, Brent Eleigh, Sudbury, Suffolk,
and is reproduced with the kind permission of Robin & Karen Turner.

Typeset in Garamond
Printed and bound by
Biddles Ltd, King's Lynn and Guildford, England.

For my mother and father
Mrs Helen and Dr C. David Johnson

CONTENTS

PREFACE
THEORY, CULTURAL HISTORY AND HISTORICAL ARCHAEOLOGY

This is a study of old houses. It is a study of why old houses were built, how they were built and used in certain ways, and why they changed in form, style and technique through time. Central to its argument is the premise that the way people think and feel about the world around them will affect the way they live in their homes; and thus, to work in the opposite direction, that aspects of past thoughts and feelings may be "read" through the form of old houses.

Such a premise is not an implausible one. If we look around us today, we see ordinary men and women expressing, arguing, working through their views of life through their control and patterning of space and the objects within it. In England, students argue with cleaners over whether the latter group have the right to enter their college rooms without knocking. Middle-class couples buy up old terraced houses and "knock through" the partitions within, often to pointed derision from working-class neighbours, stand-up comics and other social commentators.

A thousand other examples could be given of the dovetailing of domestic architecture and social meaning, and some may think the point a fairly obvious one. But in many ways it is not so apparent. In the first place, few people recognize such patterning at an overt level: it works in implicit ways, being overtly rationalized as "normal" or "natural". As Danny Miller has argued (1987), we are all adept readers of material culture distributed in space; we can all monitor someone's occupation, status, class, gender, even their political views, quite accurately from a few seconds' perusal of their homes and the material culture they possess, the objects they choose to put within that space. Further, we all know how to manipulate such impressions, creating our own identities and affiliations through our own homes and material culture. But we do so at the level of the implicit, the unspoken or rarely spoken, and the "taken for granted". This is a familiar point to readers of Bourdieu, Goffman, Geertz and others, but is an insight that has still to make its full mark on some of the less anthropologically orientated fields of study drawn upon in this book.

In any case, we often deny these potential complexities when involved in other spheres of thought and activity. Modern Western society often appears paranoid in its insistence that we live our lives and organize our space "rationally", deviation from this rationality being attributable solely to something idiosyncratic and ultimately trivial called "fashion". Of course, it is held to be self-evident in such a view that our prehistoric and historic ancestors did the same. However, the one thing we can be sure about is that the past was *different*. The past is a foreign country; there were other rationalities, other very different ways of life. To attempt the scholarly task of understanding the past on its own terms rather than imposing our own biases, it is thus necessary to seek to understand these other rationalities.

There is a still more serious problem. The study of houses embraces more than one discipline. It involves, among others, archaeology, architectural theory and history, historical geography, social, economic, political and cultural history, the study of vernacular architecture, conservation studies, social and cultural anthropology, and the history of technology. This is only to be expected in the specific period embraced by this study, western Europe in the late medieval and early modern period. As Pittock & Wear have commented (1991: 2), any study of the period must by definition move across such disciplinary boundaries if a full appreciation of past patterns of cultural life is to be attained.

A problem arising from the crossing of disciplinary boundaries is how the reader should approach this book. It is relevant to note that the reactions of critics were strikingly varied in their identification of strengths and weaknesses in the first draft of this manuscript, something which may be attributed to their particular disciplinary training. Their one common complaint was that many of the basic premises of their own discipline were detailed at excessive length, while elements derived from other disciplines were insufficiently explained. I have therefore tried to extend the explication of many basic terms and procedures at the possible cost of appearing tedious to some readers, and can only ask for the reader's patience when things he or she perceives as quite familiar and obvious are discussed in some detail.

A problem of verification as well as style is also important. It is noticeable that, in talks on my research, different audiences of prehistoric and historic archaeologists, vernacular architectural scholars, and social and economic historians are convinced (or less than convinced) by very different elements of the argument and supporting evidence. For example, prehistoric archaeologists often view the use of a statistically random sampling technique as absolutely essential, whereas many traditional documentary historians find this technique of doubtful value. Thus, in moving across traditions I have found it difficult to adopt one standard technique or method of argument, and again I ask for patience in the face of such eclecticism.

Despite drawing upon a diversity of disciplines, this study does have a central aim: to show how one class of material culture – traditional architecture – can illuminate long-term changes in the pattern of social and cultural history. It also has other concerns relevant to a much wider audience: it attempts to be a "case study" in so-called "post-processual" archaeology; it offers innovative approaches for historical archaeologists in general and students of traditional architecture in particular; it addresses an audience of historians who are interested in substantive issues of social and cultural history in the late medieval and early modern period, and who are anxious to acquaint themselves with theoretical analyses of material culture for a well documented period; finally, it addresses recent debates within ethnoarchaeology and cultural anthropology over the social meanings of space. The rest of this Preface will therefore outline some of the reasons why a wide audience may benefit from a reading of this study. Such a "ground-clearing" exercise will leave the main body of the text free to be read as a unity.

The central aim of this study is to ask the question: Why did traditional architecture in a certain area of rural England change in a certain way at a certain time? Simple economic explanations are rejected, and proximal or immediate answers to this question are sought in the changing social and cultural life of the households that occupied those houses. The houses are seen as part of a material and symbolic framework for the everyday actions that created history, the layout of house and farmstead both expressing and structuring changing social and cultural relations. Increasing "privacy" in room arrangements, changes in technical systems of house construction and decoration, changing physical relations between the house and the outside world are related to visible forces in social and landscape history. Such forces include enclosure of the landscape, class polarization and cultural centralization, and the break-up of the traditional pre-industrial community. Underlying and structuring these visible forces was a process which this study terms "closure". Closure is a term selected for its linguistic affinity with that of enclosure, its connotations as well as its precise meaning, and ultimate reference to the feudal/capitalist transition.

In many ways this study can be seen as part of an increasing concern within the "new cultural history" (Hunt 1989, Chartier 1988) to untangle from the different strands of evidence of the everyday, and from the material patterns of local communities and regions, broader patterns of cultural conflict and change that shape the larger path of history (Underdown (1985b) and Wrightson (1982) have in this respect had a major influence on my thinking. In taking one class of material culture as its primary source, however, it tries to take the story of the everyday and the material one step further. It tries to work out in practice the view that material things are not merely constraints upon human action, "the limits of the possible" (Braudel

1973), but that they themselves carry (at the level of the implicit and taken for granted) the values and messages being fought over at the level of the overt. Material things thus become important through their very ordinariness. They stand for the vast underside of cultural action, for values and aspects of their personality and world-view which men and women could not or would not express in words. Material things may therefore be very important pieces of evidence, on the general principle derived from cultural anthropology and folk-life studies that that which is not spoken by members of a cultural group is often the most vital thing the researcher needs to know. They are also important for the methodology of social and cultural history (Lloyd 1986).

Although this study attempts to contribute to English landscape and community history at a substantive and theoretical level, it also attempts to address areas of scholarship across the Atlantic. Historians of material culture and traditional architecture of the American colonies have often ascribed the complex patterning of ideas which they see in their evidence to antecedent and contemporary patterning in the Old World. House forms, ways of cooking and eating, gravestone styles change and develop in the colonies, but have had their origins ascribed to the "mother country". The empirical strength of this ascription is hard to assess, since little work of similar theoretical sophistication has taken place in Britain in particular. Many of the changes in material culture seen by Glassie (1975), Upton (1982), Deetz (1977), and the studies contained in Leone & Potter (1988), and historical changes observed by Boyer & Nissenbaum (1974) and Isaac (1983), are prefigured by changes in part delineated in this study. Indeed, a heavy theoretical debt is also acknowledged by the author to these scholars.

Among American studies of architecture, Deetz, Glassie, Leone and others have talked of "Georgianization" as a process underlying changes in house form in the 18th-century colonies. But this may be the end point, the final unfolding, of a much longer-term process of "closure" whose origins lie in the landscape of 15th-century England. Alternatively, the whole concept of "Georgianization" may be one that needs to be questioned (cf. Johnson forthcoming). The understanding of Old World architectural and material culture change presented here bears upon some of the assumptions made by these scholars. In particular, questions of historical antecedent, meaning and the individual are raised. Patterns of architecture seen by Deetz, Glassie and others as medieval, traditional and affirming individual over community are seen here as much more complex. So the meaning of the transformations Glassie and Deetz delineate has to be questioned. We must ask whether this is merely a transformation from pre-Georgian *Gemeinschaft* into Georgian *Gesellschaft*. Further, the way in which this transformation occurs in terms of architecture is presented here not simply as an inexorable, unstoppable unfolding of a deeper structure beyond conscious control, as is the impression in Glassie's account (1975: 193). Rather, it is contingent upon a particular resolution of class, status and gender interests. This is not to say that individuals were not bound up in long-term structures beyond their conscious control; society is not anarchy. However, it is to assert that their renegotiation and manipulation of those structures was more than simply noise in the background, trivial variations on a deep structuralist or materialist theme.

At a broader level, there has been increasing interest in the general field of historical or text-aided archaeology and "material culture studies" on both sides of the Atlantic. Such interest has opened up exciting, wide-ranging questions common to archaeology and the social sciences in general. This stems in part from the recent rise of "post-processual archaeology" (Hodder 1991, Shanks & Tilley 1987), a reaction to philosophical contradictions and limitations embedded within "new" or processual archaeology. Post-processual archaeology, with its stress on the importance of meaning, the individual, and historical particularity, was initially developed in the fields of prehistory and ethnoarchaeology, but is now becoming an increasing force within the archaeology of historic periods (Austin 1990: 29–35).

There has been a demand from many within archaeology to see recent "post-processual" critiques of archaeological theory backed up with case studies of archaeological practice; to see detailed empirical pieces of work which show "critical" or "interpretive" archaeology in action, tangibly deepening our understanding of particular episodes in the past. This is a valid challenge that needs to be answered. The time has come for more detailed empirical studies to accompany recent polemics. This study should be seen in that light, and consequently an apology must be made to those primarily interested in the general issues touched on in these pages, for discussions of how, in detail, that material evidence relates to the interpretations on offer. This study attempts to answer Lewis Binford's call to move away from *a priori* assumptions about what the past was like and towards an empirical exploration of whether in fact our assumptions are correct. However, it does so in a manner which Binford probably did not have in mind. To perform this function of a detailed case study an empirical discussion is needed beyond the appending of a few graphs.

The last but by no means least component of my hoped-for audience is that of Old World medieval and post-medieval archaeologists, in which class I also place students of vernacular architecture. Architecture is but one class of material culture, and standing buildings are thus but one class of the study of medieval and post-medieval archaeology. Such a classification assumes that there is no reason to expect the principles of the study of artefacts to differ fundamentally from those of the study of buildings. Buildings and artefacts have certain functions: both act as, and are utilized as, symbols. Both are created and used by women and men within a contemporary cultural world, and the changing form of both has to be understood in those terms. In particular historical periods, architecture and artefacts may play different rôles in social reproduction, and may work in different ways, but these rôles have to be discovered rather than be assumed by the archaeologist.

High and post-medieval archaeology is very exciting. We deal with a wide range of structures and artefacts: rich houses, poor houses, great parks, elaborate gardens, complex field systems, colourful pottery, mountains of clay pipes. We deal with one of the great themes of history: the rise of capitalism, the origins of modern life. Yet our work is often seen as narrow and dull by outsiders, and is little read by many historians. While I would claim that our material is much more exciting than that of prehistorians, we appear sometimes to make much less of it. In this book I have tried to broaden the range of what we as medievalists and post-medievalists can talk about, to make the evidence of material things address important and wide-ranging historical issues. Perhaps I have been unsuccessful in this instance; but I believe passionately that the attempt was worth making. And if this study is not to the reader's liking, I look forward with impatience to reading more sophisticated and scholarly attempts.

ACKNOWLEDGEMENTS

The origin of this book is research which was carried out between 1985 and 1989. As such, my first and greatest thanks must be to Dr Ian Hodder, my research supervisor during that time, who has given more than anyone else in the way of critical comment and support. Looking back at the many rethinks and changes of direction that I experienced during that period, it was Ian's advice and encouragement that was consistently the most prescient, and his comments and criticisms that were the most stimulating. I miss our discussions. Dr Catherine Hills, as my advisor, offered many words of help and criticism.

Collectively, the Departments of Archaeology at Cambridge University, St David's University College, Lampeter, and the University of Durham, must be thanked. All three departments are outstanding places to think and work, and seminars and informal discussions at all three have influenced the thinking behind this book. My time with the Public Archaeology Project in Annapolis, Maryland, influenced my thinking also. The staff of Suffolk Records Office, Bury St Edmunds, gave invaluable help and guidance to a young and naïve archaeologist in the mysteries of documentary archives.

Too many individuals to mention all by name gave help and criticism. But the following deserve special mention: Philip Aitkens, David Austin, Andy Black, Silvia Colman, David Dymond, Andrew Fleming, Rachel Garrard, Joanna and Sarah Johnson, Trevor Kirk, Mark Leone, Eric Mercer, Kate Pretty, Colin Shell, Anthony "Steam" Sinclair, J. T. Smith, Dell Upton, Todd Whitelaw and Tom Williamson. Phil Sidebottom and Pauline Fenwick redrew many of the illustrations with skill and aplomb. Simon Coleman pulled me out of several dead ends and kept me sane at critical moments; Becky Smalley eliminated many infelicities of style and thought, and made the final stages of editing an unexpected pleasure.

The late Alan Carter first sparked my interest in traditional architecture. I owe a great debt to his kindness and enthusiasm.

I thank Academic Press and Edinburgh University Press for allowing me to reproduce passages from earlier published works. Earlier versions of parts of Chapter 10 were published in a collected work copyrighted by the Board of Trustees, Southern Illinois University.

Finally, the many householders of Suffolk who let a young and slightly eccentric stranger clamber round their homes with hand-tape and notebook, and provided coffee, tea, and even lunch on occasion, are thanked especially. Their actions amply refuted the stereotype of East Anglian unfriendliness.

CHAPTER 1
INTRODUCTION

> . . . Architecture is to be regarded by us with the most serious thought. We may live without her, and worship without her, but we cannot remember without her. How cold is all history, how lifeless all imagery, compared to that which the living nation writes, and the uncorrupted marble bears! – how many pages of doubtful record might we not often spare, for a few stones left one upon another! The ambition of the old Babel builder was well directed for this world: there are but two conquerors of the forgetfullness of men, Poetry and Architecture; and the latter in some sort includes the former, and is mightier in its reality; it is well to have, not only what men have thought and felt, but what their hands have handled, and their strength wrought, and their eyes beheld, all the days of their life. (Ruskin 1880: 178)

This book is an attempt to look at a group of traditional houses, and at the women and men who built them and lived in them. It tries to study and tease out the cultural meanings embodied and expressed by architecture, and to relate traditional houses to the values, beliefs and social and economic practices of their builders and users. Since there has been little experience of such an approach in English studies of traditional architecture, it cannot be but a limited attempt: a sketch delineating only the roughest outlines. But these outlines, however rough, are very clear.

I shall argue that the structure and layout of domestic architecture relate not only to functional and economic considerations, but also to the cultural and mental life of its users. Indeed, I shall go further and attempt to demonstrate that it is not possible to distinguish these two aspects when considering the craft tradition governing the layout of traditional houses. If this proposition is at all accurate, it has an exciting implication. Study and analysis of traditional houses becomes not just an exercise in classification, but a study and analysis in its turn of traditional cultural beliefs and social practices, and an understanding of their wider historical context.

It follows that the evidence afforded by houses can, if marshalled and analyzed rigorously, tell us about traditional beliefs and practices, and help inform on wider questions of social and economic history usually explored exclusively through documents. Prehistoric archaeologists often assume that the "true meaning" of artefact variability in an historical context can be "read off" by using documents as a form of control. A brief survey of a tiny sample of the literature on the social history of rural England between 1400 and 1700 should help to dispel this illusion. It will indicate that social historians of the period are involved in a sea of contentious issues. It will also serve to set the scene for a more extended discussion of the focus of this book.

Continuity and change

Was this time one of stability or transformation? Perhaps the most fundamental debate here is the question of how far the social and economic life of rural England was transformed during this period, or how far elements of continuity dominated. At one extreme Alan Macfarlane argues that the basic structure of social relations remained essentially unchanged during this period. Arguing back from an 18th-century picture, he proposes that the existence of a widespread land market, a high degree of individualism and strong property rights can be traced back to the 13th century and beyond (Macfarlane 1978). Though his views do not appear to be widely respected in the historical community, his arguments have nevertheless had a wide impact, particularly on archaeologists (cf. Hodges 1988, Hodder 1987: 4). In many ways just as conservative in its implications is Platt's view that "England in 1700 . . . was scarcely less 'pre-industrial' than it had been in 1485" (1978: 249).

At the other extreme lie many Marxist and other historians who interpret the late medieval and early modern period as involving a fundamental transformation in both England and Europe: the breakdown of the feudal system and the rise of "agrarian capitalism", however these terms are defined. Still others, such as Wrightson, see elements of continuity and transformation, of both "enduring structures" and medium-term social change after the fashion of the Annales school of historians (Wrightson 1982: 12).

When we look at more specific questions and debates prevalent among social and economic historians of this period, it can be argued that ultimately they relate to this wider debate on the nature, chronology and degree of transformation. These more detailed questions may be explored through two dimensions: the debates over relations within and relations between households.

The family and household are not units whose structure and membership are "natural" or "universal". Their form varies between different societies and through time. The changing way in which a house is organized spatially will obviously have some relationship to the changing form of the unit occupying it, although this relationship is in no sense a straightforward one, as will be demonstrated in later chapters.

The household was the basic unit of economic, political and cultural life in pre-industrial England. It had an immediate physical structure; Lawrence Stone defines the household as "all persons living under one roof" (Stone 1977: 28). Thus it included not just the family, or "those members of the same kin who live together under one roof", but also servants. Peter Laslett (1977) asserts that in pre-industrial western Europe such a unit had four basic features which, taken together, represented a combination of phenomena unique to this area. These were, first, the nuclear family form; secondly, a fluctuating but relatively late age of child-bearing among women; thirdly, a small age gap between spouses; and, fourthly, the presence of servants as an integral part of the household. These phenomena may be taken as more or less "constant" during our period: however, within this framework, changes occurred on whose nature and precise causes there is much debate.

Masters and servants had an antagonistic but enduring relationship. Kussmaul (1981) has charted changing relations of this nature, arguing that through time we see more and more social and economic distance being expressed. For example, she notes a steady shift away from payment in kind towards payment in cash, and greater physical and social segregation between masters and servants through the 16th and 17th centuries. While the "outside" contractual nature of this bond can easily be sketched, it is less easy to explore the emotive aspect of an often close relationship – but nevertheless an unequal and exploitative one – from the few documents bearing on this aspect. In any case, such documents usually explore the master's rather than servant's side of the story: for example, in the upholding of the notion that the "family" extended over the whole household, and thus that the master has fatherly rights and duties over servants as well as family (Kussmaul 1981, Wrightson 1982: 114).

Parents and children have also been the subjects of debate. Aries (1962) has argued that children were seen as no more than smaller versions of adults up until the 17th century, and consequently that a "modern" view of childhood emerged only towards the end of the period under discussion. Stone (1977) claims that parent/child relations were characterized by distance and deference, lack of affection being partly induced by a high rate of child mortality. Pollock (1983) argues against both these positions. She finds evidence for a great deal of affection between parents and children and a highly developed notion of childhood at an early date: there were, she feels, "very few changes in parental care and child life from the 16th to 19th centuries in the home" (Pollock 1983: 268). She points out that Stone's evidence in particular is biased towards the upper classes. Again, the layout of traditional houses may be brought to bear on this question by noting the presence or absence of provision for child life and its relation to the way the house maps out the master/servant divide.

The nature of marriage relations is equally hotly disputed. Again, Stone's assertion of barely qualified male dominance and affective distance between marriage partners (Stone 1977: 136–42) has been criticized on the grounds that his evidence comes mainly from the upper classes. It has been asserted that marriages below the level of the upper gentry were often made on the basis of affection, that they were often loving and happy, and that the wife enjoyed a great deal of freedom and even equality within the marriage contract (Wrightson 1982: 72–6). In addition, the notion that women passively accepted their allotted subordinate rôle in society has been effectively challenged (Fraser 1984), while men themselves entered into a debate on what the conjugal relationship should be (Wrightson 1982: 90–3; Morgan 1944). Nevertheless, formal patriarchal authority continued to assert itself in an age where the courts routinely asserted their rights to enter into people's lives and where household order was seen as indissoluble from political order (Fletcher & Stevenson 1985: 30; Amussen 1988).

All these debates are hampered by lack of documentary information regarding "sentiment" below the level of the gentry classes. Again, this is a particular criticism raised against Stone (Wrightson 1982: 70), but it can also be levelled at much work on emotive bonds between family members by other authors (Anderson 1980: 41). Much argument is from isolated examples and often fails to deal with the middling, let alone the lower, orders of society in any depth. Again, if the picture derived from changing traditional housing could be brought to bear on these questions, it might help to add a fresh and exciting perspective to old problems.

The second major area of debate is that of the origins and definition of "agrarian capitalism". Here this will be seen in terms of the development of a specific type of unequal relation between households, in particular the transition from a feudal/"customary" village community to a class-based rural society; a shift associated with the transition from a peasant-based to "capitalist" economic structure. As noted above, some authorities (notably Macfarlane but also Postan (1983) and others) deny the existence of this shift. Others dispute the nature, chronology, and social parameters of such a transformation. Much of the debate is tied in to an internal debate within Marxist theory about the nature of class struggle and social transformation. One example is the "Brenner debate" (Aston & Philpin 1985), while other issues relate to Marxist versus non-Marxist modes of explaining the feudal/capitalist transition, as with Weber's classic ascription of the origins of capitalism to religious ethic (1930).

This controversy manifests itself in various ways, for example in the debate over the rise of the gentry and yeoman classes. The gentry were a status group below the level of the aristocracy who acted as the local landowners and usually as "an elite of wealth, status and power" through their position within the parish community and their status as Justices of the Peace: they were generally considered to be of "gentle" blood (Wrightson 1982: 26). Yeomen were generally regarded as a superior sort of farmer, generally worth over £40.00 a year (Wrightson 1982: 28; Underdown 1985b: 10). It seems clear that in terms of political dominance at least the gentry became a major force in the 16th and 17th centuries, certainly in the area of Suffolk to be discussed in this study, where it has been conclusively demonstrated that political power passed from the hands of a few great landowners in 1500 to a large body of county gentry by 1600 (Macculloch 1986: 103). Recently, historians have preferred to talk in more sophisticated terms of class polarization and centralization (Fletcher & Stevenson 1985: 10). This is an important point since it redefines the problems of developing class relations in terms of changing types and networks of social and economic relationships, rather than simply in crude terms of the rise and fall of particular classes, a redefinition that originates, it can be argued, with Stone's revision of the interpretation of the "crisis of the aristocracy" (Stone 1965). However, such an observation does not address questions of how far such changing relations were expressed materially, for example in developing physical distance and varying layout between households of varying classes or status groups.

A related debate is that concerning the chronology of agrarian capitalism: the rise of farming for profit and class relations in the countryside. This has been treated in a highly abstracted manner by scholars such as Robert Brenner and those replying to his work (Aston & Philpin 1985). Brenner argues that a particular configuration of social and political interests in 16th-century England led to the development of class relations in England that diverged considerably from those on the Continent. Others prefer to stress the interaction of environmental and socio-economic factors in producing stability and change. This debate has raised several interesting theoretical issues: the changing nature of economic rationality during this period (Yelling 1982 and others); the question of the relationship between environment and human activity (Le Roy Ladurie 1985); the issue of differing Marxist interpretations, and Marxist versus non-Marxist views of social formation and class struggle (Thompson 1963: 9–11); the definition and passive or active rôle of ideology in this debate.

This last question of ideology is worth addressing briefly. Hill (1966) has attempted to link the rise of what he calls the "middling sort" with the growth of Puritan religious belief. He has argued that "godliness" represented in part a social and political agenda for reform of all levels of society, an agenda playing its part in the conflicts underlying the English Revolution. This thesis has been much criticized, but reports of its death have been exaggerated. For example, Underdown has recently argued that in the West Country Puritans as a politically active minority did draw their support primarily from the socially middling sort, and did have a great impact on the cultural and social complexion of their communities (Underdown 1985b: 44–72), while Wrightson endorses much of Hill's thesis in terms of cultural conflict within parish communities (Wrightson 1982: 184).

However, it is simplistic to see ideological change only in these terms. Underlying overt changes in religious dogma and practice such as those associated with Puritanism (and, for that matter, related shifts in Catholic belief and practice) were more subtle and complex shifts in popular perception and belief. These were manifested in attitudes towards religion, magic and the natural world (Thomas 1971, 1983) and were not just overt political and religious conflicts. They were formed through everyday activity and material life: for example, changing conceptions of the individual and individual action being manifested and reinforced by the everyday notion of privacy, or changing conceptions of time being related to changing attitudes to work and discipline (Thompson 1967). Material life and culture will therefore relate to such shifts in perceptions and belief, for example in the nature of division between the domestic world of the house and the world of the working farm.

Aspects of these issues can thus be addressed through material culture. For example, I shall address the question of class relations by considering the layout of larger houses in Chapter 9, and consider the relationship between views of the social and natural world and changing patterns of housing in Chapter 8. However, the most notable contribution material culture studies have made so far is through study of landscape types and agrarian practices: the breakdown of the open-field system, the desertion and shrinkage of villages, the rise of the great estates. The different rates at which these processes occurred are affected by the different antecedent conditions to be found in different regions of lowland England (Williamson & Bellamy 1986). However, the way in which they tie in with domestic architecture has been less explored. In this study, they will be discussed as part of a common "process of enclosure" in Chapter 10.

These are obviously very wide-ranging debates, and it is clearly beyond the scope of this study to resolve or even adequately to address more than a small proportion of the issues they raise. To do this, however, it is first necessary to demonstrate exactly how the study of material culture in general and of traditional architecture in particular holds the potential of making such provocative insights, in both theory and practice.

The study of traditional architecture

The study of medieval and post-medieval archaeology in England is characterized by a highly impressive body of evidence, a strong corpus of detailed studies and general syntheses researched and written to high standards of scholarship. Theoretical developments have perhaps not surprisingly failed to keep pace with this body of empirical work. The reluctance to use explicit theory in any form on the part of many traditional scholars is typified by both the tone and the brevity of Helen Clarke's 13-line dismissal of the "new archaeology" (Clarke 1984: 12). Although younger students have begun to explore explicitly "post-processual" approaches, little has surfaced in print beyond discussion and applications of processual tenets (Rahtz 1983, Hodges 1988).

The comments above are particularly true of the study of traditional architecture in England. Vernacular architectural studies, just as historical archaeology in general, have blossomed only in the past 50 years: since then a plethora of regional and national studies have been produced, again characterized by high standards of recording and primary analysis. At the same time, however, scholars of vernacular architecture have often been unwilling to take up wider general issues of their work: the largely hostile reaction to Lawrence's paper "The Interpretation of Vernacular Architecture" being typical (Lawrence 1983).

We all use theory, whether we like it or not, in the sense that we all bring assumptions and wider values and aims to our work, and that these values and aims colour our observations of the evidence. The only choice we have as scholars is whether theory should be implicit and inarticulate, or clearly and explicitly stated and thought through. Thus, most work in medieval and post-medieval archaeology is apparently based on "common sense" or on "the traditional approach" (Clarke 1984: 12). Yet when the commonsensical or traditional approach is considered, its dependence on theory is immediately apparent. The driest, most descriptive study of carpentered roof forms relies on theories of typology, theories of technical competence and innovation, theories of the nature of craft tradition in pre-industrial societies, theories of aesthetics, theories of economic rationality.

The fact that these theories are often taken for granted and are rarely set out explicitly does not make such studies any the less theoretical. Conversely, the high profile given in this study to clarifying assumptions and intellectual background does not render it more reliant on theory or more "theoretical" than traditional studies.

Such a proposition can be demonstrated when considering previous work in vernacular architecture: different scholars make different sets of theoretical assumptions, although the analysis and dissection of these assumptions is rendered difficult by their implicit nature. For the purposes of defining some of the underlying assumptions in this literature, I shall distinguish two major types of approach within this mass of work: typological studies and the economic approach.

Typological studies are defined as local descriptions and classifications of house types, building materials and techniques, and decorative styles, and they aim to establish controls over dating and regional variation. Such work is a useful first step in vernacular architecture in terms of establishing basic dating parameters and guidelines; studies of excavated peasant houses have similarly moved through a phase of description and classification, although more recent work has moved beyond this (cf. Austin & Thomas 1990: 54–61). The problems with such studies, however, are strikingly similar to those raised to "culture–historical" approaches by the "new archaeology": typological studies are not easily quantifiable, involve implicit or unverifiable assumptions, and offer little potential for meaningful generalization.

It is difficult, when using regional classifications such as those of Brunskill (1981) or Harris (1978), to answer basic questions of "how many and of what type exist on the ground now?" Such studies often rely on an unsystematic sample of housing, with little explicit thought about how this relates to the studied population or to its randomness. For example, Brunskill's study of regional house types and building materials (1978) is an interesting and useful first step, but it is based on a statistically suspect sampling procedure and is of uncertain value without more intensive studies of particular regions. Again, Giles uses the phrase "fairly random" to describe a sample of buildings, when what is meant is that care was taken to look at a representative sample on a judgmental basis (though, in fairness, Giles does stop to consider this point where others have passed on (Giles 1985: xix)).

Implicit assumptions can often be detected in this approach: for example, the assumption of social emulation or diffusion (the idea that stylistic innovation starts at the top of the social scale and then "filters down") is rarely felt to be in need of qualification or justification (Jope 1973). Again, typologies are felt to be readily explicable in terms of the domestic unit's comfort and convenience, often with little questioning of what that domestic unit is, how it changes through time and space, and whether the culturally specific notion of what comfort, accommodation and convenience is may not vary between periods and societies.

Finally, such studies run the danger of giving a highly particular account of development of architecture in a restricted area which lacks comparative potential in two senses. Comparative analysis between regions is hampered by stress on the unique style of that particular area: this point parallels Binford's claim for archaeology in general that we should be studying variability rather than cultural influence and similarity (Binford 1964). Additionally, the typology appears to bear no relation to the society that produced it: crown-posts become less ornate, windows move from roll-moulded to ovolo-moulded type, lobby entries replace through-passages for no particular reason other than the internal evolutionary logic of the typology, or some vague process defined as "fashion". It can be argued that under this approach houses run the danger of becoming "fetishised" (Pfaffenberger 1988); that is, their changing form is treated as a thing-in-itself, masking the social relations – the people – that in fact cause that form to change.

Studies employing what is called here the "economic approach" take as the central theme the relation of housing to local economic trends. Again, the theorizing of this school is rarely explicit and exceptions can therefore always be found, but the underlying assumption appears to be that the numbers and size of a region's stock of traditional houses will tell us something, in a fairly straightforward manner, about the economic history of the area. Again, also, the economic approach may be interpreted as sharing much of the viewpoint of a wider school within archaeology, corresponding in many of its assumptions to a processual view.

The economic approach is undoubtedly a major advance on the typological school since buildings are being treated as historical products, indicators of past economic forces at work in an area, rather than as "artefacts-in-themselves". The classic example of this school of thought is W. G. Hoskins's thesis of the Great Rebuilding and its subsequent modification (Hoskins 1953, Machin 1977), and several outstanding studies have been written from this perspective (cf. Machin 1978, Pearson 1985 and others). There are several problems with such an approach, however. The first is the assumption often made of a straightforward wealth/houses relationship: Hoskins's discussion, for example, of the rebuilding as a consequence of the relationship between fixed rents and rising corn prices (Hoskins 1953: 50). This has to be qualified in several ways.

First, the number of houses on the ground need bear no direct relationship to past numbers of houses. This is a point made elegantly by Currie, who modelled the attrition rate of fire on a Cambridgeshire village and concluded that "apparent waves of rebuilding may be illusory. The richest areas may have the fewest old houses" (Currie 1988: 6). Although Currie may have overstated his case, any claim of past economic change made on numbers of surviving houses needs careful and critical examination. Secondly, any statement that relates wealth to housebuilding needs careful consideration both of the classes of people involved and the source of wealth under discussion. Hoskins himself (1964, 1968) has argued that wealth derived from corn harvests will be treated in different ways to wealth derived from other sources such as cloth production. He argues convincingly that the unpredictability of arable farming and fluctuations in yield make it difficult to invest year by year in a new house. Pearson (1985: 116) has argued of housing in the Lancashire Pennines that the situation was more complex than a measure of absolute wealth levels would indicate; security of tenure, social position and involvement in textile production make the situation far more difficult to disentangle. Machin has commented that in Yetminster, "whilst men [sic] required money to build . . . the degree of investment was largely determined by the answer to the question 'who will be the eventual beneficiary?'" (Machin 1978: 155). Parallel comments relating differing forms of tenure (in particular the legal niceties of copyhold versus freehold) to housebuilding rates may be criticized on analogous grounds and need to be qualified.

A more fundamental point is that the relationship between wealth levels and housebuilding is problematic in the first place. Whether or not a household will invest its money in architecture, as opposed, say, to moveable goods or the Church, is a decision that will vary from culture to culture and from social group to social group. For example, many peasant societies have been argued to have a strong ethic against reinvesting surplus money back into the household: rather, there is strong pressure to dissipate the surplus on feasts, religious celebrations and similar events bringing social prestige rather than material wealth back to the family unit (Shanin 1971: 15). This pressure derives in part from the strongly egalitarian ethic that, it may be argued, exists in many peasant communities (Bailey 1971: 19) as well as the different economic logic operating in many such communities (Wolf 1966).

If we want to understand the decision to put money into houses over other activities, we have to investigate the strength of any "peasant ethic" of this nature, the subjective level of security as well as the objective level as represented by legal terms of tenure, and the particular world-view or position of the social group or groups doing the building. We need to examine the parallel cultural and ideational changes accompanying those encompassed by J. T. Smith's (1970: 147) observation that "in a general way, farmhouses of the 16th to 17th centuries reflect a profound change in social relations involving . . . the disappearance of the peasant in the feudal sense and the emergence of a class of yeomen . . . who, by comparison with their forebears, were free men in an economic as well as legal sense".

Not only does reliance on solely economic reasoning lead to difficulties in explaining why a household, community or social group will make the decision to build, it also gives rise to problems in addressing the question of form. In other words, such an approach can answer the question "how many?" but not necessarily of "why that particular type?" The way two houses of equal size are laid out obviously varies, and it is difficult to account for that variation by economic factors alone. Even rooms giving labels referring to economic function, such as "workshops" or "dairies", beg the question, since the functions of these rooms might easily take place elsewhere or be arranged in a different pattern: different household units will have different ideas of what is functionally convenient. Rather, we can reasonably expect the layout of houses to vary according to the patterns of daily life within them: according to social and cultural factors as well as purely economic ones.

One escape from this problem has been proposed, again implicitly, by Smith and Barley. Peter Smith has argued that plan types show greater or lesser degrees of evolution according to their distance from London, though elsewhere he has traced a more complex pattern (Smith 1985: 686–9; 1988); Barley has echoed Smith's view when he ascribes the "conservatism" of houses in the north and west to "remoteness and poverty" (Barley 1967: 760). Geographical and social diffusion of form certainly play a rôle in traditional architecture (Jope 1973). It is important, however, to follow up the raising of such geographical questions with studies of cultural attitude: why Wales and the North and West of England chose to remain conservative in plan, what social factors caused the area to lag behind the lowlands, why it eventually gave way to the national trend when it did, and so on.

It can therefore be concluded that economic factors are themselves often proximal rather than ultimate causes – only part of the story – as indeed Hoskins himself recognized (1953: 53). We have to question why wealth was accumulated in a particular area or by a particular group at a particular time. Later I shall argue that wealth accumulation may well have been conditioned by a cultural attitude or ethic that in its turn has to be related to other social and cultural factors.

It is important to stress the underlying disciplinary and social factors surfacing in these debates. The typological approach appears very often to be taken by scholars trained in art history and architecture, and also to draw upon the work of amateurs and local groups. Consequently the interest is in the "artefact-in-itself" and in the immediate context of the village or town. What I have termed the economic approach has very often been articulated by professionals trained in historical or geographical disciplines. Such scholars very often assume a "commonsensical" approach to the question of cultural meaning and identify the process of understanding the wider historical context exclusively with the technique of documentary analysis (e.g. Machin 1977: 56).

It is also important to stress that such approaches were appropriate to a young sub-discipline. The typological approach succeeded in establishing the basic parameters of the objects of study, while economic factors are obviously important and are a logical first place to look for the historical context of housing changes.

A third approach, now to be discussed, is similarly dependent on ideas and influences from other disciplines. It attempts to draw together work in folk-life studies, historical and symbolic anthropology, and social and post-processual archaeology. The starting point for this approach is the proposal that material things are more than simply tools for coping with the environment. Artefacts are social products: that is, they are produced and have meanings assigned to them in a social milieu. The way meaning is assigned in this process is a highly complex one and will vary from culture to culture, particularly with the development of mass production and consumption (Miller 1987; see also Chs 3 & 7 below). However, it is sufficient to note here that all artefacts clearly do have cultural meanings attached to them by societies and that the meaning of the same object can be reassigned through time.

It is therefore possible in theory to write an account of material things in terms of the meanings they carry and how these might relate to social and cultural change. If such an account involves questions of community or class values and ethics, it can begin to address the criticisms of the economic approach raised above.

What is true of material things is equally true of the form of enclosed space. This has been realized by architectural theorists for some time (Preziosi 1979, Rapoport 1982), but this insight has taken time to filter into the mainstream of British vernacular architectural studies.

It would be unfair, however, to claim that such an approach has no antecedents in British vernacular studies. There are such antecedents and these are worth reviewing. First and most notably is the work of S. O. Addy (1898), based on research in the Sheffield area. Addy noted the distinctive "Englishness" of the bay system of design of timber frames (see Ch. 3), and attempted to relate this to "Anglo-Saxon" systems of measurement and thought. As a pioneering effort this was a classic work, although it now appears quite ahistorical and unsystematic in nature. Innocent (1917), although interested more in techniques of building construction, accepted Addy's basic thesis.

Sir Cyril Fox and Lord Raglan are usually noted for having laid out the definitive methodology for vernacular architectural studies in their three volumes on Glamorgan houses (1951), a work that also contained interpretive elements of importance in this context. Fox and Raglan classified their houses into three phases, medieval, sub-medieval and Renaissance, and in addition to environmental and economic factors saw underlying cultural change as a force behind the transition. In particular they identified what they saw as a rise in the need for material comfort and privacy arising from "Renaissance" ideas. The architectural result was more segregated house plans and symmetrical facades through time. They did not go on from this to ask why Renaissance ideas gained in popularity at this point in history and how this might relate to contemporary social change either within Glamorgan or in a wider sense. Many of these ideas can also be seen later in the work of Eric Mercer (1975), who although using the definition of "comfort and convenience" noted above, discussed the transition between medieval and post-medieval plan types in social terms.

Raglan was also interested in social evolutionary theory, and went on in a paper entitled "The house: shelter or temple?" (Raglan 1957) to claim that all houses could, fundamentally, be seen as a union between the Earth Mother and Sky Father. Like Addy's work, this paper was ahistorical and unsystematic by modern standards, but raised some interesting points (e.g. relating tidiness and the concept of the sacred) and is worth mentioning in this context.

All these early writers were influenced to a greater or lesser extent by the tradition of folk-life studies. I therefore suggest that as the economic approach developed and the study of traditional architecture became more rigorous in its methodology, the intuitive leaps of faith and lack of historical specificity involved in studies such as Addy's or the observations of Ewart Evans (1966) became more readily apparent. Relating houses to economic changes needed ever tighter date brackets which the folk-life tradition was unable to supply. Houses were also seen – quite correctly – less and less as part of a living cultural tradition and more as indicators of past historical change. Consequently such ideas lost currency as the economic approach became dominant.

However, cultural approaches have been further developed in other countries. In France, the Musée des Arts et Traditions Populaires has produced a series of regional volumes (e.g. Bucaille & Levi-Strauss 1980) whose basic approach claims to be derived from Claude Levi-Strauss's thought on the transmission of culture in traditional societies. Houses and farmsteads are treated as embodiments of cultural values: their layout expresses the timeless cultural order of the pre-industrial rural community, and accounts of housing change have been integrated into wider interpretations of changing material life (Braudel 1973: 192–226). Again, however, the same sorts of problem are readily apparent. It is difficult to find an explanation of change through time rather than an ahistorical and sometimes naïve description of the unchanging nature of rural lifeways. As a result, analysis tends to degenerate rapidly into a rather dry typology. In addition, similar methodological problems recur: selection from the sample frame of farmsteads to study appears in the case of the Musée volumes to be haphazard rather than truly random.

A stronger body of research has been carried out on the east coast of the United States. Here the influences and interpretations have been more various, but an underlying stress has always been on architecture as carrying cultural meaning. Upton & Vlach, for example, comment that

> the study of intention becomes the ultimate one in vernacular architectural studies, because it is the study of people acting. It shows us people . . . engaged with their surroundings in a critical way, people making their own histories in the face of authorities trying to make it for them (Upton & Vlach 1986: xxiii).

Studies of traditional architecture are carried out under the general heading of "material life" and have stressed the house as the centre of cultural and social values and activities. The best known example of such work is Henry Glassie's classic, *Folk housing in Middle Virginia* (1975). A critique of this book is offered in Chapter 3.

Such studies have often stressed the central problem resulting from the introduction of Georgian principles of architectural order into 18th-century vernacular architecture, relating it to social and economic factors via its "restructuring of architectural authority" (Upton 1982: 95). Through its stress on cultural meaning in everyday life this work finds a ready home within the study of American material life as a whole (St George 1988) and within social history. Isaac's classic study of 18th-century Virginia, for example, draws on the work of Glassie and other writers to put together an "ethnography" of everyday life, drawing on the methodology of symbolic anthropologists such as Geertz (Isaac 1983).

The approach taken here is an eclectic one, which may be labelled as "contextual". This word has many related meanings (Hodder 1991: 118–145). In one sense it means no more than the proposition that houses must be placed in their social and historical context. However, it is also more than this: it is necessary to propose that houses should be treated as cultural products, but that culture is not some kind of disembodied "folk mind"; rather, houses are the product as much of divergent and conflicting social interests as of a unified community ethic. This insight owes a great deal not only to the American approaches outlined above but also to ethnography and ethnoarchaeology (Cunningham 1964, Humphrey 1974, Bourdieu 1977).

Structure of the study

It was noted above that one of the major problems with social approaches to traditional architecture is very often the lack of rigour with which they have been carried out. Chapter 2 therefore sets out the rationale for the region examined here, namely an area of western Suffolk in England, the relation of its housing population to both surviving and past sample populations, and the use of a random sampling technique. Basic questions of distribution and chronology will also be resolved as a prelude to the core of the empirical discussion of the houses in Chapters 4 to 6. In particular, the period 1400–1700 will be divided into three basic units.

Chapter 3 will examine in more detail the theoretical basis of the analysis. It will do so through a general critique of various approaches to the study of domestic space and specifically through a discussion of Henry Glassie's use of Chomskian concepts (Glassie 1975). It will then outline the justification for a simplified "grammar" for the houses under discussion. The concept of "craft tradition" is seen as central to an understanding of this "grammar". Arguments are put forward for the coherence of this approach, supported by discussion of the "bay system" of design and of the nature of craft production and social meaning in pre-industrial communities.

Chapters 4 and 6 go on to delineate "open" and "closed" systems of competence, corresponding to the early and late periods of the three under discussion. The way in which these systems express both corresponding and varied social meanings (these meanings relating in turn to the patterns of social relations at the family and household level) is discussed. Chapter 5 examines in more detail the central, "transitional" phase, and explores the wide range of plan forms in this period through a series of specific examples and their manipulation of old and new forms. The range of building innovation is related to changes in structural detail and society as a whole.

The conclusion of these core chapters is that while significant elements of continuity are present, traditional houses in western Suffolk underwent a fundamental transformation between 1400 and 1700, and that a full understanding of this transformation must be sought in cultural terms. Chapter 7 further amplifies the content of this transformation. In particular, the changing nature of traditional technical systems is cited to support the thesis of a shift from "openness" to "closure" of the house.

Chapter 8 attempts to provide a synchronic, "snapshot" analysis of the closed house and farmstead. It relates house and farm to 17th-century values of the family and household in an attempt to get closer to the specific cultural changes underlying the architectural transition previously outlined. Chapter 9 outlines changes in "polite" architecture, again seeking an understanding of its nature in cultural and social terms. Evidence from "polite" and gentry houses at the one end of the social scale, and labourers' cottages and shared houses at the other, is then marshalled to support the proposition that a shift from quantitative to qualitative spatial variation is evident during this period. In other words, houses develop from being larger and smaller versions of the same spatial system to being very different things. It is suggested that this development has very direct implications for the chronology and nature of developing class relations within rural communities in this period, as mentioned above.

So far a detailed analysis of changes in housing has been offered, and related to wider social changes. But little hint has been given of causality, of the reasons behind the transformation argued for. Chapter 10 attempts to fill this gap. It draws a contrast between "wood-pasture" and "sheep/corn" areas of western Suffolk and argues for a relationship between the changes of forms of houses and the enclosure of fields. It is noted, however, that churches present a more complex picture, appearing to present an apparently reverse transformation to that of the houses and fields. It is thus suggested that a contextual account of the relationship between secular and religious belief is necessary at this stage. This goal is approached through a consideration of Puritan belief and its secular impact, but this analysis is qualified and deepened by a more sophisticated consideration of changes in conceptions of the self and the social and natural world.

Changes in the cultural and the symbolic therefore emerge as a central part of any understanding of why the pattern of housing, and the pattern of rural society, changed so fundamentally at this time, although in parallel with the famous arguments of Max Weber only one side of the causal chain is being put forward. Only a limited causal explanation is therefore being given.

The explanation is also limited in space and time. The Conclusion attempts to sketch out the context within which these changes took place. It also examines the implications of this study for a much larger project, a deeper understanding of the archaeology of late and post-medieval England. In this way the final chapter is not just a conclusion, but an exciting and, I hope, promising beginning.

CHAPTER 2
AN INTRODUCTION TO WESTERN SUFFOLK

In order to study houses, it is first necessary to select a period and an area. The period dealt with here is that of the transition between the late medieval and early modern worlds. In many areas of England, the 15th century saw the erection of thousands of houses built to a medieval design, houses that, in contrast to their predecessors, survive in large numbers to this day. By the end of the 17th century, as we shall see, the layout of these structures had been transformed, a transformation that pointed the way towards the emergence of the Georgian and modern house. The period 1400–1700 is thus also one well suited to comparative treatment with contemporary documents, as well as the wider interpretations of social historians.

The region selected is part of the English county of Suffolk, in East Anglia (Figs 2.1 & 2.2; Plate 1a & b). The county of Suffolk has a reputation as one of the sleepier corners of England. It is a predominantly rural area, the two centres of Bury St Edmunds and Ipswich not qualifying as anything more than market towns and county centres. It is also one of the less spectacular landscapes of Britain. No part of Suffolk is over 200 m high; the main body of the county undulates in a general and unhurried fashion, echoing the farmer's bumper sticker, "Don't rush me – I'm from Suffolk." Within this landscape villages, hamlets and farmsteads sit, the changing composition of the inhabitants now reflecting the social changes and community tensions of the present. Smart, restored cottages owned by "yuppies" sit next to more dilapidated farms that have been owned and worked by locals for generations.

As one gets to know this landscape, however, its apparent uniformity and dullness fades away. The more subtle rises and falls of the arable fields can be seen as more aesthetically pleasing than the barren hills of other parts of Britain; certainly they were seen this way in the pre-industrial period (Thomas 1983). Still closer inspection reveals that subtle changes in altitude and drainage correlate with village and house forms. The Stour Valley villages of Cavendish and Glemsford, densely packed round greens and with several large gentry houses, contrast with dispersed settlements and hamlets devoid of larger houses a few kilometres to the north. As one becomes more familiar with such a landscape, changes such as these stand out; as one walks or drives between such areas, they assume a perceived suddenness and importance quite equal to that between mountain and valley, hill and plain.

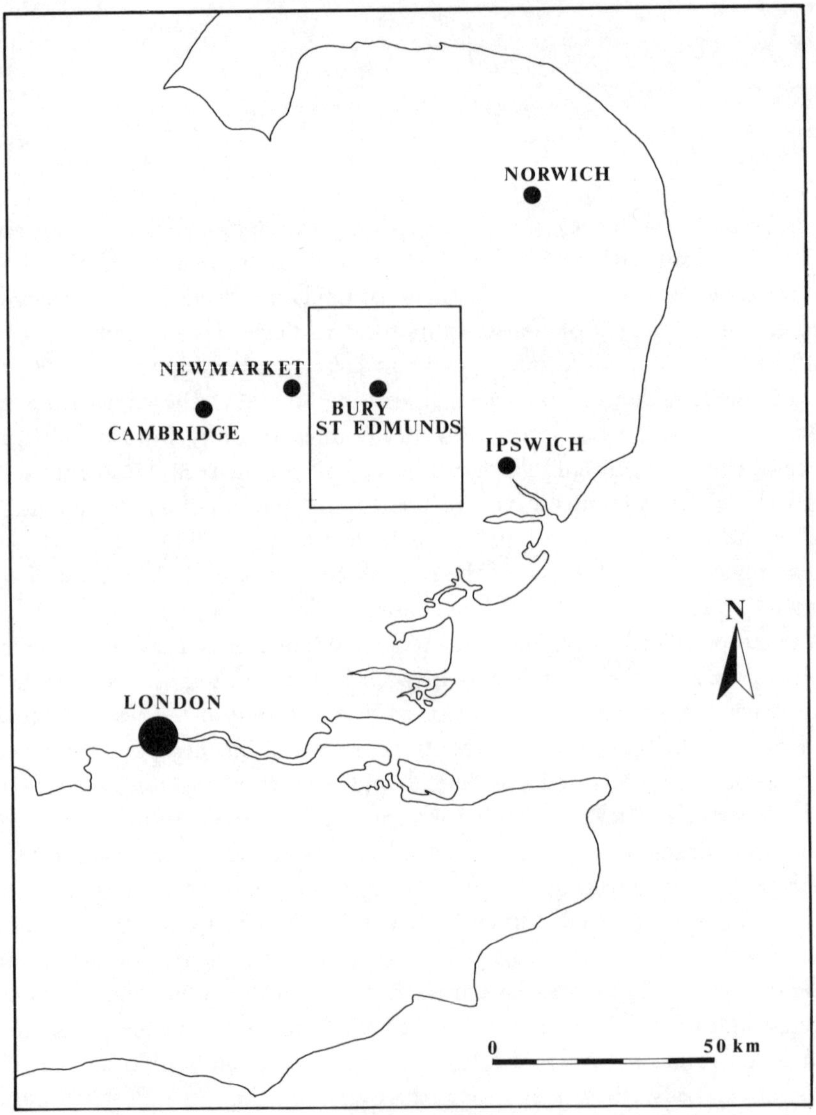

Figure 2.1a Regional location of sample area.

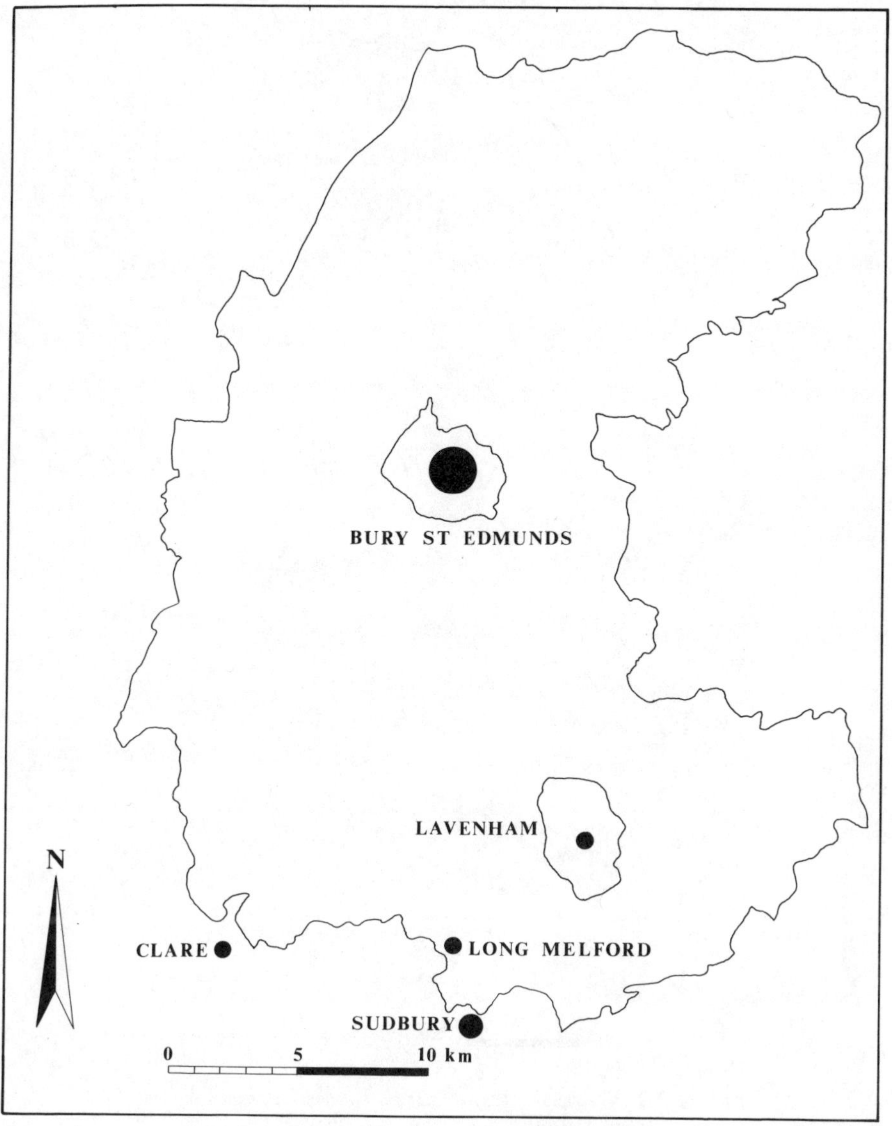

Figure 2.1b Location of sample area.

As this knowledge of the Suffolk landscape deepens so its appearance of stability and timelessness is also revealed as a myth. In the 15th, 16th and 17th centuries the county of Suffolk was socially and economically "progressive" and religiously radical, and at the forefront of a set of social, economic and political changes affecting England as a whole. During the English Revolution, this was evident in Suffolk's rôle as part of the core of the parl-

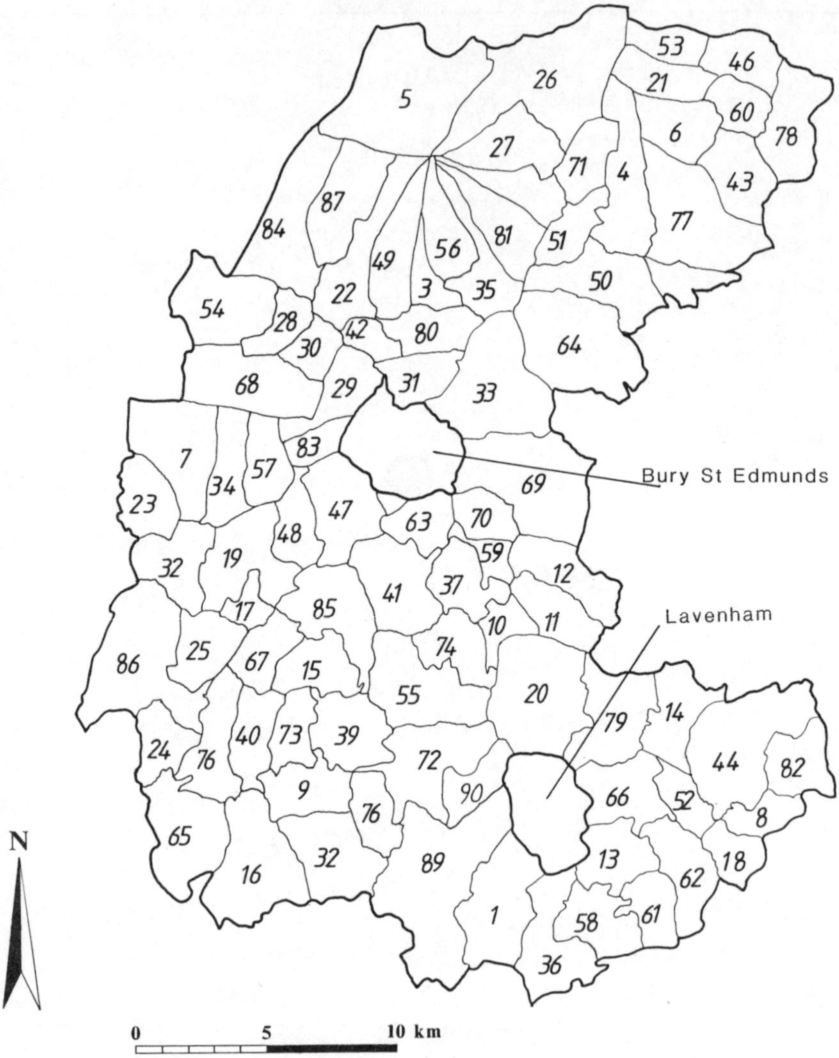

Figure 2.2 Western Suffolk: parish names and boundaries.

1 Acton
2 Alpheton
3 Ampton
4 Bardwell
5 Barnham
6 Barningham
7 Barrow
8 Bildeston
9 Boxted
10 Bradfield Combust
11 Bradfield St Clare
12 Bradfield St George
13 Brent Eleigh
14 Brettenham
15 Brockley
16 Cavendish
17 Chedburgh
18 Chelsworth
19 Chevington
20 Cockfield
21 Coney Weston
22 Culford
23 Denham
24 Denston
25 Depden
26 Euston
27 Fakenham Magna
28 Flempton
29 Fornham All Saints
30 Fornham St Genevieve
31 Fornham St Martin
32 Glemsford
33 Great Barton
34 Great Saxham
35 Great Livermere
36 Great Waldingfield
37 Great Welnetham
38 Hargrave
39 Hartest

iamentarian Eastern Association (Everitt 1960). Economically, the growth of textile production as a rural industry from the 1460s onwards around Bury St Edmunds, Long Melford and Lavenham brought a degree of wealth and industry to the area unsurpassed in pre-industrial England (Dymond & Betterton 1982, Dymond & Northeast 1985: 41–8; Unwin 1907).

Farming itself was also changing: 16th- and 17th-century Suffolk saw the rise of arable and dairy farming for profit, fostered by its relative proximity to the growing giant of London, and hence its growing involvement with the "pull" of London's markets. Tax records testify to the economic wellbeing of the area (Pound 1986, Redstone 1904). In terms of religious radicalism and change, Puritanism was a powerful force in Suffolk society by the English Revolution; many of the Puritans of New England came from Suffolk (St George 1984, 1986).

Traditional houses populate this deceptive landscape more densely than any other area outside south-eastern England. A rough estimate based on the statutory lists of buildings of "historic and architectural importance" suggests that between 5,000 and 8,000 houses in the county as a whole survive from before AD 1700, a number too large for the most ambitious of studies. I therefore decided to cover a smaller sample area in the west of the county, away from the coast and around (though not including) the market centres of Bury St Edmunds, Long Melford and Lavenham. I also omitted towns from the sample, again for reasons of sheer numbers.

This area of western Suffolk contains several of the subtle but important contrasts in landscape mentioned above (Fig. 2.3). To the north of Bury St Edmunds stretches a "sheep-corn" area of glacial soil of poor fertility and drainage called the Breckland. The Breckland had few inhabitants and even less wealth before the 18th century. It suffered badly during late medieval desertion and contraction of settlement and was to be reorganized drastically in the 18th and 19th centuries with enclosure and the introduction of sugar beet farming. Today, much of this land is under an ugly conifer forest while the

---

40 Hawkedon
41 Hawstead
42 Hengrave
43 Hepworth
44 Hitcham
45 Honington
46 Hopton
47 Horringer
48 Ickworth
49 Ingham
50 Ixworth
51 Ixworth Thorpe
52 Kettlebaston
53 Knettishall
54 Lackford
55 Lawshall
56 Little Livermere
57 Little Saxham
58 Little Waldingfield
59 Little Welnetham
60 Market Weston
61 Milden
62 Monks Eleigh
63 Nowton
64 Pakenham
65 Poslingford
66 Preston
67 Rede
68 Risby
69 Rougham
70 Rushbrooke
71 Sapiston
72 Shimpling
73 Somerton
74 Stanningfield
75 Stansfield
76 Stanstead
77 Stanton
78 Thelnetham
79 Thorpe Morieux
80 Timworth
81 Troston
82 Wattisham
83 Westley
84 West Stow
85 Whepstead
86 Wickhambrook
87 Wordwell

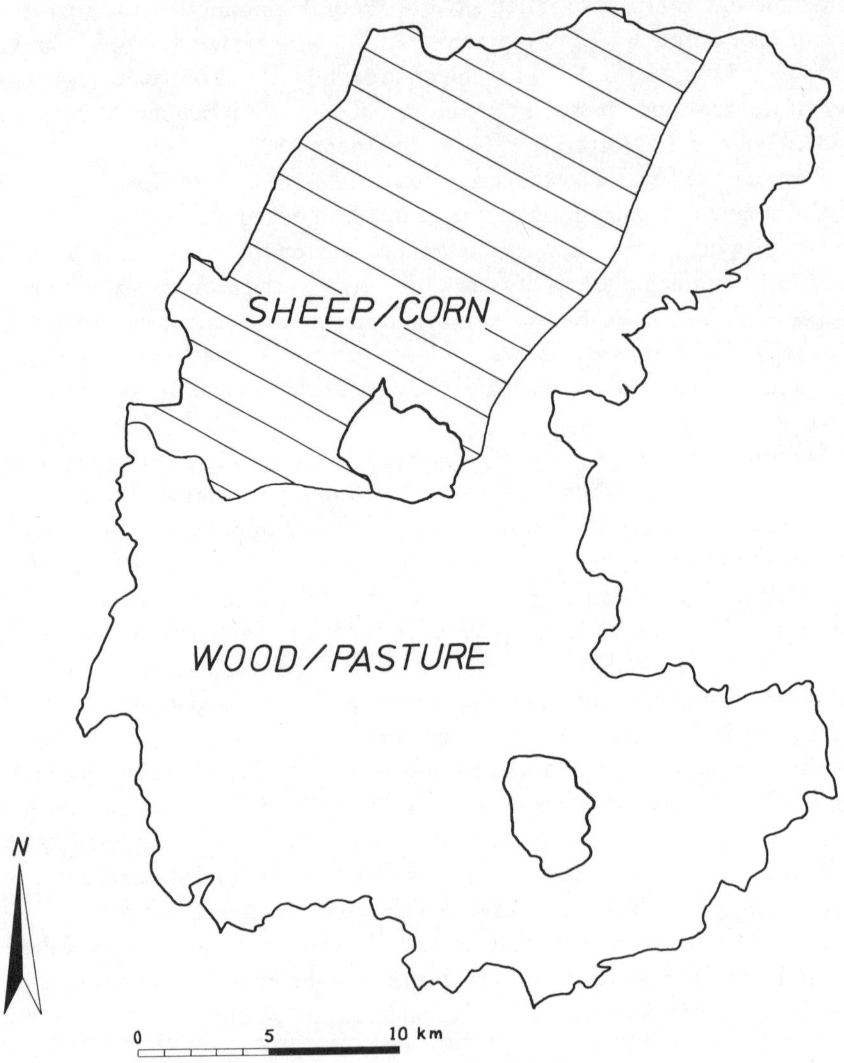

Figure 2.3 Western Suffolk: landscape type.

remainder was under uglier American air bases at the time of research. To the east of the Breckland, the large nucleated villages of Great Barton, Ixworth and Stanton stand on the divide between the Breckland and "High Suffolk"; and to the south of Bury, a large area of classic "High Suffolk", "ancient" or wood-pasture landscape stretches through Suffolk into the county of Essex to the south. This High Suffolk landscape is fertile, mostly devoid of large villages outside the river valleys, with dense but dispersed settlement.

The overall division between the north and south of this strip of Suffolk was clearly seen by contemporaries to have social and economic resonance, as acknowledged by Reyce in his 1618 Breviary of Suffolk (Hervey 1902: 26). *The chorography of Suffolk*, written between 1600 and 1605, describes this division under the heading "The Nature of the soyle":

> The nature of it is as divers . . . That p't of it which is called the Woodlande and High Suffolck is exceeding fruitfull comparable to any p't of Englande for pasture for oxen & kine, not so good for sheepe. In this p't of the countrye are made butter & cheese in exceeding great quantitie of wonderful goodnes comparable to any in the Realme. The commoditie thereof is unspeakable to the inhabitants of the same amongst which are very many yeomen of good credit & great liberalitie, good housekeepers, but the wayes & common roades in this countrye are very fowle & uncomfortable in the winter tyme to travayle in. The other p'ts westerlye of the countrye are very fruitfull also, but the woodland carryeth the chief creditt for goodness of grounde. . . . The soyle also about Burye to Newmarket warde, Mildenhall, Elden [Elveden, near Euston], Barton &c. is heathy & barren fit only for sheep & conyes although in some places of the same there be some spots of good and fertil groundes as their botomes & medowes (Macculloch 1976: 19–20).

One way in which this division was reflected was in terms of the type and security of land holding and tenure. The wood-pasture area was one of "copyhold by inheritance", reasonably secure against exploitative rack-renting and arbitrary fines to the extent of being as secure as freehold tenure (Kerridge 1969: 37–9, 64). In the northern Breckland area the power of the landlord over the tenant was more pervasive (Dymond & Martin 1988: 100). This division between north and south was a microcosm of many of the landscape divisions of England as a whole; it had social, economic and cultural implications, as Reyce comments. Some of these will be touched upon in Chapter 9.

Within this area a total of 794 traditional houses are thought to date from the 15th, 16th and 17th centuries;[1] a huge figure, but possibly a biased one. It is a tedious but necessary question to ask how biased, and in what way. Fortunately it is possible to compare the picture of the modern housing population against that in later 17th-century Suffolk by use of the Hearth Tax Returns, a tax record drawn up in 1674 giving numbers and owners of houses together with numbers of hearths within the house. Figure 2.4 shows the numbers of houses per parish recorded in the 1674 returns, together with the number of pre-1700 houses mentioned in the county listings. The totals are 2,831 houses from the returns and 794 mentioned in the lists, giving an overall survival rate of just over 28 per cent.[2]

In other words, three out of ten of the houses standing in 1674 still stand today. Such a rate of survival of traditional houses over three centuries is better than expected: Christopher Currie has argued for an expected survival rate in neighbouring Cambridgeshire (based on destruction by fire alone) much lower than this (Currie 1988: 7). It could be that huge numbers of smaller, less substantial houses standing in 1674 have completely vanished, but this is unlikely (see Ch. 9). We may safely assume that the existing sample is not grossly biased towards one tiny subset of the housing of 1674.

From this total of 794 houses, a random sample of 79 was taken – an unusual step in studies of traditional houses, where a more usual procedure is to take a complete sample of a small area or simply a haphazard sample of a region. The use of a sample of this nature is necessary, however, given the first principles of sampling theory: namely, that a random sample is the only way to obtain a statistically valid picture of the characteristics of the frame under study (Flannery 1976: 131–6). In addition, a "judgemental" or haphazard sample of houses was added. These included a few houses to which firm historical dates could be attached, houses in the area surveyed by other groups, and an exhaustive survey of one parish, Brent Eleigh. The total number of houses listed in Appendix 2 is 127.[3]

How old are these houses? Most dating of fabric within traditional architecture is done intuitively on the basis of typology. In particular, Cecil Hewitt has erected a complex classification of joint forms used in timber framing. However, doubt can be cast on the reliability of such classifications empirically (Mercer 1975) as well as in a wider sense (Wilson 1959). Briefly, in order to extrapolate from known to unknown dates the typological method has to assume a fairly uniform rate in the evolution of the typology. Qualifications to this assumption must be made: the pace of change may vary according to social or regional factors or the conservatism of the individual craftsman or client.

In the course of this study it proved almost impossible to found a systematic typology on "hard evidence" such as historical dates in the absence of tree-ring dates.There was also a related danger of circular reasoning inherent in assigning dates on the basis of plan type. Consequently I am inclined to be cautious about precise dates. I view Machin's caution at dating any building within a 50-year period (Machin 1978) as entirely justified. Given this lack of hard evidence for absolute dates, comments on the chronology of housebuilding rates must be made carefully.

Between 1450 and 1700, building continued at a more or less continuous rate in western Suffolk, at least when taking building century by century. (It will be argued in Chapter 4 that the bulk of surviving 15th-century houses are post-1450 in date.) Within centuries, there may have been quite significant rises and falls in building activity, but overall this broad picture of continuous rebuilding seems accurate.

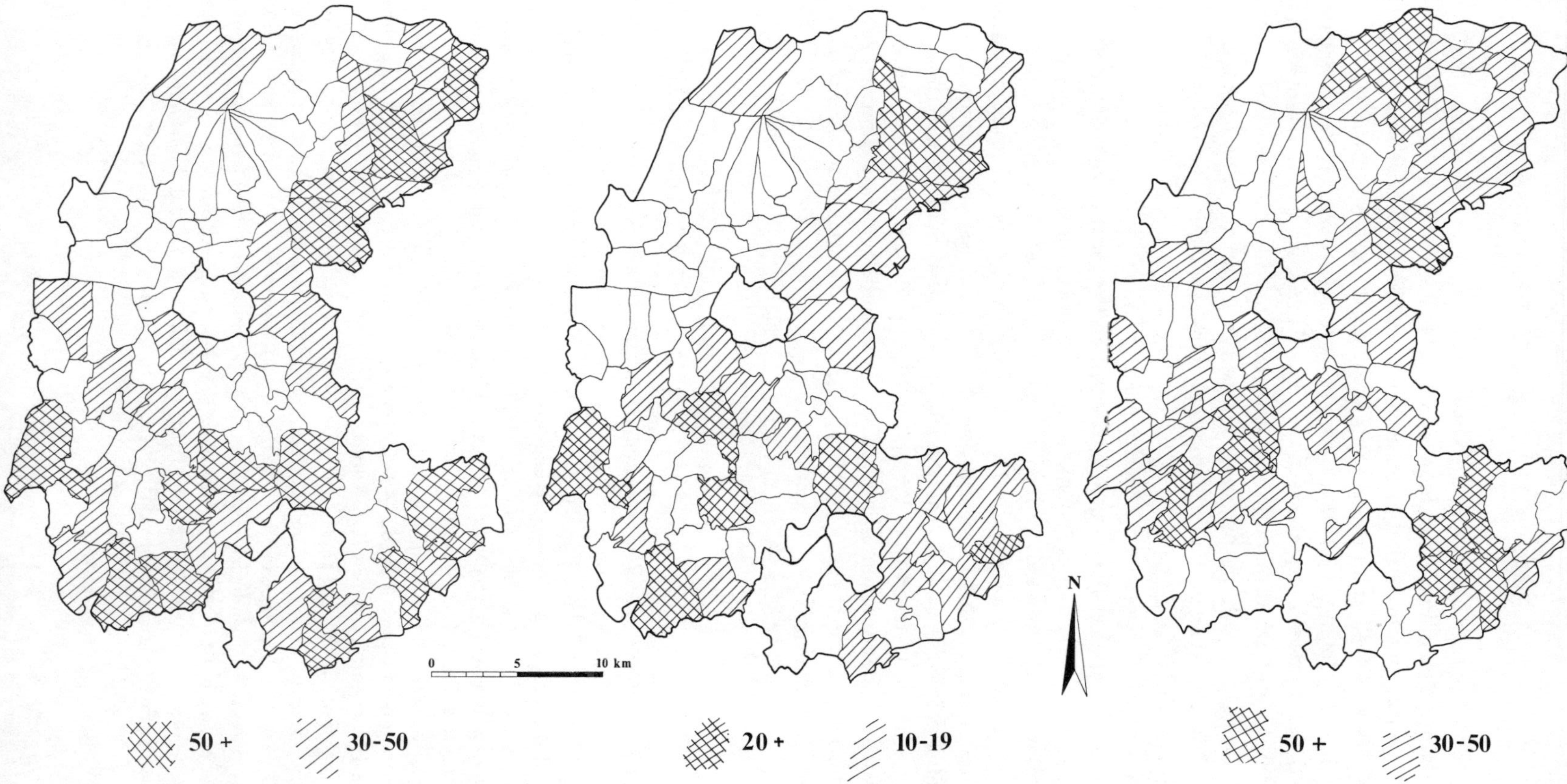

Figure 2.4 Numbers and survival rates of houses per parish: (left) 1674, (centre) present, (right) percentage survival rate.

If this is so, then Machin's (1977) reassessment of W. G. Hoskins's concept of a "Great Rebuilding" must be accepted for western Suffolk. Hoskins argued for a central, pivotal period of rebuilding across lowland England as a whole from 1560 to 1640 and included Suffolk in his thesis (Hoskins 1953: 47). In Suffolk, one would expect such a rebuilding to be early since the underlying social and economic causes are also early. Machin argues for a much more drawn-out process than Hoskins's narrow 60 to 80-year band. In western Suffolk, partly due to the problems of dating, it is difficult to pick out specific waves of rebuilding within the period spanning the 15th to the 17th centuries with certainty.

However, as has already been argued, it is not sufficient to interpret changes in traditional architecture, whether in the form of a constant rate of rebuilding or a building boom, simply in terms of numbers of houses. Accompanying this steady process of rebuilding lay a transformation in form, structure and decoration of these houses. I shall argue that this transformation is a quite fundamental one and is linked to social causes and consequences of parallel importance. It is this transformation that will be described and dissected in Chapters 4 to 6. Before this description can take place, however, I shall examine the assumptions and principles underlying the construction of traditional buildings; I shall also look at the approach taken to their interpretation in this analysis.

Notes

1. This figure was produced by consulting the Department of Environment lists of historic buildings for the area. Copies of relevant computer print-outs have been lodged with the Haddon Library, Department of Archaeology, Cambridge, and the Suffolk Records Office, Bury St Edmunds.

It should be noted that although in theory the listings record every building surviving in a "reasonable state" before *c.* 1700, omissions and errors are sometimes made, often due to lack of time available to examine the interior of the building. This is largely untrue of the north and middle of the sample area but is valid for the south. For example, in Brent Eleigh, 14 houses were recorded as pre-1700, of which three were 15th-century, five had 16th-century origins and four were 17th-century. Detailed internal analysis changed these figures to five 15th-century plus six 16th-century and one unsurveyed house. Of the 30 houses overall subsequently sampled on a random basis in the south of the sample area, eight were found to be inaccurately listed; in five cases these were open-hall houses listed as 17th-century, one was a building listed as 17th-century but probably 100 years older (Clarkes Farm, Acton) while the other two were exceptional buildings being dated too old. The general impression is that whatever the vagaries of individual interpretation of housing, overall we may expect a modest rise in the numbers of open-hall houses in particular.

However, whatever the errors of the lists within the pre-1700 period, the identification of most buildings as constructed before this date can be assumed with some confidence. Only one unlisted building was discovered to be worthy of attention in the course of the entire research. I am grateful to both Silvia Colman and Philip Aitkens for discussing the merits and the limitations of this evidence with me.

2. This assumes, of course, that bracketed entries in the publication of the returns are single houses subdivided into tenements, an assumption argued for in Chapter 9 and supported by Dymond & Martin (1988: 78). There are 767 double entries, 198 triple entries, and 19 quadruple entries, giving 767, 396 and 57 extra houses respectively if they are not treated in this manner; the total is 984 to be added to the previous total of 2,831, giving a modified total of 3,815 and a modified survival rate of 20.8 per cent. This figure is still much higher than that modelled by Currie (1988).

3. One published house (Mercer 1975: 202) was not included as it was not on RCHM files in either the London or Bury St Edmunds archives and was discovered too late for the purposes of inclusion in the sample.

CHAPTER 3
HOUSES, TRADITION AND SOCIAL MEANING

How should we study houses? I have argued that purely typological or economic approaches are inadequate in dealing with the interpretation of traditional architecture. Further, I have stressed that it is necessary, therefore, to look at what buildings meant, how they may have expressed or related to cultural values, in order to understand them fully. Having examined the specific context to be explored, this chapter will sketch out the theoretical issues in more depth. It will look in detail at the question of exactly how buildings may be expected to carry social meaning, and how this meaning may vary between region, time and social group. The literature on the general question of the meanings of architecture is vast, since this subject has already been tackled with some sophistication by the different fields of architectural theory, archaeology and ethnoarchaeology, symbolic anthropology and structural and semiotic theory. However, none of these fields has had to deal directly with the problems raised here of combining both diachronic and synchronic analysis, in other words of both change through time and of a particular point in time. Some discussion of the various perspectives available is therefore necessary, although this must involve covering some difficult theoretical ground.

Functional perspectives

A series of writers, dealing mainly with the problems presented in understanding the modern built environment, has tried to understand the layout of buildings by seeking to map out how architecture structures space in terms of how it controls encounters between people. These encounters are understood either in terms of functionally interrelated behaviours or in terms of communication in the overt sense: in other words, what people do and their overtly expressed reasons for so doing. These relations and communicative behaviours are taken to be more or less directly observable. Rapoport (1982, 1990), for example, outlines a general and cross-cultural model proposing that architectural design integrates four elements: space, time, communication (defined as "who does what with whom" (Rapoport 1982: 180)), and meaning. "Meaning" in this view is directed by visual cues in architecture and moveable goods. It is decoded both for the participant and the observer by repeated behaviours and observation of the social context. From Rapoport's model we can understand social behaviour as a system of activities, and architectural form as a system of settings, that will vary in a predictable way according to the organizational characteristics of the society. For example, Rapoport predicts that an increase in cultural complexity will lead to a rise in the number of specialized architectural settings and a rise in the number of "visual cues" needed to communicate social messages. Rapoport views his model as standing on the same theoretical ground as Binford's (1988) conclusions on the interpretation of activity areas (Rapoport 1990).

Hillier & Hanson propose a method of "discovering house genotypes" that makes little explicit reference to Rapoport's work but appears to share many of the same assumptions and to be formally compatible with it. Starting from the proposition that "there is always a strong relationship between the spatial form and the ways in which encounters are generated and controlled" and that "in principle the spatial organisation is a function of the form of social solidarity" (Hillier & Hanson 1984: 18, 143), they map the topology of houses through penetration diagrams, showing wide differences in the layout of superficially similar houses. Again, this model is a cross-cultural one, explicitly drawing on Durkheim's global and evolutionary distinction between mechanical and organic solidarity, and again it depends for its explanatory power on relating apparently observable behaviour to an ostensibly observable spatial pattern.

Both these models are powerful ones, in that they provide straightforward sets of methods that enable interesting attacks to be made on otherwise intractable problems. For example, Brown has applied penetration analysis to 17th-century London with interesting conclusions about precisely when the internal layout of London housing moved from a sub-medieval to modern pattern (Brown 1986). On a broader scale, McGuire & Schiffer have used a similar set of assumptions to "advance a preliminary but general theory to explain the design of vernacular architecture"; they go on to use such assumptions to give a convincing account of architectural change in the American Southwest (McGuire & Schiffer 1983: 272). Nevertheless, the two models share theoretical flaws in several respects.

The core set of problems is Rapoport's and Hillier & Hanson's assumption of a functional view of the social world with its emphasis on behaviour and system, the assumption that social activity is directly observable, and a naïve view of the question of meaning. This is not the place to rehearse the already worn theoretical criticisms of such a view (cf. Shanks & Tilley 1987), but some of the specific assumptions to which it leads can readily be seen to be limited. For instance, it is difficult to see how architectural change can be explained within this framework. Explaining change would pose no problem if architecture simply changed with pre-determining social change, but as Hillier & Hanson (1984: 9) themselves point out, "through its ordering of space the man-made physical world is already a social behaviour". Similar problems occur with the question of the generation of meaning. The meanings of built space clearly change: what a 16th-century house meant to its builder is clearly different to what it means to its 17th-century modifier and 20th-century owner. Meanings also change between groups: a house may be the centre of a working farm to its yeoman owner but may host a constellation of different meanings to its gentry visitor or to the labouring classes. Meanings of architecture may also change between overt and implicit, official and unofficial levels.

If we want to address exactly how social meanings are assigned to built form and how change through time occurs, we must look not at behaviour but at action. In other words, we must stress the activity of building and using houses as taking place with reference to prescribed cultural rules existing only between the ears of men and women rather than purely as externally observed behaviour (Giddens 1985). We can start with the basic proposition that the relationship between spatial form and social and ideational structure (between the form of the house and what that form means) is not straightforward or unproblematic. While culture conditions space, it does so not in a simple way regardless of the specific context being considered. Put simply, in some societies social relationships may be overtly expressed through layout; in others they may be masked, for example in an unequal, class-based society with an apparently egalitarian form of architecture (Miller 1984).

One possible way to understand this problem is through the Marxist view of ideology, as developed through Western Marxism. This holds that the overt view of a society, as expressed, for example, by the layout and form of its architecture, will by definition misrepresent the real nature of exploitative relationships in that society. It will do so by masking inequalities, making the historically particular form of that society appear natural, or by making the dominant sectional interests of the ruling classes appear universal (Leone 1984, Shanks & Tilley 1987: 75–8; see Dickens (1980) for an example of such a type of critique and analysis within the realm of architectural theory). One does not have to be a Marxist to see that this view holds much truth in terms of "overt", vulgar ideology. Its very powerful implication is that we must seek misrepresentation at covert, non-vulgar levels as well. At the very least we cannot assume a direct, unproblematic relationship between space and society that is predictable regardless of cultural context. We must allow the possibility that meanings are not assigned in a straightforward manner, and that they are not predictable or functionally related. In short, this relationship between space and society can and must be theorized.

Questions of meaning

One attempt to theorize this relationship between space and society is derived from linguistic theory via the structuralist and semiotic tradition initiated by Saussure (1983). In this tradition, particularly as developed in structural anthropology, culture is seen as a system of signs, the rules governing the articulation of which are formally analogous to those governing language (Levi-Strauss 1963: 31–54). Preziosi, for example, has developed a comparison of "architectonic and linguistic semiosis", claiming that "the fundamental semioses of both systems are clearly homologous" (Preziosi 1979: 67).

However, again the central problem of the assignment of meaning is not solved by this project. According to Saussure, the linguistic sign is arbitrary: the relationship between signifier (the word "pig") and signified (the thing with four legs and a little curly tail) is not a logical or metonymic one. This is clearly inadequate for material culture in general and architecture in particular, for two reasons. First, the sign is rarely purely arbitrary. For example, the signifier of crenellation has a non-arbitrary and metonymic relationship to the specific signified of military defence. Secondly, the elements are not purely communicative or symbolic: in this case, crenellation may have a function beyond that of display. It is not surprising, therefore, that Preziosi cannot move in his theoretical discourse beyond the rather opaque statement that "the semiotic nature of the built environment is saliently [*sic*] through a consideration of the multifunctional nature of the architectonic tradition" (Preziosi 1979: 63). We are therefore faced with the same gap between space and meaning which we started out with.

More recent developments within post-structuralism, Western Marxism and "contextual archaeology" have suggested that meaning is not a single or unitary thing. Meaning is variable: it is produced by individual people working within a given cultural structure, by renegotiating and transforming that structure by creatively manipulating existing meanings to produce new combinations. Central to any understanding of this manipulation is the question of power (Shanks & Tilley 1987: 73). This conception retains the notion of linguistic analogy though in a looser sense and links this with questions of the individual, agency, and social conflict and inequality.

The most sophisticated study yet of the links between this general view and the specific problems involved in the study of domestic space is that by Moore (1985) of the Marakwet of East Africa. Moore identifies these problems and argues that space should be treated as a form of text. Space, just as a text, has both overt and hidden meanings, and it is possible to reinterpret or reread that text. Thus Moore argues that the organization of houses and compounds does encode a series of messages relating to male dominance in Marakwet society, but that women neither reject the system totally nor blindly accept the dominant reading of it. Rather, they reinterpret it in an analogous manner to the way a text is reread and reinterpreted. Thus, just as a text, space can have different meanings for different people.

Moore's argument is much more complex than this summary, but it is worth stressing that if "cultural forms are produced, like language, from an underlying set of relations according to rules of combination and articulation", then it is equally true that "to understand how the organisation of space comes to have meaning it is necessary to relate that meaning to the economic and social realities that both produce and are produced by the ordering of domestic space" (Moore 1985: 1, 107). In other words, the structure of domestic space will be organized around, and will express the world-view or mentality of, the society that produced it, and will express that view, but this world-view in turn has to be understood in terms of that society.

This is an important statement. In the first place, we should pay attention to the structure of society: given the nature of the changing social forms in England sketched in Chapter 1, we can expect the organization of space to relate to factors such as master/servant relations, to gender and to parent/child relations. Secondly, we will not be looking at a monolithic, culturally disembodied message about an ideology or world-view. Houses are built and rebuilt by individuals, ordinary men and women, who have their own view of the world, even if that view is a rereading or restatement of the dominant or socially accepted view. The houses they build and the space they thus create can have their meanings assigned and reassigned by other individuals, and it is essential to realize and accommodate this possibility in our understanding. It may, however, be difficult to detect this purely through the material evidence, and may make for a necessarily complex, deep, many-layered understanding rather than a "simple", superficially more satisfying, single one.

For example, I shall argue in Chapter 8 that the layout of 17th-century houses related to a system of values that acted to legitimate the position of the male head of household. But this was an historically particular system just as its expression is particular. It was expressed by different individuals in different ways; yeomen's houses are different to humbler cottages, although similar principles may be at work in both cases. We must also allow theoretically for the possible development of women's perspectives on these values and their renegotiation of the meanings of household space, however difficult these might be to identify directly in the archaeological evidence alone. The result of all these qualifications is that 17th-century houses probably meant different things to different people, and the necessity of exploring these meanings militates against a simple reading of those houses.

I do not want to establish a formal set of ground rules constituting yet another universal model for the production of meaning through architectural form. I suggest, rather, that the way meaning is produced is historically particular: that is, it will vary from culture to culture. In this sense we have to allow empirical analysis to examine the way meaning is produced as well as what meanings are produced. (I will in fact argue that the interdependence of these two questions declines through time and the decline of this interdependence, one aspect of what will be termed "closure", is associated with the historical context.) However, it is useful to discuss the application of one such group of models to architecture, namely, concepts of generative grammar. These may serve as a very direct introduction to an understanding of the wider parameters of the specific craft tradition to be analyzed.

Grammatical approaches

A generative grammar, according to Chomsky (1965: 8), is "a system of rules that in some explicit or well defined way assigns structural descriptions to sentences". In terms of material culture, this may be seen as a set of rules generating, first, a set of shapes or basic geometrical entities, and then manipulating those entities to form a set of artefacts. Examples of such grammars in material culture range from flint arrowheads to pottery decoration (Deetz 1967: 87–94; Washburn 1983).

Such a grammar therefore seeks to model or to make explicit the often implicit and unspoken process of design in the mind of the maker. In this case, it models the way the final form of the building is thought out in implicit stages in the mind of the builder. This process is seen as a "competence" in linguistic terms: a "system of generative processes" that generate actual sentences from base components (Chomsky 1965: 4). A grammar is therefore an explicit description of a competence held at an unspoken, intuitive level, Bourdieu's level of "practical consciousness" (Bourdieu 1977: 72–8).

If competence is a system of generative processes, then structure consists of the sets of units competence generates and transforms: a group of sentences may be generated by a competence from an underlying deep structure, just as a set of houses may be generated from an underlying set of geometric shapes.

Chomsky demonstrates (1957: 30) that there are more than just "deep" and "surface" structures involved in the levels of components implicated in sentence formation. Without automatically extending this proposition to material culture, we may propose that an artefactual competence may be divided into subsets of rules, the beginning and end of each subset corresponding with a certain structural level of the creation of the artefact.

There are two related questions here that are not of primary interest to Chomsky but are crucial for students of material culture. First, how is meaning generated in this framework? Chomsky assigns this function to a separate rule set, the "semantic component" (Chomsky 1965: 16). This is not adequate for material culture, however; rather, meaning must be established via context. So whereas it is useless to expect some inherent meaning to appear, genie-like, from within the compositional rules behind the artefact, that artefact may be assigned meaning by the archaeologist from its various functions, its appearance in similar contexts, or from documentary references. As suggested earlier, the way meaning will be assigned by social actors may vary historically; medieval patterns of signification may be as different from our own as the meanings they signify.

It is therefore important to stress that it is impossible to understand the function and meaning of the artefact fully by analysis of the competence alone. However, the competence is the vehicle by which the artefact is created and meaning thus initially assigned; the two aspects are thus interrelated and cannot be considered in isolation.

Secondly, where does change come from? This question is closely related to the question of absence of a theory of practice within structuralist studies. When is language variability simply a random or insignificant shift in "parole" or "surface structure", and when is it a deeper, underlying change in competence? Chomsky is not interested in these questions since his purpose is a synchronic one, in other words concerned with analysis of the present rather than with historical change.

In the context of analysis of material culture, however, it may be possible to use an artefactual grammar to begin to elucidate these questions. A rigorous examination of when and where certain rules and rulesets are applied or rejected may isolate real periods of change and continuity, much as Washburn (1983) suggests that such factors may isolate group interaction more effectively than consideration of specific attributes.

Bourdieu (1977) points out that it is inadequate to regard the actions of people in general, and consequently the creation of material culture in particular, as simply the execution of some rules or models. He argues that mental "deep structures" do exist, but that while they control the individual's actions in one sense, they can be actively reinforced, renegotiated, or transformed by those actions. Shanks & Tilley (1987: 71), following Giddens (1979, 1985), point out the implication that material objects are not so much structured as "structuring", that is, that through artefacts their makers actively negotiate or enforce social categories and relationships.

The conclusion of both Bourdieu's and Shanks and Tilley's critiques can therefore be argued to be that the essential nature of competence is not being disputed. Rather it is the unchanging, ahistorical nature of that competence and the consequent passive stance of its user implied by Chomsky and orthodox structuralism that is at stake. At this rather rarefied level, therefore, the project of writing a grammar to describe that competence is not rendered obsolete: rather, it is made to share the stage with questions of meaning and the individual. Put another way, Levi-Strauss's fundamental categories are still there, but they are open to renegotiation, to use as instruments of oppression or subversion, and change.

The implications of the necessarily abstract and difficult issues raised above are made more readily apparent when one considers how spatial grammars have been used in the past. One example is Stiny's use of "shape grammars" (Stiny 1976, 1978). Stiny's concern is to develop a sophisticated geometrical model for the replication of architectural styles and systems, for example those of Palladio, rather than to understand the social reasons for the rise, stability and decline of those styles. His is therefore the study of "form for itself", legitimate in its own terms but one corresponding to artefact fetishism when considered as a means of doing archaeology. To clarify: the grammar serves Stiny's purpose in simulating certain architectural styles but does not lead to an historical or archaeological understanding of those styles. The second study I want to consider will be treated in more detail, as its concerns lie closer to the present project both empirically and theoretically. The key work in this context is Henry Glassie's *Folk housing in Middle Virginia: a structural analysis of historic artifacts* (1975).

Glassie's evidence is that of around 300 "folk houses" in two counties of Middle Virginia. Of these, around 150 were left out of the analysis, as being of modern, prefabricated construction. For the rest, Glassie composes a "generative grammar". He argues that the mind of the Virginian folk builder worked from a base component of a set of geometric units, themselves transformations of the square, to form first ground plans and then three-dimensional, real buildings. This formulation of the artefactual grammar is then set in its context. First, the grammar is used to arrive at a fresh classification of folk housing in the area. Secondly, innovations and variations within the rule sets are examined by taking individual exceptions and showing how they stand at particular points within the grammar. Finally, the temporal context is examined. Changes in house design over time are shown to relate to a much larger shift in cognition and society during the 18th century: from a low to a high emphasis on privacy both within and between households; from complex, open design of architectural detail to simpler, closed forms; and, thus, from the architecture of a small-scale, face-to-face community to a more private, alienated form of society.

This is a huge achievement, especially since it has been extended by others, in particular James Deetz (1977), to cover a wide range of colonial American material culture. However, a series of criticisms may be levelled at this work. Relatively few of the houses visited were properly surveyed; of the rest, many were not even examined internally. Glassie is not clear about numbers of houses examined in the text, and Stone (1988) concludes that in fact only 12 houses form the core of the analysis. In addition, the selection of just two counties for analysis in the vast area available means that it is unclear how far Glassie's findings are accurate for Tidewater Virginia as a whole, particularly when his disregard for documentary sources makes the sample socially as well as geographically suspect (Stone 1988: 69).

Of theoretical importance is Glassie's characterization of the "transformational grammar". Post-Chomskian linguistics has moved on from the notions of transformational grammar which Glassie has borrowed. It can be argued that Glassie has not composed a transformational grammar at all, but rather what Chomsky has termed a "phrase structure grammar" (Chomsky 1957: 26). In more practical terms, the grammar as put forward is ahistorical: both pre-Georgian and Georgian houses are lumped together in one formulation. This one model has to take in over a century of housebuilding and enormous variability in plans, including both sides of the very transformation Glassie later delineates. This has several consequences. First, the grammar as formulated is unneccesarily cumbersome: one suspects that the variability in spatial form could more simply be covered using two grammars. It is also difficult to see how the first half of the book, putting forward as it does a unified supra-historical account of the Virginian folk builder's competence, relates to the second half, which outlines a massive change within this period of folk culture.

The third problem relates to the specifics of the craft tradition under study and its relation to wider social change. Glassie never explores relations between builders and clients, and apparently assumes a close and unproblematic relationship.

Fourth is the criticism that Glassie makes little or no use of documentary sources in his analysis. His central thesis is that, given the lack of documentary information for ordinary people at this time, history can only rid itself of the charge of elitism by "reading" the artefact. But in fact such documentary information is not lacking. For example, Dell Upton has shown how patterns of room naming, and hence overtly expressed conceptions of aspects of the meaning of space within houses, can be related to the Virginian "social molecule" (Upton 1982: 98–107). Secondly, broader information has been drawn together in a book examining the very social and ideological changes Glassie himself infers, *The transformation of Virginia, 1760–1820* (Isaac 1982). In this work, Isaac ascribes the social changes in 18th-century Virginia primarily to the growth of Baptist and other radical religious beliefs. He does so by using the evidence of church and estate records, and more particularly information on ideas and sentiments contained in planters' diaries, sermons and newspapers to construct an "ethnography" of Virginia both before and after its "transformation". Mark Leone has argued that the adoption of the Georgian architectural and landscape style is related to industrialization and changing class relations in 18th-century Chesapeake society (Leone 1984).

This last point is worth expanding in relation to questions of grounding and of causality. The logic that Glassie argues lies behind the houses is never "grounded"; in other words, it is never related back in a rigorous or systematic fashion to the everyday life of the society that produced that logic. This could be done by showing how that logic might have functioned as an ideology, as a system of ideas that legitimated and reproduced the existing social order, and thus by relating it to unequal social relationships within and between households as argued above. Only brief reference is made to how the Virginian farmer might have held his family – as he held himself and the forces of nature – "under fearful control" (Glassie 1975: 162).

Thus causality is also brought into question. What caused the great shift from "pre-Georgian" to "Georgian" house forms? Glassie attempts to tackle this question in his last chapter, significantly titled "A little history" after a quotation from Levi-Strauss; as we move from page to page, this shift is first related to developing class relations in Virginia, then to Europe and America as a whole, then outwards. In this way the study of Virginian folk housing is fitted into a much wider set of themes encompassing, for Glassie, the whole of human history, which is seen as the steady extension of human control over the chaotic forces of nature (Glassie 1975: 193).

Relating the specific architectural components of Virginian house form to the whole of human history in this way is a massive achievement; but we are still left asking why this occurred, and why it took the specific form it did in 18th-century Virginia. To relate traditional housing to some wider change does not necessarily lead to an understanding of why that wider change occurred, an understanding which must be sought in historical terms.

To summarize, many of the substantive problems that can be found in Glassie's analysis rest in turn on the theoretical criticisms already noted: an inadequate notion of change and causation; a related need for a theory of social practice and thus a consideration of the immediate social context; and a need for greater detailed verification. These in turn relate in part to the need for an analysis of social relations and historical change.

Towards a conception of craft tradition

So far, the practical and theoretical limitations of a range of approaches have been outlined. It is worth repeating that they are seen not so much as invalid as inadequate on their own, and that therefore other factors such as context, function and overt and covert semantics need to be examined to achieve a fuller understanding. I now want to turn this statement on its head: to argue that, if related to these other themes, an artefactual grammar could and should be part of an enquiry into past social change.

At a general level, a grammar may achieve three aims. First, it may serve to prompt new questions. An attempt to formulate a grammar is an attempt to uncover the compositional rules underlying the artefact, and as such may assist, for example, in selecting the key features whose variability will be central to a typology. Secondly, it may be an accurate description of the competence of the maker/builder, and thus throw light on questions such as the degree of craft specialization or distinctive craft tradition (see below). Thirdly, it may allow a fresh classification in terms of rules and rulesets.

How might such a competence work in the specific realm of traditional architecture in a pre-industrial period? Ingold (1990) has argued that it is misguided to think of other historical periods or social or ethnic groups as having a technology in the sense of a *logos*, an abstracted body of technical knowledge related in a systematic and "rational" way and independent of social context. He argues, for example, that hunter-gatherer groups have no formal concept of production of tools, and that such activity must be seen as embedded in other social activities such as ritual and hunting itself. He continues by arguing that the development of social complexity can be related to the abstraction of techniques from their context, culminating in the development of a "pure" technology under capitalism. It follows that when conceiving of a specialized craft such as the construction of timber-framed architecture in pre-industrial Suffolk, it may be useful to think of its underlying system of rules or "competence" as lying midway between the two extremes Ingold delineates. This position, in the middle of the spectrum between technology and unspecialized production, holds true in three senses. We are first dealing with a state society, but not a "developed", industrial society. At the same time, late medieval and early modern traditional architecture is that of a group or groups within society between the top and the bottom. "Polite" or elite architecture had its own, more explicit rules and meanings. We are dealing here with socially middling timber-framed buildings. Thirdly, the relationship between builder and client is much closer than the distant one of modern times, but a specialized profession does exist and houses are not simply built by those who live in them.

In such a situation it may be asserted that there is indeed a specialized body of practical knowledge, belonging to a skilled or semi-skilled group of craft specialists, but that this knowledge and its associated competence is not necessarily overtly articulated or acknowledged. This is clearly true in terms of the skill of carpentry seen in the buildings considered here, as well as in terms of what we know of the organization of the craft tradition from the documents (Salzman 1952: 195–210, Quimby 1984: 89–125). Here, this body of knowledge is designated the "craft tradition" in deference to Richard Harris (1978: 3), and to make the link between the craft tradition and the buildings associated with it clear the subject matter of this study has been termed "traditional" rather than "vernacular".

Harris (1989) argues that when we look at timber-framed architecture in lowland England as a whole we can see certain salient features of the craft tradition. He also adopts the metaphor of language, arguing that within this national "language" of building there are "regional dialects". He notes four basic rules, and demonstrates that they are not "commonsensical" ones: alternatives exist to all four rules in the vernacular traditions of other areas and countries. I have listed Harris's rules; the comments are mine, and will be clearer to non-specialists in consultation with Figures 3.1–3.

(a) The tie-beam lap-dovetail assembly as the standard way of treating the joint between post, wall-plate and tie (see Glossary and Fig. 3.3). The major exception to this technique is cruck construction, in which a pair of curved timbers are raised to form an inverted V. Examples of cruck-framed buildings are not known from East Anglia, however.

    The only exceptions known from this study are at Shrub End, Great Barton, and two ties at Drift House, Sapiston. In these houses lateral support is provided by anchor-beams at cross-rail level only, and in both cases the intention appears to have been to leave the upper floor of a one-and-a-half storey house free of barriers at first-floor level. Examples of this practice are also known nationally in both cruck and box-frame construction (Drury 1984).

(b) The bay system, and its congruence with house plan. By this is meant the technique of dividing the frame into separate trusses linked by the wall-plates, cross-rails and sill-beam, and the homology or formal correspondence of bay and room divisions. Addy (1898) postulated that bays were often 16 ft apart, and that this related in historical terms to the space required for stalling a "yoke" of oxen in the Anglo-Saxon house. As a rule, most bays in Suffolk are much narrower than this.

(c) The placing of the "upper face" of the truss towards the heated room or towards the higher-status end of the building. The upper face is that which is "fair" or away from the possibly waney edge of the timber and

Figure 3.1 Simplified sketch of timber frame of a house with clasped-purlin roof, with specialist terms indicated (see Glossary for definitions).

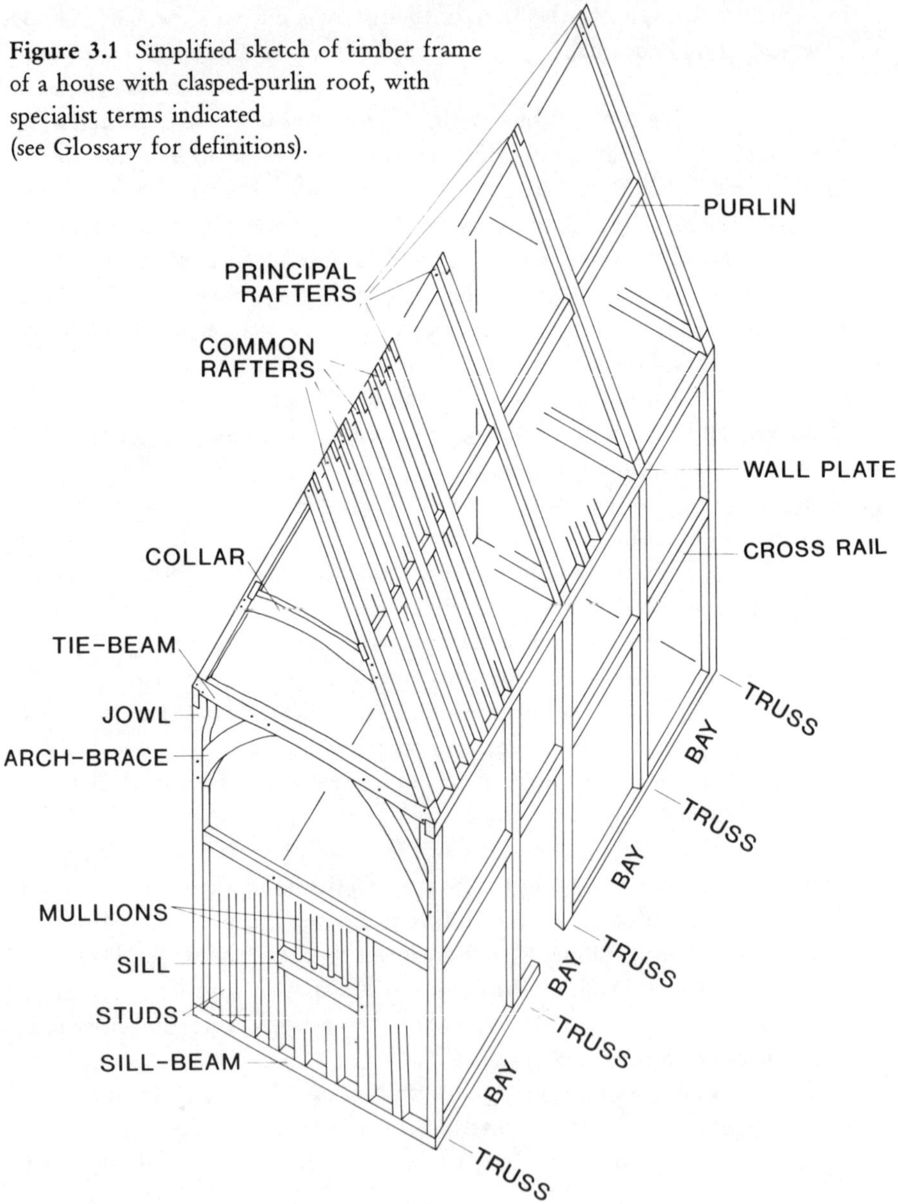

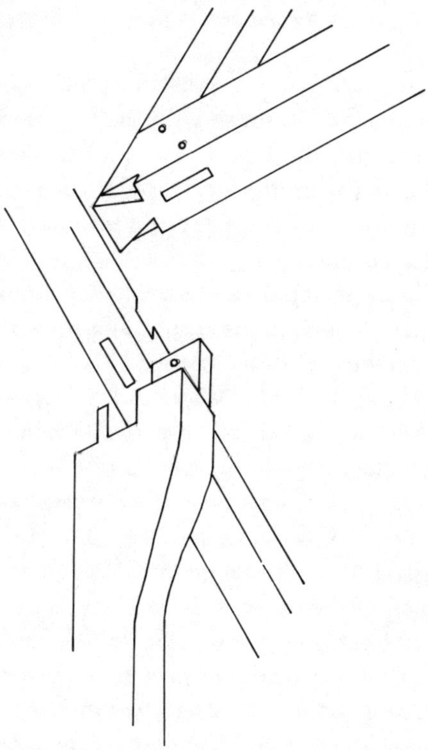

Figure 3.2 Tie-beam lap-dovetail assembly.

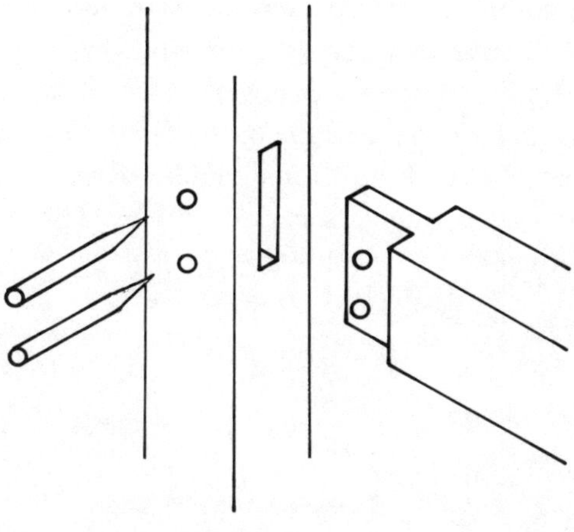

Figure 3.3 Mortice-and-tenon joint "faced-in" towards the viewer.

which has pegging driven into it, so that the points of the pegs are on the other side while the bases are flush with the timber (Fig. 3.3).

(d) The "quiet and orderly translation of trees into buildings" so that the symmetry of timbers within the tree is reflected in the building.

For the 15th- and 16th-century buildings dealt with here, these rules may be taken as more or less constant.

The dominant building material in pre-industrial Suffolk was wood, and more specifically oak: of all the houses, only Sparrows Hall, Stanstead, was built of another wood (elm) and only Stanstead Hall is of brick. The framing of a building is best thought of as a Meccano kind of construction, a rigid timber skeleton carefully jointed together with the joints held – but ideally not supported – by wooden pegs. Nails were rarely used until the later 17th century. The frame would then be covered or infilled with panels of wattle and rendering (Plate 2a). Timber framing and a box-frame method of construction require expertise in both precise measurements, fine carpentry technique and considerable prefabrication, with each truss being "reared" on site.

In what follows only the most basic rules of layout will be given. The resolution will consequently be less fine than that given by Glassie, but will cope with minor variations more easily and be more accessible to the reader and flexible to use. An account of changing technical competence will be given in Chapter 7.

While generally conforming to the rules given above, houses may be divided into three groups within the period 1400–1700: open, transitional and closed. This is a typological classification that corresponds roughly to temporal divisions in the early and late 16th century. The logic of these titles will become clear in Chapters 4, 5 and 6.

A fairly simple competence characterizes open and enclosed houses (Fig. 3.4, overleaf). Open houses are all centred around the layout of a central hall open to the roof and its upper and lower ends. Closed houses vary little around a plan with lobby entry backing onto the chimney-stack with separate chimney-bay in the timber frame. The middle period is one of transition between these two related though separate systems. The story of this transition is the central theme of this study.

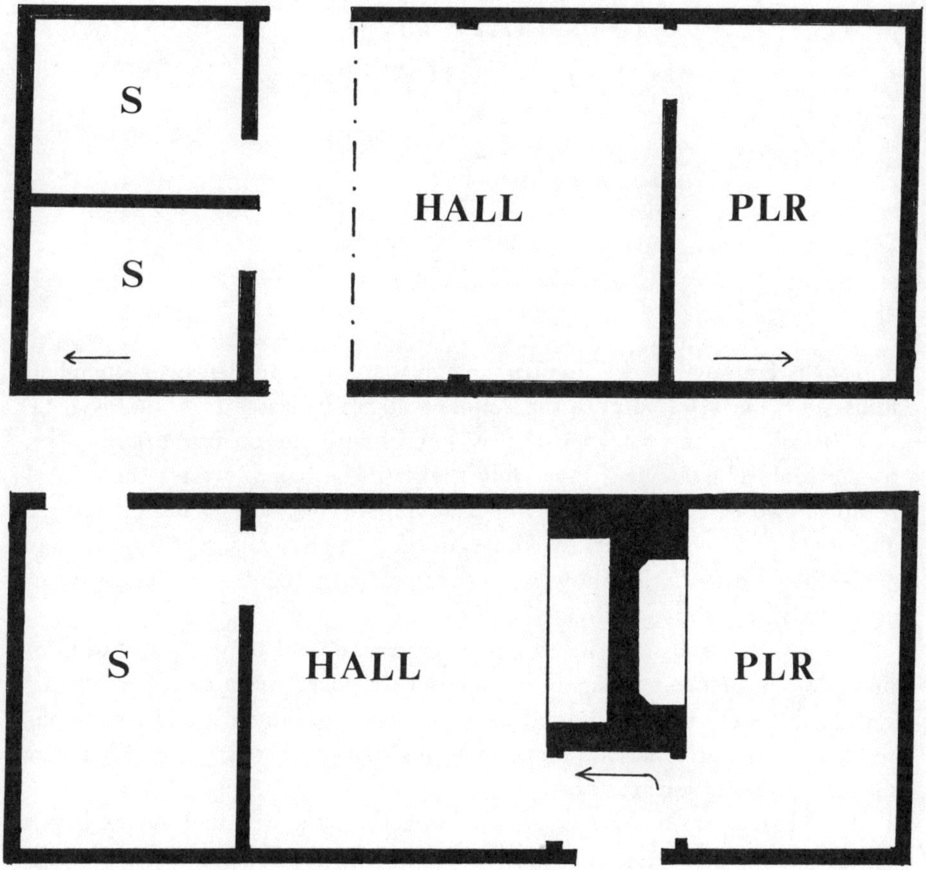

Figure 3.4 Simplified plans of open-hall house (above) and three-cell lobby-entry house (below).

CHAPTER 4
OPEN HOUSES

Suffolk is famous for the number and quality of its medieval or open-hall houses. Of the 116 houses in the sample that can be classified with any accuracy, 40 fall into this category, that is, houses with one or more rooms open to the roof. This room is invariably the hall; the hall is always the central room of two or three. Such open-hall houses survive, usually heavily altered and converted into modern dwellings, in their thousands across England and Wales. Their distribution, however, is strongly clustered. One of the strongest concentrations is found in wood-pasture Suffolk.

This chapter will first sketch out a "grammar" and basic classification of open houses, before moving on to consider the social meanings of the spatial system thus delineated. The outlines of an open grammar are fairly simple, resulting in a fairly narrow range of forms or rules listed below. There are only a few exceptions to these.

1 The "base unit" is the *bay*. At this level the structural unit of the bay is congruent with the spatial unit of the *cell*. Both parlour and service cells are of one bay while larger rooms such as the hall are formed of aggregates of bays. The base unit, therefore, combines construction with layout.

2 Two bays are combined to form the *hall*. The only known exception is the small single-bay hall at Depden, the only house built with aisled construction; since aisled construction is a rather different affair technically from post-and-truss framing this house is unique within the sample. A one-bay open hall is also known from Pebmarsh in neighbouring Essex as well as from other areas of Britain (cf. Smith 1975: 41), but other examples of early smaller houses in Essex usually have open halls of two bays (Hewitt 1974). The bays may be of similar or different lengths, and the result may or may not approximate to a square; the sample is too small to draw consistent rules on this clause.

Semantic elements, in other words elements assigning meaning to the space created, have already entered the competence at this point since the two bays are traditionally designated as *upper* and *lower*, with these words having social as well as architectural resonance. Rule 3 applies to the lower bay.

3 A pair of *opposed doors* is added. This can either be within the lower bay of the hall, with no permanent partition, or as part of a "screens-passage", with a spere truss or more frequently a screens partition dividing the doors and passage from the hall. The choice between these rules is probably partly a matter of relative status and/or size. Traditionally, a spere truss is composed of screens but with a wide central opening and is used in conjunction with a moveable partition (Mercer 1975: 232). This use of a moveable partition may be the case also with opposed doors with no screens at all, although this is unlikely in smaller houses.

4 A *service end* is added. This is as either:
   (a) a *one-bay cell*. This is usually divided into two symmetrical rooms, and has symmetrical service doors leading onto the screens passage or hall immediately on either side of a central post in the truss. Since such cells have very often been rebuilt, it is difficult to demonstrate this rule absolutely. However, all the open houses with some evidence of service cells had positive evidence that this arrangement was the rule.
   (b) a *service wing*. This last has the symmetrical arrangement of two doors flanking a central post, but the arrangement of rooms behind this may be asymmetrical. The wing may extend to the rear rather than to the front.

Layers Breck, Rougham, is the only example of a house where the symmetrical arrangement is broken by a stair running directly off the screens passage into the upper floor of the service wing, rather than access being through the lower floor. This pattern is more frequently seen in other areas and may be a feature confined to larger houses. Layers, however, is unusual in other ways; it has an extended service wing running back in a house of otherwise "Wealden" type, and a series of serving-hatches by the rear external door (Fig. 4.1). These may relate to the provision of a smoke bay at the end of this wing and hence possible baking functions,[1] also seen in a separate serving hatch at Mill House, Alpheton (Fig. 4.2). In these two houses separate access may be required by the household to a separate suite of well proportioned, possibly high-status set of rooms over.

At this point the ground plan of the simplest houses is complete. For example, Frogs Hall, Barrow, is a large high-status, three-bay, two-cell house of this type. At the other end of the scale, the tiny house near Manor Farm, Monks Eleigh (Plate 6a), has room within its gutted, collapsed frame for only two cells.

5 A parlour or chamber is added to the upper end of the hall. Again, this may be in one of two forms:
   (a) a one-bay parlour, the door being at one end of the hall partition (the

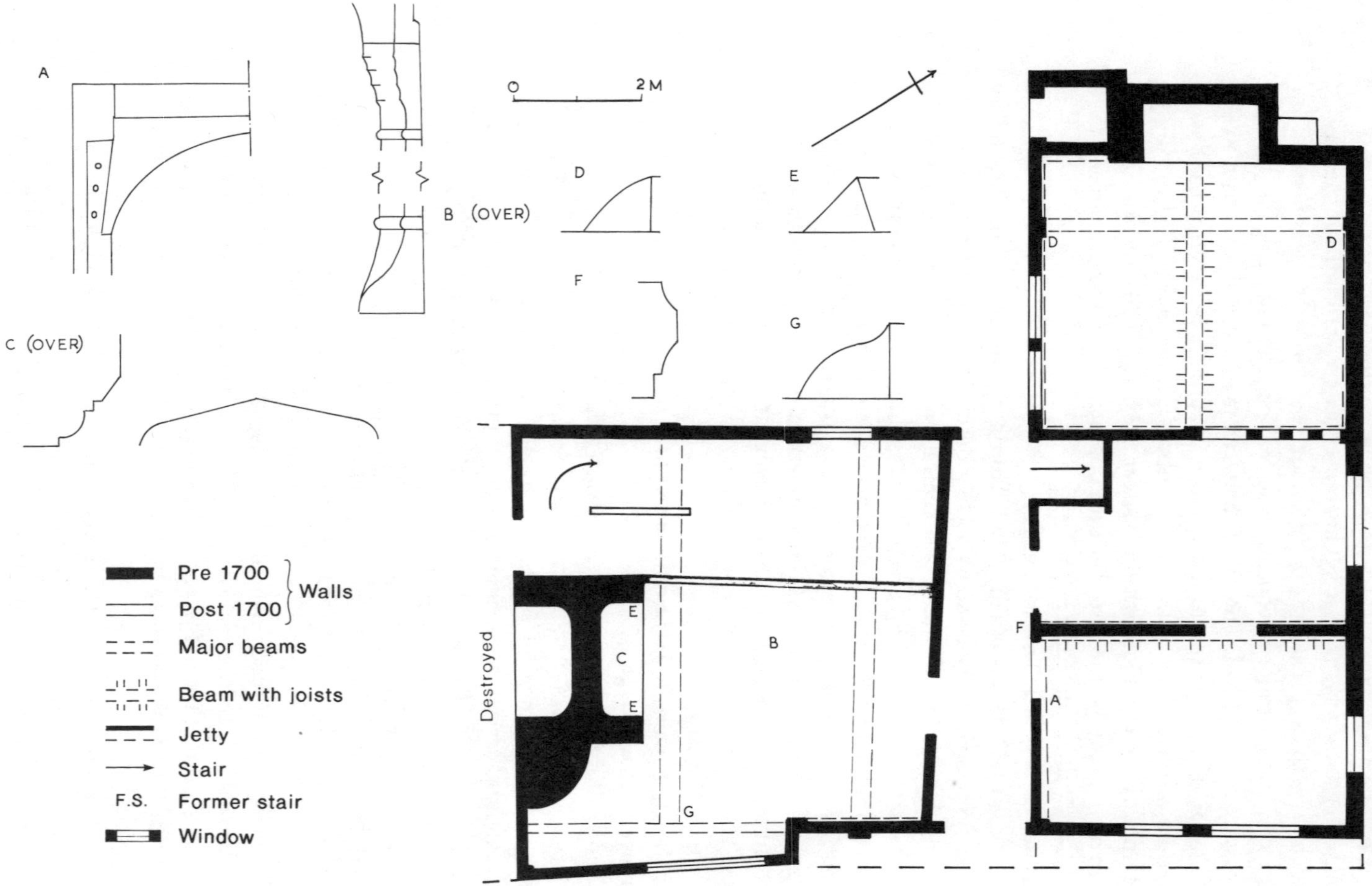

Figure 4.1 Layers Breck, Rougham: a 15th-century "Wealden" house with service wing of the same phase. The parlour wing has been destroyed, but the rest of the main range has exposed framing with close studding, moulded bressumers, and plain joist ends and brackets. The hall has a sooted crown-post roof (Plate 3a). Screens passage has a moulded cross-rail to S, and indications of a spere truss. The front door has mortices in posts and cross-rail over for probable porch. The wing has a fine pair of four-centred arched doors. Door into central partition is inserted. A smoke bay to E; crown-post roof over. In the later 16th century, a stack and ceiling was inserted into the hall. Probably at this point the hall wall-plate was underbuilt and a stack inserted into the smoke bay in the wing. The date of the destruction of the parlour end is uncertain. C18/19 partition inserted into hall along with stair.

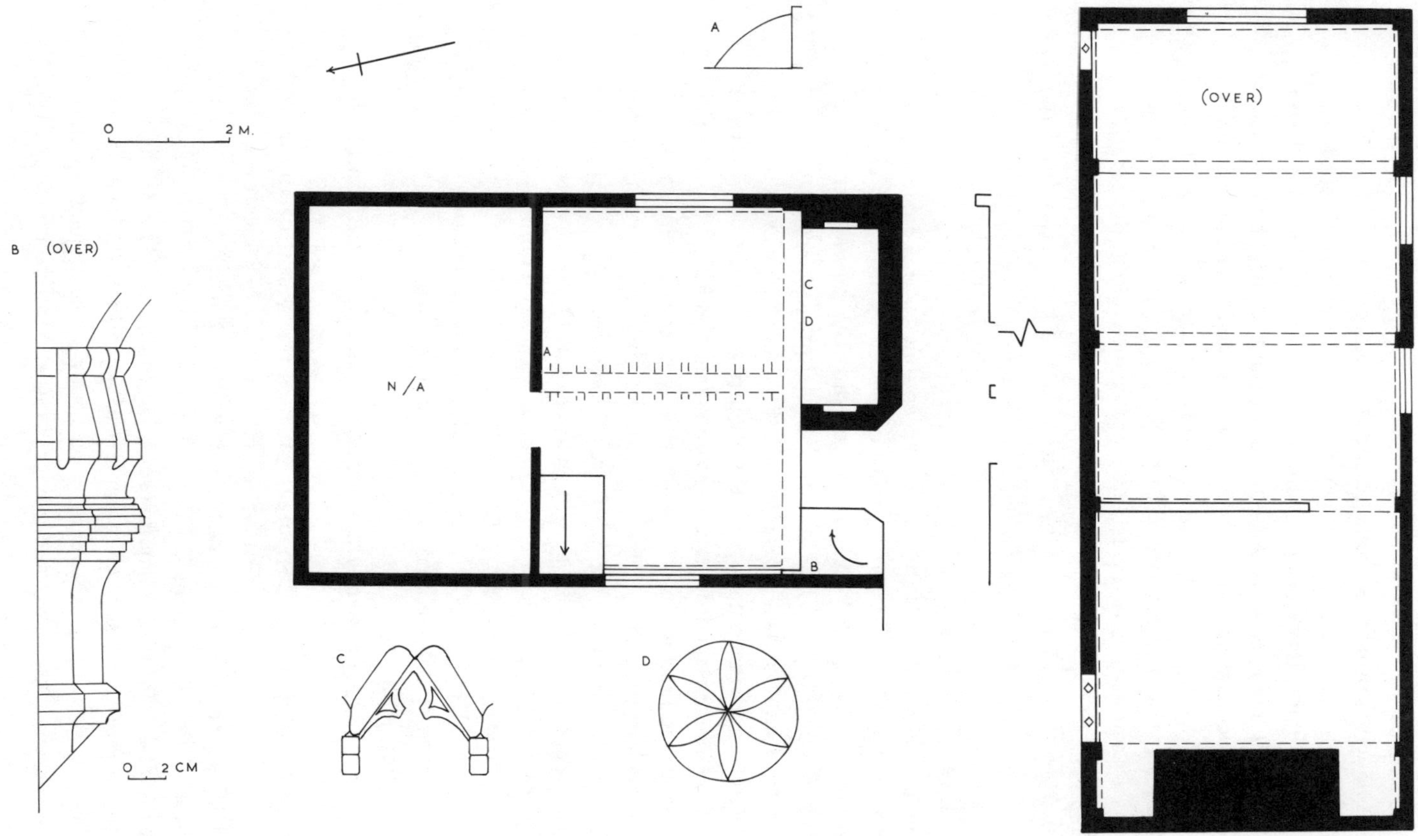

Figure 4.2 Mill House, Alpheton: a large, early 15th century open-hall house. The first phase is a hall with cross-passage and service cross-wing. The hall has a fine arch-braced tie with ornate crown-post and corbels to the arch-braces. The rafters are sooted. At the upper end of the hall there are traces of a raised dais end, now destroyed. The cross-wing has the site of a stair in the W service room, and a four-centred arched door to E. It has four irregular bays. There are four crown-posts. A late 15th-century stack was inserted into the hall, backing on to the through-passage. It has arched recesses, arcading over the lintel, and remains of a castellated top. Around the same time, a smoke bay was inserted at the western, rear end of the service wing. The mid-16th-century ceiling in the hall is carried on inserted cross-rails and spine beam. The parlour may have been rebuilt in the form of a wing at this or a later date. There are several later alterations, including 17th- or 18th-century outshuts on the N side of the crosswing and the insertion of a 16th- or early 17th-century stack into the smoke bay.

only exception is Shepherds Cottage, Hawstead, where the parlour was of two bays);

(b) a parlour wing, usually of two or more rooms.

Most parlour wings are of two or three bays, although two (Street Farm, Brent Eleigh; Honeyhill, Little Saxham) are probably longer than this. Extra bays or cells seem simply to be added on behind the parlour. Some of these rooms at both service and parlour ends may well be workshops, particularly in and around the cloth producing centres south of Bury.

It is well known that the practice within "Wealden" houses is to lay out the parlour as an ordinary jettied cell, but to place a tie along the length of the cell rather than across it. The movement of this one beam by 90 degrees, therefore, changes the cell into a wing, marks off the high-status from the low-status end, and divides it conceptually if not spatially into two bays.

6 Upward extension: the hall has no chamber above it, and is open to the roof; all other rooms have a chamber above.

There are several houses which may be exceptions to this rule. Poplars Farm, Brettenham (Fig. 4.3), has no evidence of partitions or of ceiling at the service end; all the ceilings have been inserted into the house near Manor Farm, Monks Eleigh (Plate 6a), Seldom In, Poslingford (Fig. 4.4), and Swan Cottage and the Old Cottage, Brent Eleigh (Fig. 4.5). This is admittedly negative evidence, and in some if not the majority of these cases former ceilings may be either masked or have been removed and reinserted at some point. Lack of any ceilings is almost certain at least at the house near Manor Farm, where much of the frame is exposed. It is certain that no partitions ran above tie level at Poplars, since the whole roof is sooted.

Parallels to these houses may be sought in a series of Devon houses, which have remains of head-height partitions under a formerly completely open roof. These partitions were subsequently preserved when upper storeys were inserted over them (Alcock & Laithwaite 1973). It is likely that two or three of the houses mentioned above were of this or similar form.

7 *Jettying*: jettying is the practice of having an overhang at first-floor level (see Ch. 7, Fig. 7.2). Crosswings have jetties and a gable at the front. Cells are not jettied.

Examples are known from other areas (such as the Weald of south-east England) of houses jettied on the end wall (Harris 1978: 67). However, this does not appear to be commonly practised in western Suffolk, either at this or later periods: the only example from the sample is the 1607 phase of Thurston End Hall, Suffolk, a supravernacular building. (The Guildhall, Laxfield, a few kilometres east of the sample area, is another supravernacular example.) The only examples of a wing with no evidence of jettying are at Swan Cottage, Brent Eleigh, and the service wing at Mill House, Alpheton;

however, evidence for later underbuilding may be obscured in the latter case.

8 *Roofing*: ends of roofs are either gabled, hipped, or a variety of the two. Many wings have gables at the front and hips at the back, suggesting that gables were used for display and hips where this was not a factor. This contrasts with later houses, where gabled roofs predominate (see Ch. 7).

9 *Piercing*: except where otherwise stated, windows are in the centre of the walls of the cells they pierce. The hall is lit by a window or windows in the upper bay.

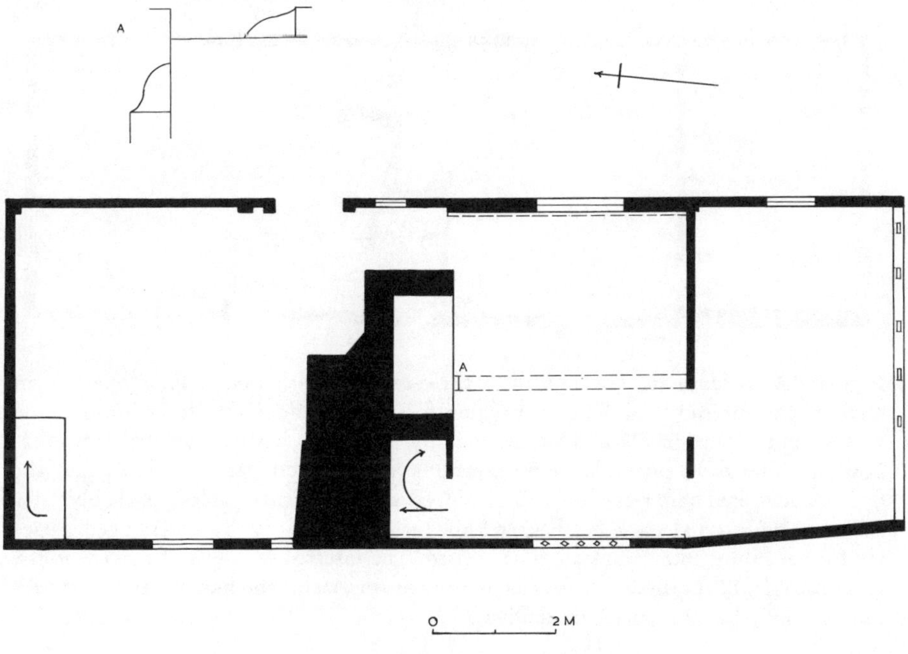

Figure 4.3 Poplars, Brettenham: a smaller three-cell open-hall house, standing within a moated site. There are four bays. The parlour end has a studded partition with arch-braces, and probably former external door. The two-bay hall has five mortices for a diamond-mullioned window in its upper bay. The lower bay of the hall and service area is obscured by later alterations. Crown-post roof, partly rebuilt and sooted all the way along: no partitions above tie level. In the later 16th to early 17th centuries, the stack was inserted backing on to the cross-passage.

This relatively simple set of rules will generate all and only the forms of open-hall houses found. The only exception is the hall-plus-service wing type, which is theoretically possible but which has no definite examples from the sample of houses studied.

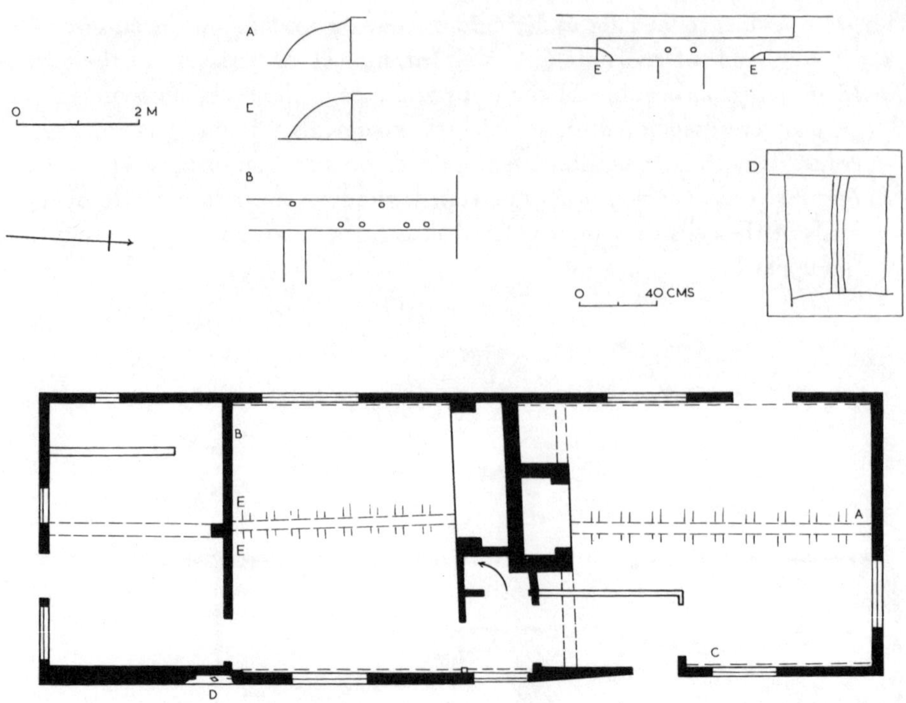

Figure 4.4 Seldom In, Poslingford: a three-cell open-hall house. First phase form unclear: parlour end to S. There is pegging for a former door into the parlour at the W end, and it is probable that the door frame now to E has been moved from that position. The roof, probably coupled-rafter type, has been largely rebuilt, but the occasional sooted rafter survives. One hipped end; the other gabled, probably later rebuilt. The inserted stack has been rebuilt to N; an oven has been destroyed. Space for former lobby entry and stair thus created. The inserted ceiling is of narrow joists, and probably 17th century. It may be later than the stack. The house was extensively renovated in the 19th and 20th centuries.

If we look at the numbers of different types of house produced (Fig. 4.6), the dominance of the three-cell type without wings is clearly seen. If only the randomly sampled houses are taken dominance is even more marked. This pattern could not be expected from the national literature: the majority of examples in Mercer's national survey (1975), for example, have wings of some form. I suggest that this biased perception is due, first, to the difficulty of identifying open-hall houses from external evidence in the absence of crosswings and, secondly, the bias towards larger open-hall houses with wings inherent in any sample that is not undertaken on a random basis.

The class of smaller houses thus identified is of a distinctive date as well as form.[2] Where early 15th-century houses have been identified, they are usually larger houses with wings that appear to be of high, probably manorial, status.

We are left, therefore, with a sudden growth of housebuilding at the level of medium- to small-sized farmhouses without crosswings in the later 15th century.[3] This growth is paralleled in other areas of England, for example by that noted by Giles for the aisled houses of the southern Pennines, which are probably no earlier than 1475 (Giles 1985: 27).

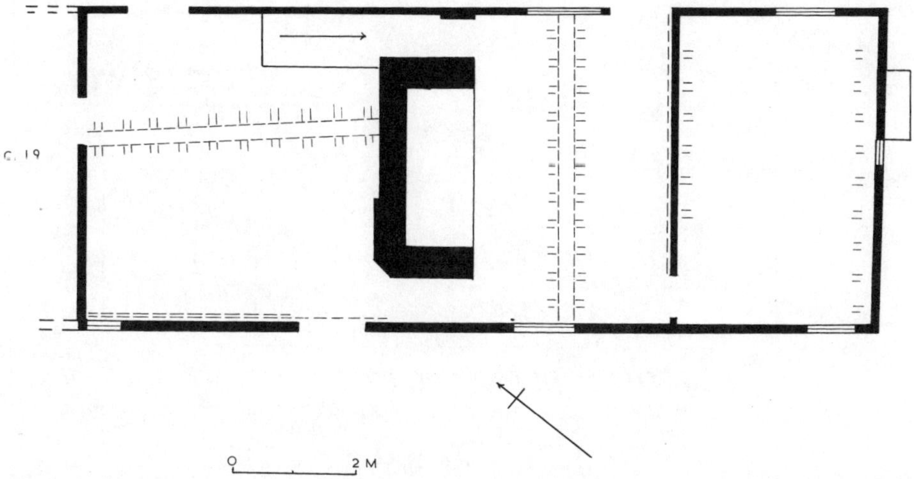

Figure 4.5 Old Cottage, Brent Eleigh: a three-cell house with 15th-century core, much modified. Probably a simple coupled-rafter roof. It is possible that former partitions only rose to cross-rail height. The stack was inserted probably backing on to the cross-passage, into the lower end of the hall. The inserted main cross-beam is carried on lintels over modern windows. The ceiling to NW has also been inserted, with sooted rafters reused as ceiling beams.

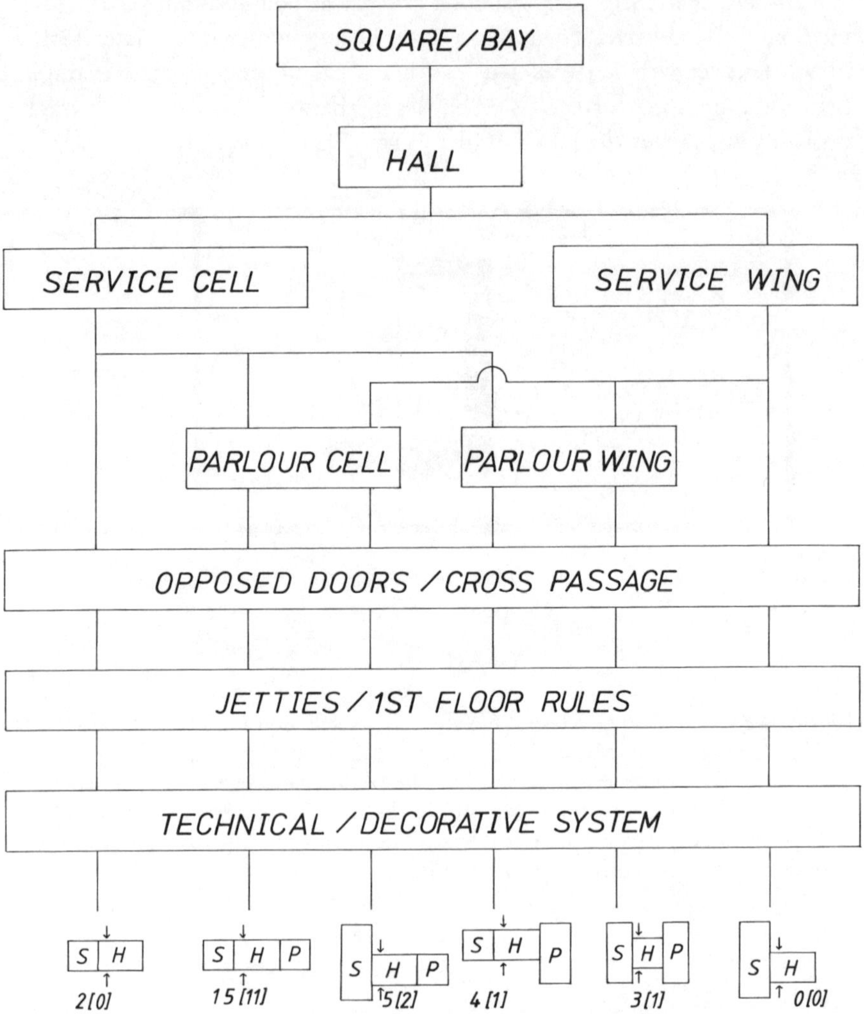

Figure 4.6 Sketch of competence for an open-hall house.

Interpretation

It is . . . clear that changes in the nature of the open hall coincided with changes in late medieval society, that the open hall disappeared as the modern world came into being, and that medieval social relations were essential to it. To establish the precise rôle of the open hall is one of the essential tasks now facing students of vernacular architecture (Mercer 1975: 22).

The form of open-hall houses is so familiar to most scholars in the field that few stop to ask why such a form persisted in popularity for so long. The conventional explanation for the open-hall form is related to the central hearth. It is argued that in the absence of a brick chimney stack, the smoke needed space to disperse among the rafters, leaving the atmosphere of the living space reasonably clear.

Objections to this view are very powerful. First, it is unclear whether such an upper space is in fact needed. Other cultures are able to use open hearths within much lower roofed areas, such as the "black houses" of the Scottish islands. Secondly, if such a commonsensical view is taken, there are two drawbacks to the open hearth: the cold, draughty and smoky interior produced (as the medieval writer Langland comments: Goodridge 1959: 215), and the high fire risk involved in letting the sparks and smoke disperse in the rafters and thatch of the roof. Occupants were clearly aware of the fire risk since a few houses had plaster laid between the rafters to reduce this; an example is known from Wattisfield, just east of the area discussed here (Colman 1967). In other areas of England, houses had timber and plaster "firehoods" over the hearth but retained the hall open to the roof (cf. Giles 1985). If this explanation is to be convincing, therefore, it is necessary to postulate that a brick stack was either beyond the knowledge of the East Anglian builder or could not be afforded at this time.

It is difficult to believe that brick stacks were unknown. The principle of the chimney had been known in England since at least the 12th century, and they were present in larger buildings all over Suffolk. In any case, there is some documentary evidence to refute this notion. Two letters written around 1446 in the archives of the manor of Havering-atte-Bower, in neighbouring Essex, ask for a "ducher or a flemying" brickmason to be sent over, or failing that a young Englishman ("for a yonge man is sharpest of witte and cunning"), to "make a Dowble Chemeny of Brykke". This is clearly not a major piece of work, since it is requested that he finish within a fortnight (quoted in Ryan 1986: 112).

The proposition that stacks were too expensive involves the corollary, that their eventual introduction in the 16th century was caused by the falling price of brick and/or rising wealth levels. This is difficult to prove or disprove. Falling brick prices must be as much a consequence as a cause of rising demand in the long run, given economies of scale in production. In any case, it is doubtful that brick prices would conform to a normal supply-and-demand model at the local level, since the bulk of consumption of brick was taking place at the elite level (Howard 1985, Smith 1985). The availability of bricks for use in socially middling houses probably depended on social and spatial proximity to a high-status builder employing a brick manufacturer rather than on market forces. This seems to have been the case at Havering, where the writer suggests he go to nearby Witham to get a brickmason, probably from the building works going on at Faulkborne Hall there (Ryan 1986: 113).

It could be argued that traditional builders simply did not know any other way: that they built open-hall houses because they were naturally conservative. However, this begs the question of why they then chose to change when they did. The technique of framing with ceiling joists supported on cross-rails and beams is fully present in the service and parlour ends of open houses; many houses have cross-rails running across the open hall. Therefore the technical knowledge and ability did exist. Builders simply chose not to utilize that knowledge in the context of the hall.

Clearly, other explanations are thus either inadequate or partial. We therefore have to return to Mercer's proposition that the open hall must be seen in the context of the social life that went on within it and the social meanings it carried. The social meaning of the open hall, and the way that structure carried that meaning, is not difficult to find at the upper levels of society. It carried the meaning of a social structure that has been variously termed feudal, *Gemeinschaft*, or "peasant traditional" (Dobrolowski 1971: 277) but here will be termed patriarchal: a structure based around the unit of the household, around "good governance and public rule" (Mertes 1988), within which the members of the household were bound together by asymmetrical ties of kinship and dependence.

Following the demographic and structural changes of the later 14th century, the 15th century saw shifts in the relationship between landlord and tenant, employer and labourer, and master and servant (Hilton 1975: 239–45). In particular, the ranks of the upper peasantry in many regions became a distinctive group, with security of landholding and employing a varying number of servants and day-labourers in their own right. As Hilton has commented (1985: 252), the ambivalence of the contemporary literature towards this group indicates its potential threat to the established medieval order and its attempted cooption into the established view of society.

These national shifts can be seen particularly in wood-pasture areas such as the southern part of the sample area, where the upsurge in building at the socially middling level in the later 15th century has already been noted. Wood-pasture areas may have been more conducive to housebuilding, given the weaker restraints on individuals within parish communities (Williamson & Bellamy 1987: 28) and consequent polarization of village society with a growing class of richer peasants able to build permanent houses. However, "despite the growing polarisation of village society [in wood-pasture areas] its cohesion and solidarity were maintained" (Razi 1987: 388) and this distinction should not be overemphasized.

Within his house the family head was in an ambivalent position. His relations to his social inferiors (women, servants and day-labourers) were governed by established rules of medieval patriarchy. These rules made the household the centre of political life, in the sense that it was the central setting for the playing out of unequal social relations (Walzer 1966: 149). Thus tension was created. On the one hand there were new social forces producing an upper class of peasantry, and enabling this group to build substantial houses surviving to the present day. On the other hand the way in which this group manifested its relation to the world was an older one, expressed in their houses in terms of established patriarchal values.

There was also a tension between the ideal community expressed by those values and the actual behaviour of the social subordinates involved. Over half the late medieval population of East Anglia was made up of servants or day-labourers. Shortage of labour meant that the day-labourer could command a high wage, and he did not scruple to enforce this (Hilton 1975: 31). The scale of reports of servant insubordination is probably only limited by the nature of the documentary evidence. The rôle of women in brewing, dairying and other activities gave them a considerable degree of independence within the household. It has been suggested for a later period that this was particularly true in wood-pasture areas (Amussen 1988: 90).

It is therefore interesting to find that the layout of the peasant house bears a strong resemblance to its larger counterparts in its basic tripartite design and the layout of the open hall. I suggest that this is due to the continued use by the builder of the rules and meanings of medieval patriarchy, a use noted by scholars in other spheres of discourse (Hilton 1975: 17), and thus the architectural system that went with them. Thus architectural conservatism is explained in terms of the meanings it carries and their manipulation by social actors, in this case by the socially middling builder of the house. Archaeologically this system of meaning can be examined in two ways: through a consideration of segregation and of symmetry.

It is commonly asserted that the open-hall house lacked segregation. While holding some truth, this statement is simplistic and needs further exploration. There are just as many divisions at ground-floor level as in many later houses, and many upper-floor rooms, away from the main areas of circulation, are treated elaborately in architectural terms.

The more complex reality is that the layout of the open house encodes a pattern of circulation that involves a tension between what Girouard, in dealing with "polite" or elite medieval architecture, calls "centrifugal" and "centripetal" forces (Girouard 1978: 30; Mertes 1988). As Langland complained, the master and wife enjoyed differential privacy; the convention was to eat in the hall at the upper end, after which they had the option of withdrawing. The servants and others presumably had to bed down in the hall itself. In addition, the upper floors of parlour wings in particular, and the rooms over the service that may have been used as solars (upper-floor retiring rooms), have large windows, and framing exposed internally (Figs 4.7 & 4.8). All parlour and service wings have two full storeys and what appear to be fine suites of rooms above, though no definite examples have a ceiling at wall-plate level (i.e. between the first floor and the roof space).

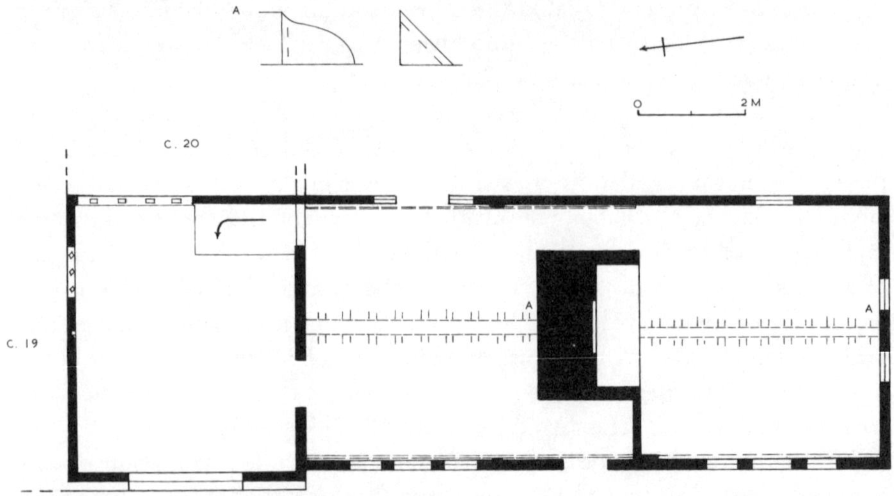

Figure 4.7 Tudor House, Hitcham: an open-hall house with service crosswing. The two-bay wing has a sooted roof above and had a further cell to S; there was also a narrow jetty, now underbuilt. Stair in SW corner probably in former position; arch-braced tie over. This phase had cross-rails in the main range and a crown-post roof, sooted throughout. The stack was inserted in the 16th century. The hall fireplace is blocked but the other fireplace is large and possibly a kitchen fireplace, in which case the house was "turned round" at this point. The lobby entry created has no room for a stair; there was a former stair on the other side. At the same time the hall ceiling was inserted and the room to S of stack rebuilt. The room to S of stack was damaged by fire and renovated in the late 19th / early 20th century. In the 19th century the house was refronted.

At the other end of the house, the service rooms were separated even from the hall by the screens passage or space between the opposed doors. They thus had more spaces and doors between them and the central room than later, post-medieval service areas. The activities of the lower orders were probably separated from the upper by the walls of the house itself, as in later periods (see Ch. 8). The hall provided a central focus or place for interaction between the members of the household, a place for eating and a general work area. The key point is that it was necessary to pass through the hall to get from one end of the house to another: it had centralizing functions.

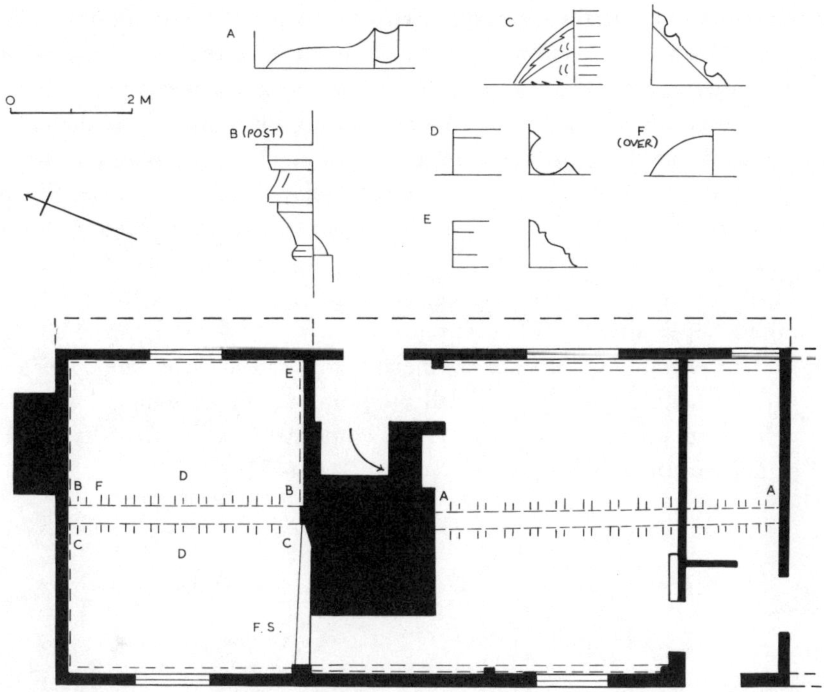

Figure 4.8 Oaklands, Stanstead: there are two separate structures on this site, both 15th century: one was formerly the Guildhall, later reused as a farm building to Oaklands. The Guildhall is not illustrated; it is in the form of a medium-size, three-cell open-hall house. Oaklands itself is an open-hall house with fine parlour crosswing. The roof is well sooted and there are mortices for a crown-post. The main range wall-plate projects in "Wealden" form; two ties are carried on brackets. The hall space appears unusually large. There is no service end, although there is just enough space for a possibly destroyed service end between Oaklands and the Guildhall. The two-bay crosswing has two jetties at the front with projecting brackets, carved bressumers, and moulded arch-braces to the gable collar. Former stair in SW corner. In the 16th century the stack was added and hall ceiling inserted (Plate 3b). A fine lintel in the hall may be taken from another building. Probably at the same time a ceiling was inserted over the parlour. The clasped-purlin parlour roof may have been rebuilt at this point.

If open houses are not unsegregated in any simple sense, neither are they simply asymmetrical. The facade of a Wealden house (Fig. 4.9) or the plan of a three-cell open house (Fig. 3.4) in fact shows a great deal of symmetry, particularly down the long axis. The short axis, across the hall, deliberately uses asymmetry to indicate asymmetry of status through the organization of space. I suggest that the elements of asymmetry are deliberately placed within this framework by the craft tradition to stress social hierarchy. There is no obvious difference in status between the pair of service rooms, probably the dairy and buttery, so they are symmetrically placed to one another. The doors are placed at the lower end of the hall, making the lower bay of the hall draughtier and establishing an equivalence between upper and lower and host and guest for visitors upon their entry to the house. The doors are symmetrical along the short but asymmetrical along the long axis. The hearth is placed centrally and individuals place themselves spatially and socially on either side of it. The windows are in the upper bay, again marked by a projecting oriel window in high-status buildings. Symmetrical raised benches may have lined the walls. Only one house, of probable manorial status, has traces of a raised upper end termed a dais (Mill House, Alpheton: Fig. 4.2). The only known example within the sample area of a canopy over the upper end of the hall, a feature again symbolically stressing the upper end and found in other regions of England (cf. Giles 1985), comes from a house in Lavenham not included in the sample (RCHM records: TL916491).

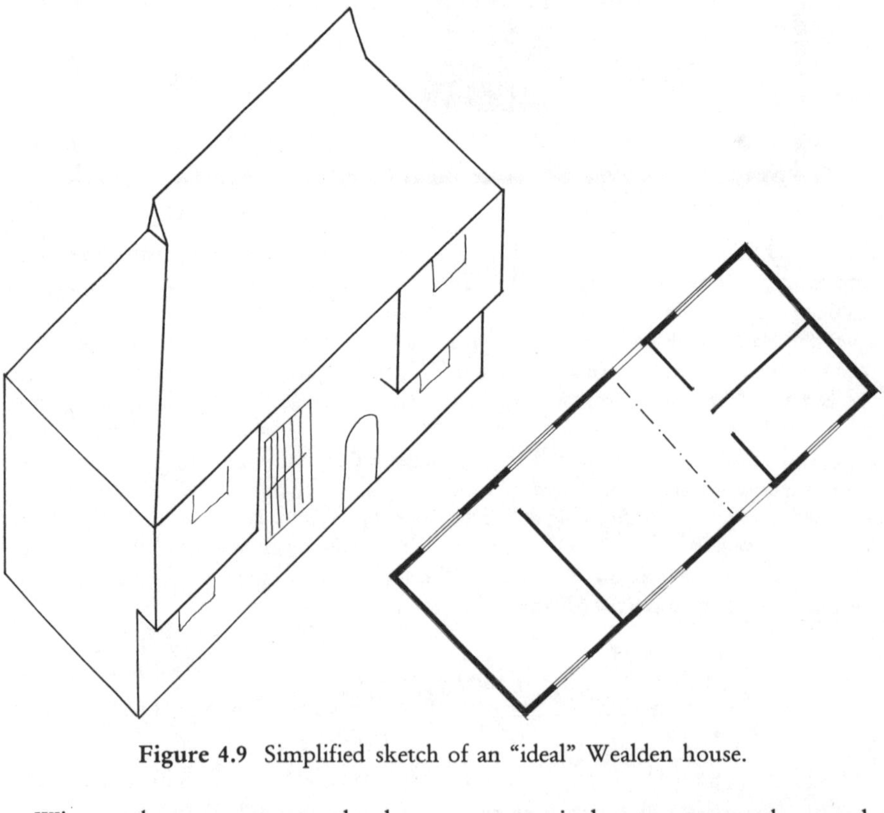

Figure 4.9 Simplified sketch of an "ideal" Wealden house.

Wings, where present, are clearly an asymmetrical arrangement; the sample has roughly equal numbers of parlour and service wings. The service wing, however, still has a pair of doors symmetrical to the hall whatever the arrangement behind (as at Layers Breck, Rougham, and Mill House, Alpheton, where pairs of service doors lead into long service wings running back). Both parlour wings and halls have doors at one or other end of the hall partition, again jarring the symmetry with an indication of status.

It has been suggested for Sussex and Kent that the upper bay of the hall was deliberately made slightly (i.e. one rafter) longer than the lower (Harris 1978: 49). It is not clear whether this was the case in western Suffolk. The evidence from the houses surveyed is not conclusive either way. Five have larger upper bays while four are roughly equal. The average lengths are also roughly equal. However, the space taken up by screens passages is also included in these figures. In other houses, insertion of stacks and other alterations makes it unclear whether these houses had screens passages or opposed doors, although the weight of negative evidence suggests the majority had the latter. Whether equal or not, the division between the upper and lower bays was marked with a fully visible and often impressive open truss surmounted by a crown-post (Plate 3a).

Although mealtimes and other activities were not the occasions for ceremony in smaller houses, it is easy to see how the hall framed everyday action in such a way as to enforce the playing out of socially asymmetrical rôles. At mealtimes the servant would show deference to the master, the wife to husband; the everyday rhythms of work and life would involve movement through the hall, the giving of commands and the showing of implicit respect and subordination.

The open hall, however, did not merely encode the values of the medieval household in a physical form; it also acted, as Moore (1985) might argue, as a text, to both present and misrepresent. The open hall appears an undivided space: it appears open to all; hence the misconception of the lack of segregation. But if the architectural detail marks out the upper bay as the area of the master, this openness is not so much an egalitarian one as a platform for the management of unequal relationships at the everyday, face-to-face level.

I suggest, therefore, that the open hall carried meaning at at least three levels. At the physical level, it directly moulded circulation patterns within the house around its centrality. At the level of formal symbolic code, it acted as an explicit structuring of space along socially hierarchical, patriarchal lines. At the level of spatial text, it signified several different things: it asserted communality and community, but also denoted inequality and segregation at the same time.

We can see now how important it is to allow for the play of different levels of meaning stressed in Chapter 3, since the open hall derived its symbolic and social power through this play.

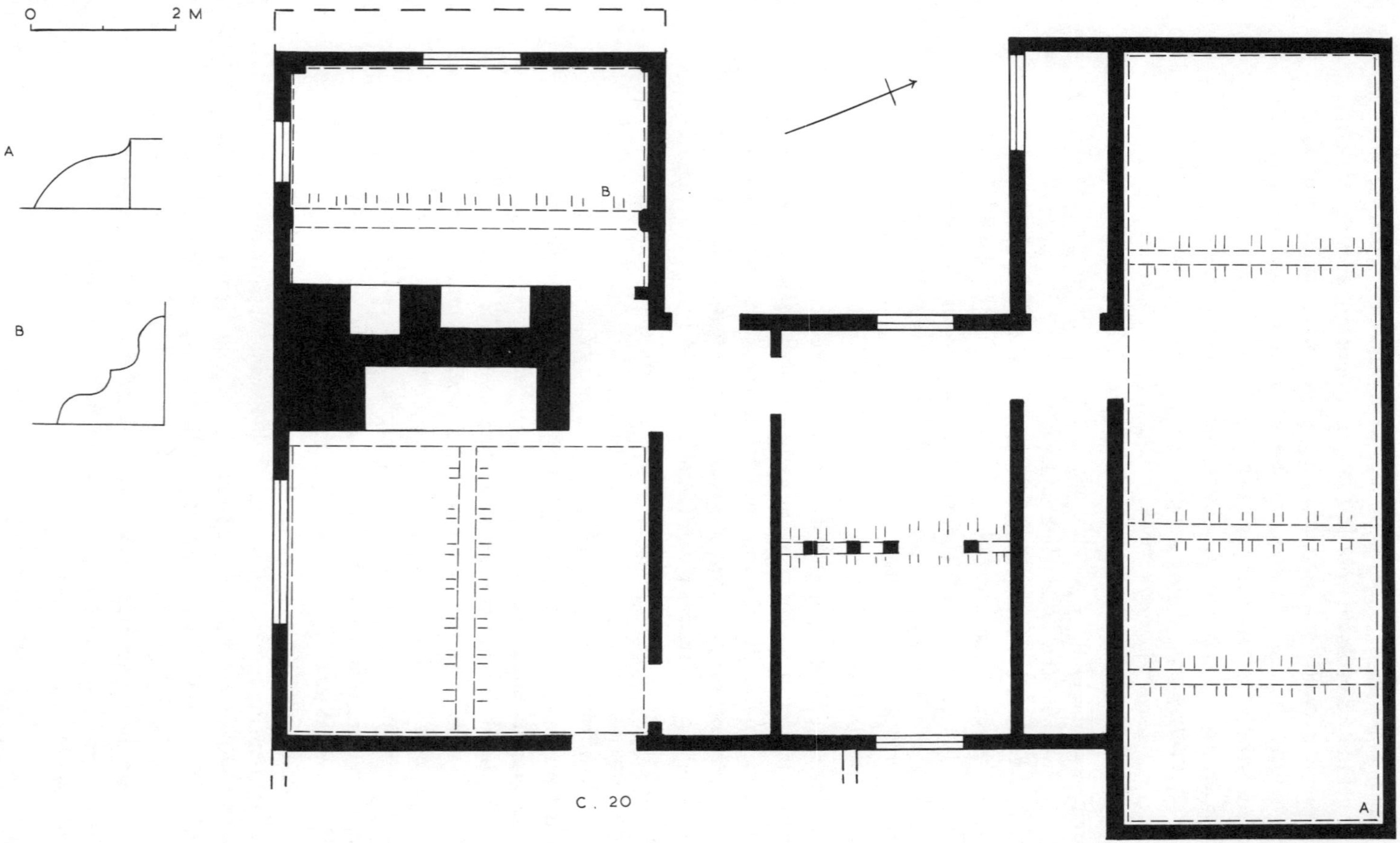

Figure 4.10 Malting Barn, Great Waldingfield: an H-plan, open-hall house, subsequently altered in a complex sequence. The first phase is what is now the wing to N. Three bays; that to E has mortices for a partition. There are unchamfered joists of large scantling and traces of a former jetty at the N end. Roof of coupled-rafter type, with the upper parts to NW sooted. At the NW end, there is a surviving sliding shutter. This is possibly the shell of an early hall-house. The hall and this wing are of different phases. Over the hall, a lightly sooted roof and open truss with wide arch-braces and simple crown-post. Shutter grooves in wall-plates in bay to N, indicating that this was probably the upper end. The cross-wing to S has a jettied front, with plain brackets and bressumer, arch-braces over and close studding. The cross-rails, beams and joists have unstopped, roll-moulded chamfers. Former external door in the NE corner. Wing has an unsooted crown-post roof. Alteration in the 16th century involved conversion of the hall into a service area and insertion of a stack into the parlour wing. The parlour stack has carved lintels, diagonal offsets and an oven. In the C17 the E end of the N wing was partly rebuilt and the outshut to S of the N wing added.

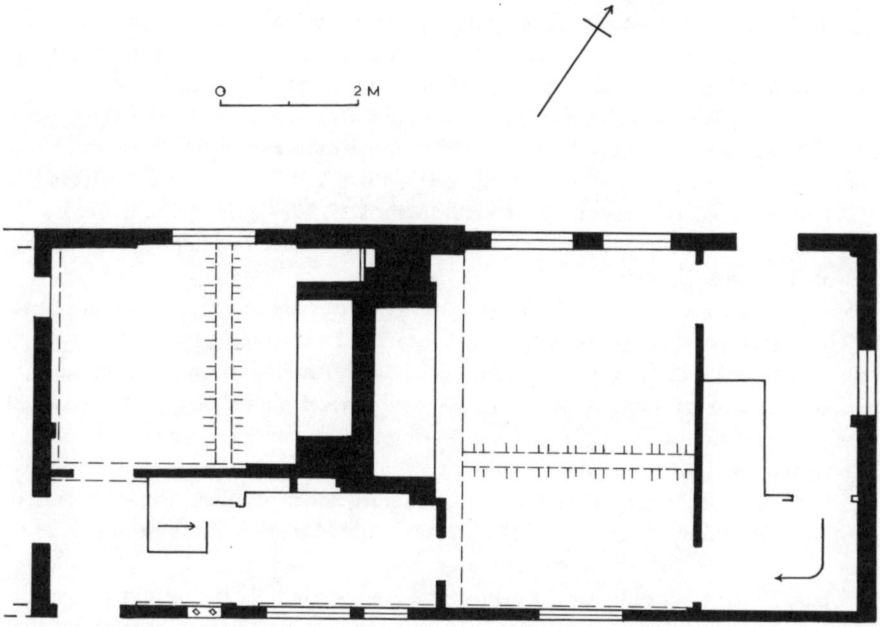

Figure 4.11 Chestnuts, Preston St Mary: a two-phase open-hall house, later modified heavily. The medieval frame includes a blocked door just S of the stack, traces of a diamond-mullioned window to N, and wide divergent tension-braces in the W wall of the hall, defining its upper end. The frame has butt-joints to N and S of stack, and the blocked door appears to have two phases. The roof is masked. A two-phase stack was added and hall ceiling inserted in the 16th century; the house was "turned round" at this point. There are traces that the ceiling to E of the stack is also inserted. In the 17th century a partition was inserted in the room to E. The gabled, thatched roof was probably rebuilt in side-purlin form at this point. Later, the house was converted into two cottages before being converted back into one dwelling in the 20th century. Some traces of herringbone pargeting.

Notes

1. This interpretation was suggested to me by Philip Aitkens.

2. Dating of an individual house is problematic in the absence of evidence. However, I suggest that as a group we can consider whether open houses are later or earlier, and conclude that the bulk of housebuilding activity took place in the latter half and towards the end of the period between *c.* 1400 and the earlier 16th century. There are several reasons for arguing this.

First, wealth levels within the sample area show wide fluctuation within the 15th century. Dymond & Virgoe (1986) demonstrate that, overall, wealth levels did not rise appreciably until the 1460s (at the earliest) after an early 15th-century depression. The wealth generated by the development of the cloth industry at Lavenham appears to rise towards *c.* 1500 according to Dymond & Betterton (1982: 6–14), and by implication this is probably true for the Bury/Lavenham area as a whole where many open houses are located (see Fig. 10.2). Certainly on a national level the wool and cloth trade was hit by disease, low prices and trade embargoes with the continent from the 1420s onwards before recovery in the 1460s (Mate 1987: 526–7). It would, therefore, be surprising if the early 15th century was a period of intense building activity in this area at the vernacular level.

Such a suspicion is confirmed by the stratigraphic evidence. If the rate of housebuilding were constant from, say, *c.* 1350 onwards, we would expect a fairly large number of open houses to be of two or more phases. After all, during the transitional period it is unremarkable to find a house with several phases of rebuilding spaced barely a generation apart. In fact such a development is rare: only three examples are known (Figs 4.9, 4.10, 4.11).

Re-use of timber from earlier houses is almost entirely absent at this point, in contrast to transitional and closed houses. The only exception is Cawston's, Hartest (Fig. 4.12), where the crown-post roof re-uses a few rafters from an earlier building. This suggests that not only are the majority of houses relatively late within the period, but that the framing of the structures they replaced was not worth reusing: thus, that earlier houses were probably of the lighter framing known from 14th-century building in the area. Framing style, crown-post shape, joint forms and similarity to 16th-century framing styles support such a view (Johnson nd: 61–4). Consequently, where surviving crown-posts are of a simple type, edge-halved scarfs are present, and/or the style of the timber framing is late, the house has been interpreted as "mid or late 15th century".

3. One exciting implication, not central to the argument here, is that of a sudden rise in demand for good quality timber in the later 15th century; a demand which continues through the 16th century "building boom". Direct documentary evidence for how woodland was managed to cope with this is lacking, but a study of surviving woodland outside the well known estates of the Abbey of Bury St Edmunds has great potential (Dymond & Martin 1988: 50). Another implication is that Dyer's (1986) arguments for a steady period of good quality housebuilding from the mid 14th century onwards do not appear to apply to western Suffolk.

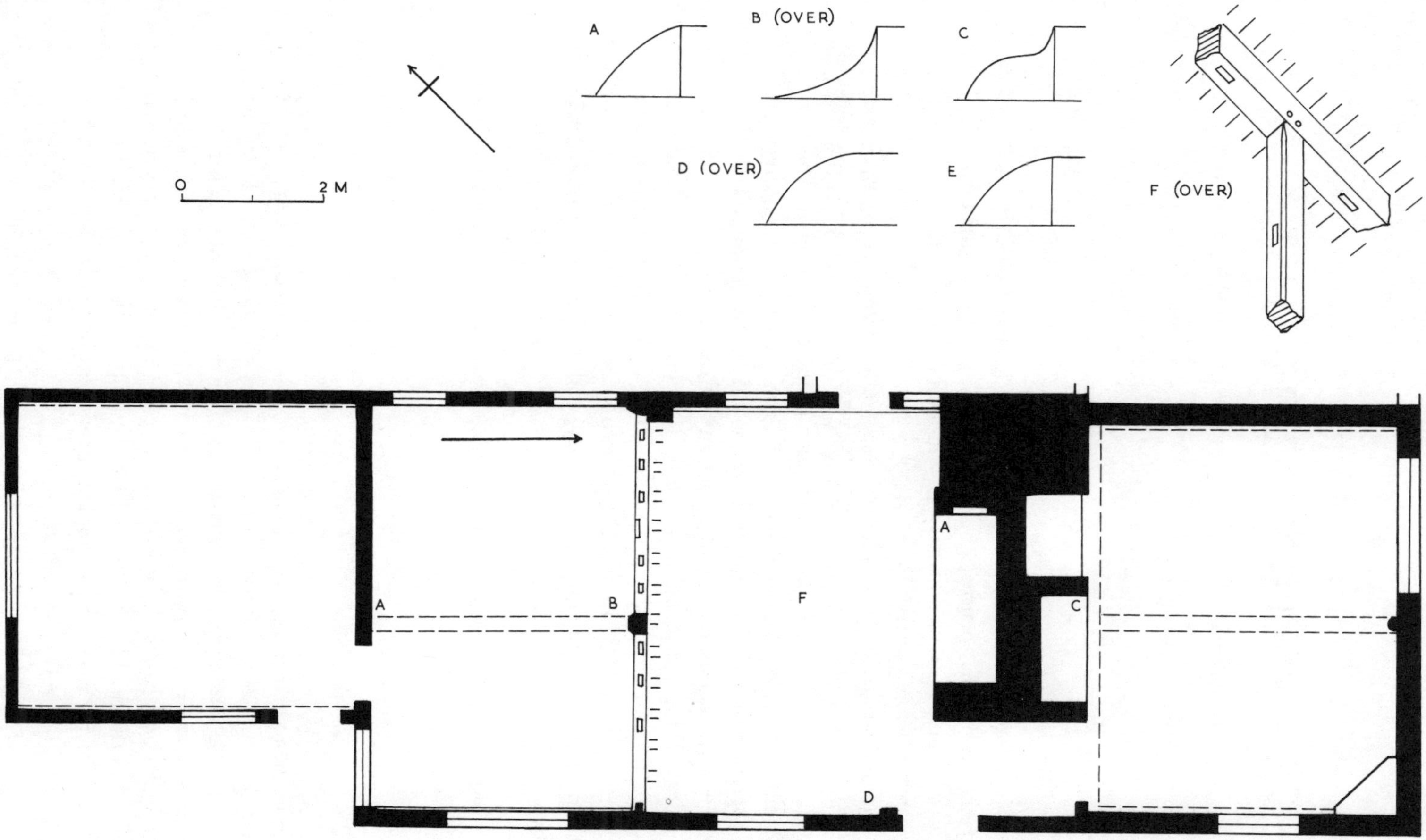

Figure 4.12 Cawston's, Hartest: a three-cell open-hall house. The crown-post roof is preserved down to the sooted slats between the rafters, a few of which have been re-used from a coupled-rafter roof. The hipped end to W has rafters stopping *c.* 60 cm below the apex, probably to form a vent for smoke. The house was "turned round" when ceiled over. The inserted hall fireplace has arched recesses and "herringbone" niches at the back. A lobby entry was inserted by cutting back one of the posts to the former open truss. Stairs were inserted running from the hall N of the stack. The service end was rebuilt as a parlour cell and the tie S of stack moved, either contemporary with or after ceiling-over of hall. A ceiling was subsequently inserted at collar level into this cell. There is a one-storey 17th-century dairy or backhouse to W, largely built of waney wood.

CHAPTER 5
TRANSITIONAL HOUSES

The open-hall tradition came to an end in Suffolk after the early 16th century. By the end of that century, most houses were of the closed, three-cell lobby-entry form (Fig. 3.4). This chapter will look at the picture of change in the intervening, transitional period.

The transitional period saw a great range of building forms produced. House forms range from extreme conservatism in their similarity to open-hall plans to early examples of the dominant form in the closed period. The technical system and decorative details employed show corresponding diversity. This is therefore a period of unusual forms, diverse techniques and often lavish decoration. The rate of building activity of the later 15th century continued unabated through much of the 16th century;[1] some houses show signs of rebuilding or alteration every generation (Plate 4a, Fig. 5.1). Again this rate of building may be related to economic factors: the continued prosperity of the cloth industry up to the mid 16th century, and its decline from the 1560s onwards, in particular (Dymond & Betterton 1982: 32; Dymond & Martin 1988: 112). So the transitional period is remarkable for a continuation of a rate of house-building established from *c.* 1460 onwards.

Conversion of open houses

It is important to remember that all surviving open-hall houses are also by definition transitional and closed houses. That is, almost all the houses discussed in the previous chapter were converted to a plan with ceiling throughout the house and had a chimney stack inserted at some point during the 16th century. Such conversions show as much variation in the way they were carried out and in the final form of the converted house as the newly built transitional houses themselves. The final plans produced, however, do correspond closely with the layouts of new houses.

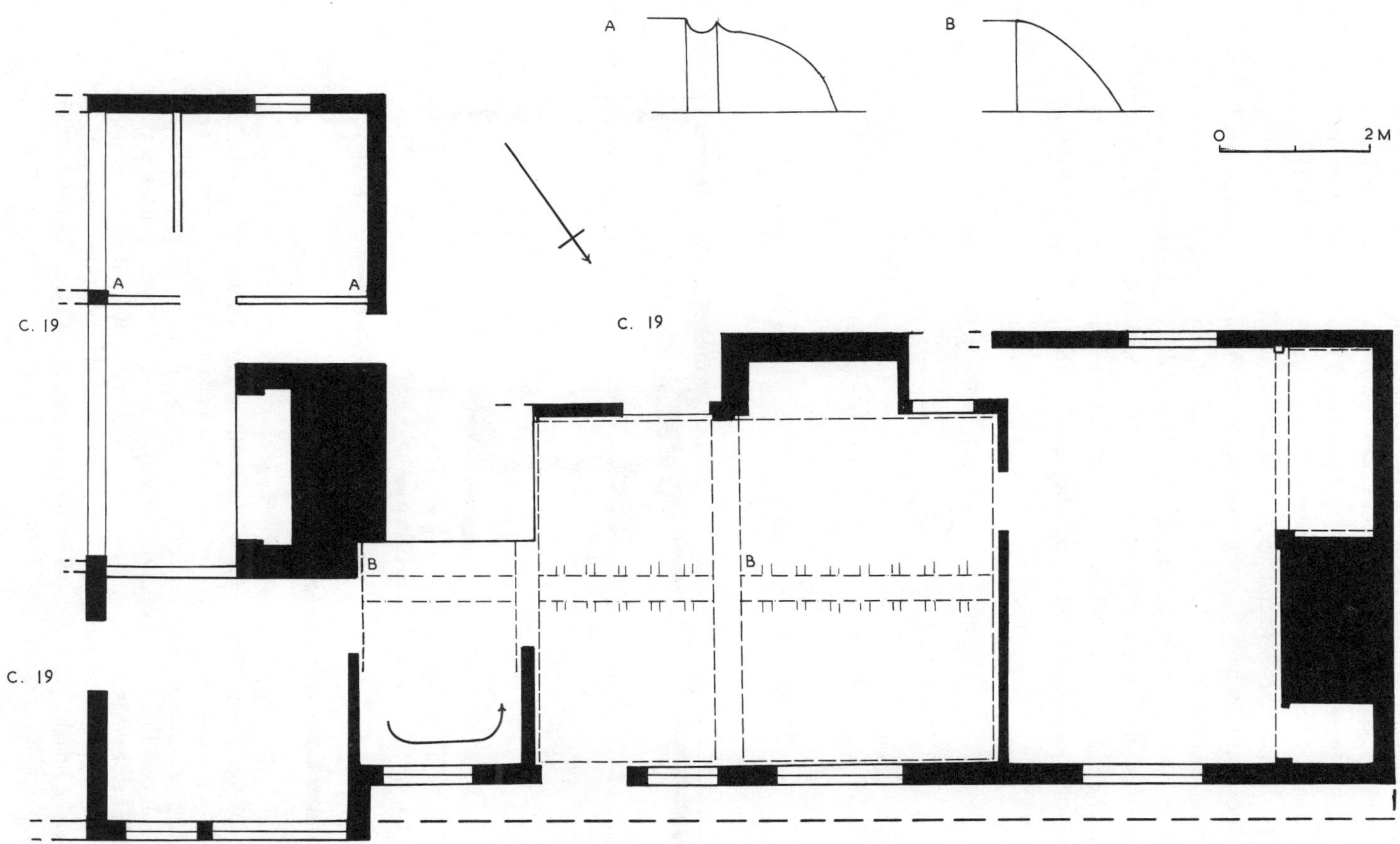

Figure 5.1 Corner Farm, Brent Eleigh: a house with brick nogging, rapidly rebuilt and extended in the 16th century; it may be a piecemeal but complete rebuild of an open-hall house. The first phase is probably the two-bay jettied wing to W, with the stack housed within the frame and four-centred arched doors to N of fireplace at both levels. The mid-16th-century three-bay jettied wing to E is probably also earlier than the main range; the stack in this wing is inserted. The jettied three-bay main range is of two cells. Former opposed doors at W end of hall. The cell to E is obscured by a 19th-century inserted stair. Arch-braced tie and clasped-purlin roof over; the roof is reached by a 16/17th-century stair over the lower bay of the hall. There are large roll-moulded and ovolo-moulded mullioned windows. The date of this final phase is unclear but not later than *c.* 1600. Much of the sequence is obscured by extensive 19th-century restoration; many of the details may have been plundered from other houses.

The simplest method of conversion was to take the whole house down and start again, not necessarily on the same site. Obviously such a method is difficult to detect by the analysis of standing fabric, and does not come strictly under the rubric of "conversion". However, it is worth noting, for example whenever the new house is found upon a site with an older moat (see Fig. 8.3) or as a possibility where framing from an open house has been re-used. A more visible technique was to build a new hall or main range and re-use parts of the open house as a service range. At Church Farm, Brettenham (Fig. 5.2), and possibly also at Lower Farm, Risby (Fig. 5.3), the crosswing was retained but the old hall completely demolished and replaced with a fine new main range; such a form is also a possibility at Clockhouse Farm, Shimpling (Fig. 5.4).

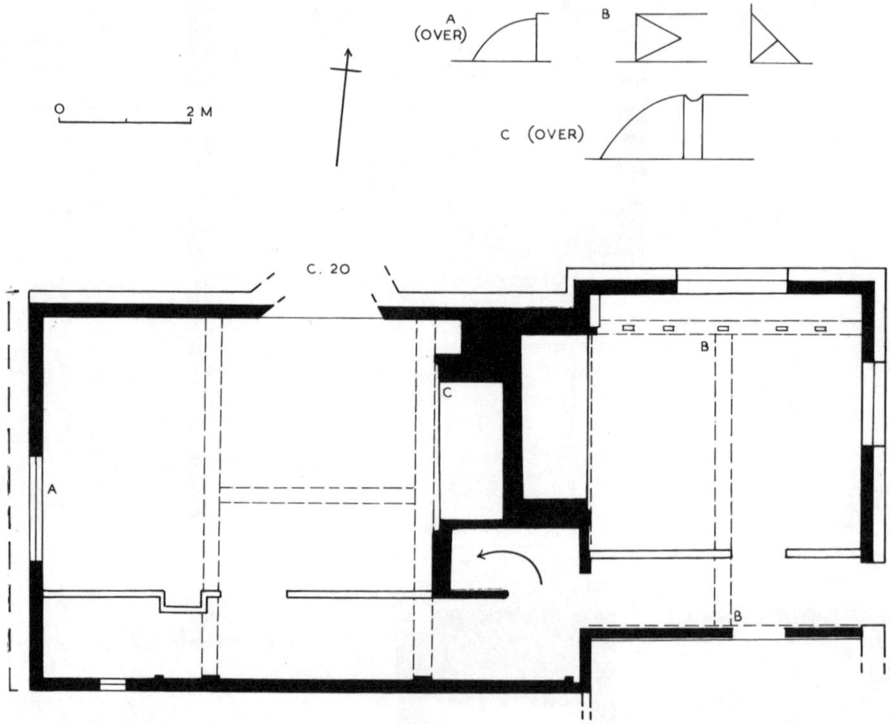

Figure 5.2 Church Farm, Brettenham: a house with a 15th-century wing and 1587 main range. The two-bay wing had an arched door to S and a jetty to N. There was no window to N over. Shutter groove in cross-rail immediately to S of stack, indicating that former hall could not have extended this way. The main range consisted of two bays plus chimney bay. Space for lobby entry to S of stack, in front of newel stair. The gable end of the main range has bressumer with the date 1587 and initials R. M. R. Marshe bought the manor of Willishams from Sir William Spring in 1585 (Fine, Mich. 27-8 Eliz.; Copinger 1909, Vol. 3, 145).

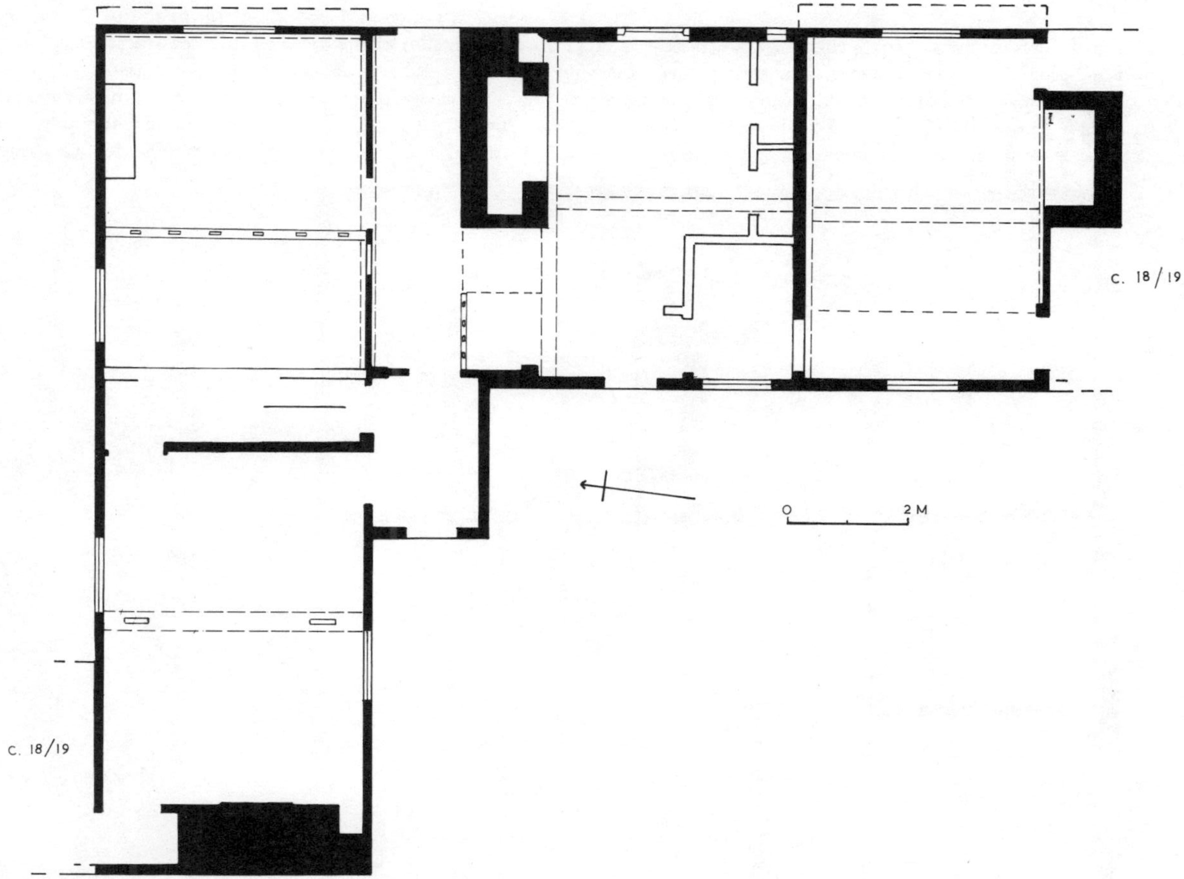

Figure 5.3 Lower Farm, Risby: a complex house of open-hall origins. The hall had a screens passage at the lower end. Beyond this the service end has frames for service doors, a cross-rail framed into a central post, and studding over this. This appears to have fronted an open hall. The roof over the hall has been rebuilt, but a few sooted rafters survive. The service wing runs back; at the rear, it reuses a formerly arched-braced beam with octagonal chamfer. The inserted stack has arched recesses. The main ceiling beams have mid-16th-century leaf stops, and are impressively high. A parlour wing was added at this point or later in the 16th century, with a jetty and gable to N with stud-braces, three-window ranges and an external stack. Also at this point the service wing was remodelled, with a rail inserted into the cross-passage cut at its E end to receive a bressumer. The front was rebuilt above the cross-rail in jettied form, with studding and windows similar to the parlour wing. The whole roof was rebuilt in clasped-purlin form. A stack was added at the W end. The porch at the angle of main range and wing is well framed but of uncertain date.

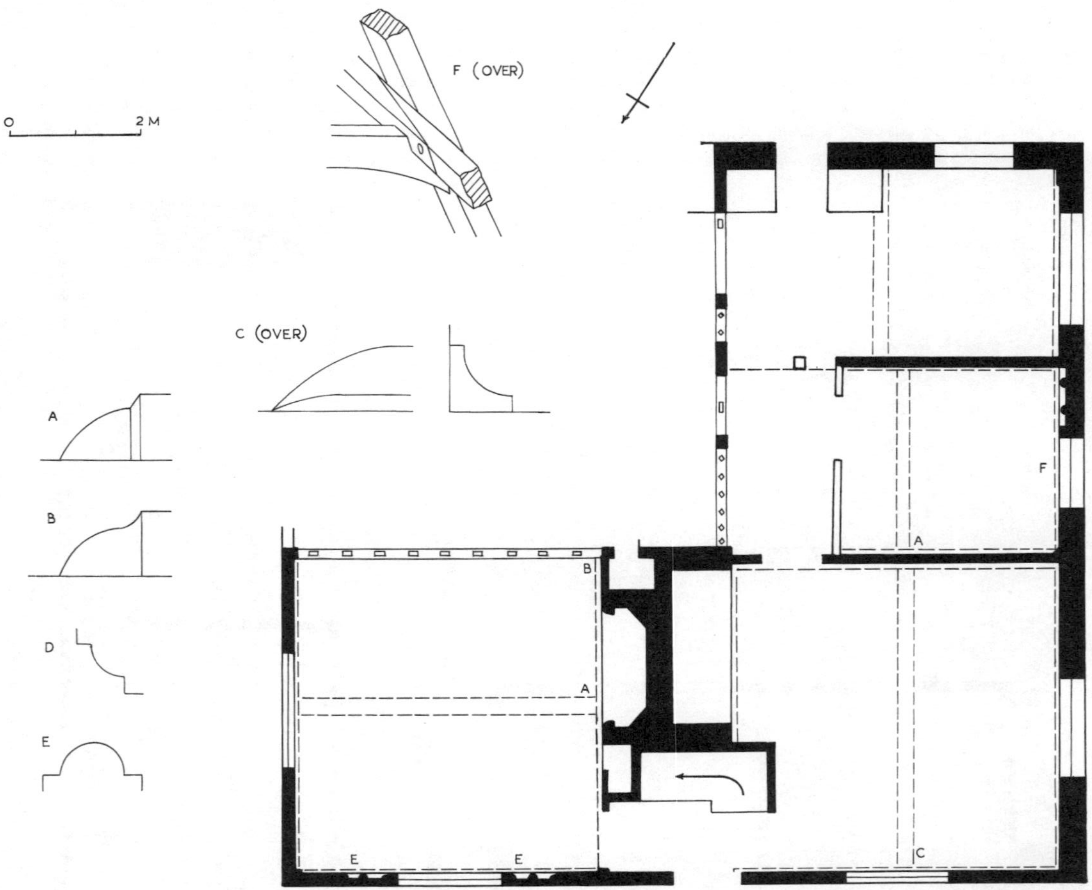

Figure 5.4 Clockhouse Farm, Shimpling: a house of early/mid-16th-century origins, extended in *c.* 1600. Uncertain whether the NS range is a later 15th century cross-wing to a destroyed hall or a transitional house. Fully ceiled, with two full stories. Probable site of an external door at the S end of the E wall. The tie over the partition to S had wide arch-braces; there was a partition to N. Clasped-purlin roof. Mortices for diamond-mullioned windows and shutter grooves. Pargeting in the form of rows of dots. Parlour added to this structure; ovolo-moulded three-window range in N wall. Wall-plates to N and S have another roll-moulded plate over. Clasped-purlin roof, with the purlins stopping short of the chimney bay. Stack rebuilt or extended at this time, in the form of back-to-back fireplaces and a lobby entry with stair. Stair to loft in SE corner of the NS range was probably inserted at this point. Partly refaced in brick in the 19th century.

However, the most common solution to the problem of conversion was to insert the stack into the interior of the frame of the old house, and to insert a ceiling into the hall at the same time. This involved least effort and destruction of the old fabric, since the stack could be inserted between two tie-beams: in some cases the upper part of the stack is sloped or battered to one side to avoid the collar-purlin of a crown-post roof. Insertion of a stack and ceiling thus could be done in various ways, several of which are noted below:

(a) Into the lower bay of the hall, with a single-fireplace stack backing onto the cross-passage. This is the pattern at Mill House, Alpheton, the only known example where the open hall was retained; the hall was subsequently given a fine ceiling in the mid-16th century. Such a pattern barely alters the ground-floor layout or heating pattern of the house. However, it does remove some of the centrality of the open hearth and allows circulation around the house at first-floor level.

(b) Into the lower bay of the hall or the cross-passage, but with a pair of back-to-back fireplaces, "turning round" the house (moving parlour end to service end and vice versa) in the process. This is the most dramatic method, since in addition to completely reversing the orientation of the house a lobby-entry plan is created. No definite examples are known of "turning round" and creating new opposed doors at the former upper end of the hall, and still less of new service ends.

(c) Into the upper end of the hall, with back-to-back fireplaces. The opposed doors at the lower end could thus be retained, or a lobby entry inserted; it is difficult to detect which option was taken since in most cases a subsequent lobby entry was inserted and the opposed doors blocked at that later point.

These three procedures all involved insertion of the stack into one end of the hall or passage. Two houses vary from this pattern. At Old Cottage, Brent Eleigh, the stack was probably inserted into the service end, and at Shepherds Cottage, Hawstead (Fig. 5.5) into the parlour.

To some extent the choices outlined above were governed by technical factors such as the presence or absence of existing cross-rails, or the width of the space between the ties available for the inserted stack. However, the explanation of "commonsense" and convenience is again inadequate or partial. The easiest imaginable method is to place an external stack against the side wall of the hall; the resulting plan is known from new transitional houses such as Riverside, Chelsworth (Fig. 5.6), or the larger houses of Hawkedon Hall and Thurston End Hall, Hawkedon (Figs 9.2, 9.3), and the option was taken up elsewhere in England. So these insertions were only partly governed by what was technically possible or easy: the widely varying final layout produced shows the degree of choice that was possible. Where the stack was inserted

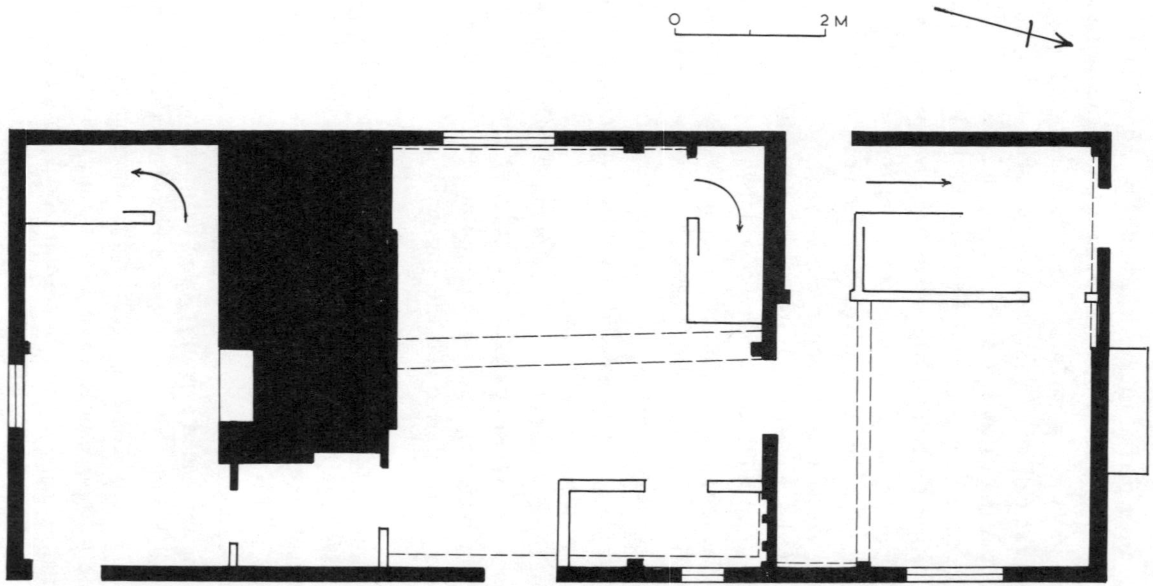

Figure 5.5 Shepherds Cottage, Hawstead: an unusual house, probably of 15th-century origins; interpretation uncertain. Two unequal bays in the hall area. Below this, mortices indicate a former cross-passage and "medieval" service arrangement. Over, the now absent central tie was formerly arch-braced. Several of the cross-rails are inserted. The framing is of good scantling but of poor carpentry. The hall was ceiled with an inserted beam and unchamfered joists. The stack is of back-to-back type, and apparently inserted into one bay of a two-bay parlour. Conversion was to a three-cell lobby-entry form. The house was extensively altered in the 18th and 19th centuries in the process of division into three cottages.

within the structure, and whether the stack had a single fireplace or back-to-back fireplaces, produced a new house-plan. This new plan corresponded to one or another of the new house types seen in this period. It is now necessary to consider these new house types and their social meanings.

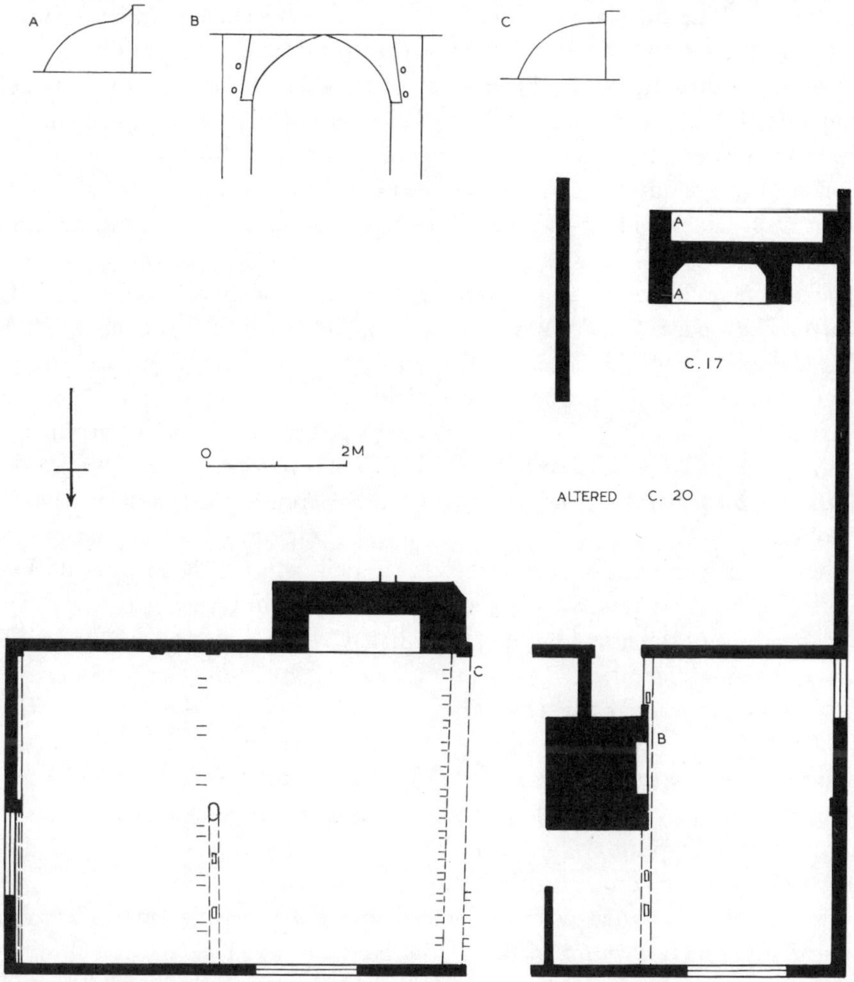

Figure 5.6 Riverside, Chelsworth: a 15/16th-century three-cell house with 16/17th-century wing and external side-wall stack. The hall is of two bays. The stack has a plain back and a tapering elevation. The cell to E has traces of a former stair to S. Over, the N wall has a central post, with diamond mullions and shutter grooves on either side. Former "medieval" service arrangement at this end. The roof over is probably of coupled-rafter type; no trace of sooting. The date of this phase is probably *c.* 1500. The 17th-century service wing has a stack with back-to-back fireplaces, but is otherwise obscured.

Interpreting transitional houses

Chapter 4 tried to understand the popularity of the open hall both in terms of its layout and in terms of its persistence through time, when alternatives were available. It did so through discussion of the social meanings the open hall carried. The corollary of this argument is that the abandonment or modification of the open hall must relate to the abandonment or modification of those social meanings and changes in the underlying social form to which they referred. The variation in layout of altered and new houses can be understood in terms of the piecemeal and varying nature of this abandonment.

Transitional houses vary from "conservative" to "radical" plans. This variation is difficult to relate to other factors such as size, social status, or time. It is true that some larger houses have conservative plans and this question is touched on in Chapter 9. However, smaller houses such as Riverside, Chelsworth, The Lodge, Coney Weston (Fig. 5.7), and No. 32 Pages Lane, Higham (Fig. 5.8), for example, have equally "conservative" plans. Conversely some larger houses, such as Newbury Farm, Bildeston (second phase) and Vaiseys, Brent Eleigh (Figs 5.9, 5.10), have fully developed three-cell lobby-entry plans.

Variation in layout is also not a distinction between early and late houses. Both Newbury Farm second phase and Vaiseys are pre-1550 in date, whereas Cooks Farm, Hartest (Fig. 5.11), with stack backing onto through-passage and sub-medieval service end, is probably not much before 1580 in date. Rather, therefore, we must try to understand this variation in terms of the intended specifications of the house-builder as mediated by the limitations and possibilities of the craft tradition.

Thomas Hubka has suggested that innovation within the craft tradition does not generally involve completely new ideas: rather builders "accomplish change by reordering the hierarchy of ideas . . . contained within the known grammar" (Hubka 1986, 430). This observation on the general process of vernacular design appears to be accurate here, given the close similarity of date and style of open and transitional houses. So what did innovation in this period involve and what were its antecedents? The specific elements of innovation were the full ceiling of the house, the chimney stack and the chimney bay with lobby entry. The end product of innovation was the "truly post-medieval house", which, Hewitt comments, "was planned as two parts having a chimney bay between them" (Hewitt 1973: 60).

We have seen that ceilings, and cross-rails to support ceiling joists, were present in most ends of open houses. Both insertion of ceilings into open halls and construction of new houses required no change in the grammar other than that concerning open halls specifically, but it did require some change in the technical system, namely the introduction of cross-rails, cross-

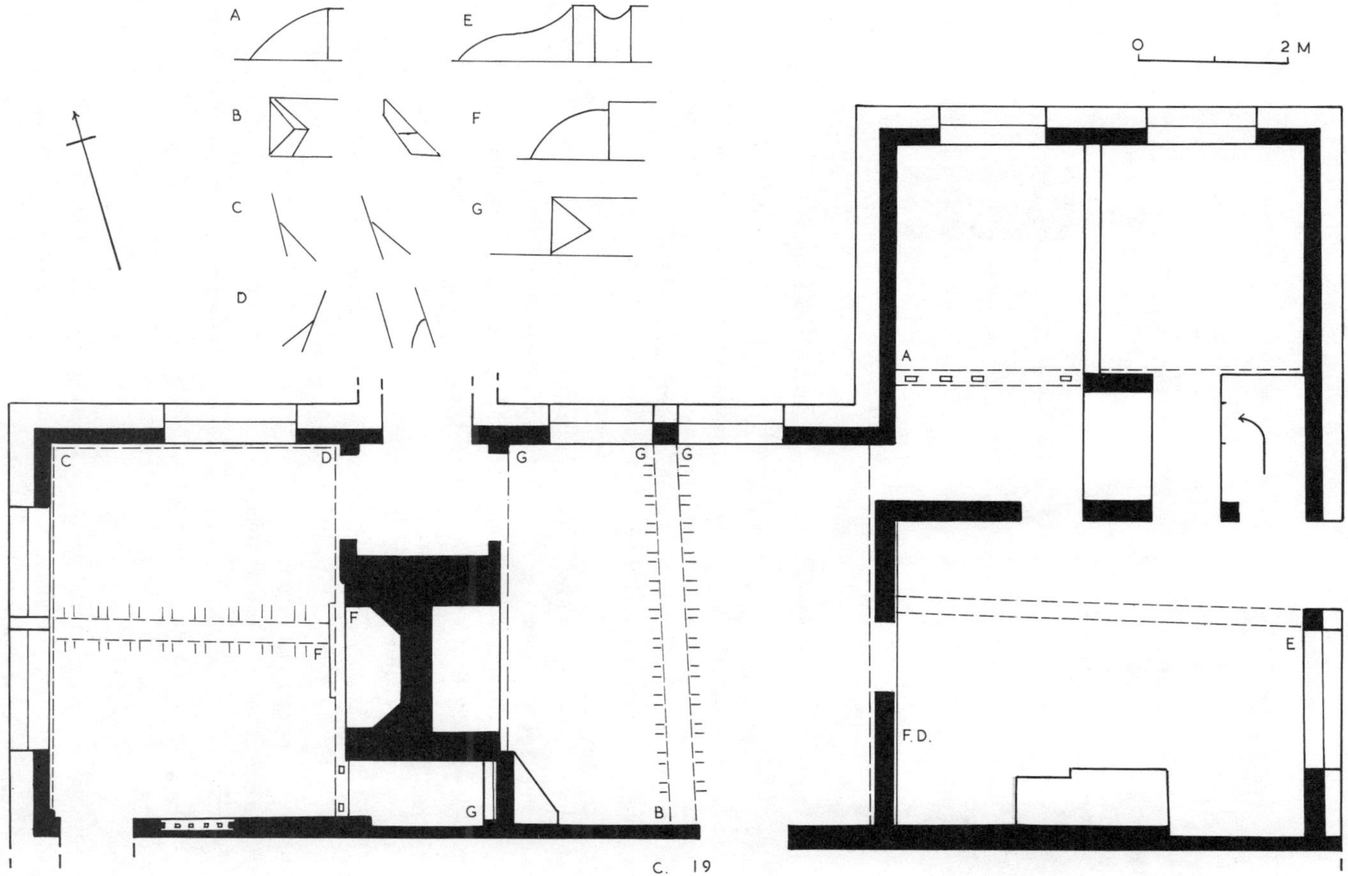

Figure 5.7 The Lodge, Coney Weston: a 16th-century three-phase house (Plate 4a). The first phase was a two-bay ceiled hall with end-wall stack. This probably had a further cell at the service end. The hall cross-beam is jointed into its posts; there is no cross-rail. A further cell to W is possible, the door position uncertain. The parlour was rebuilt or more likely added in the mid-/later 16th century. This end of the building was heightened and a fireplace added. The joists are unbroken so there was no stair up from the parlour. This now formed a typical three-cell plan, although the door position is uncertain. The service wing was added and the main range heightened at *c.* 1600 or later. Probably at this point the house was converted to a lobby-entry. A brick front range was added in the 19th century.

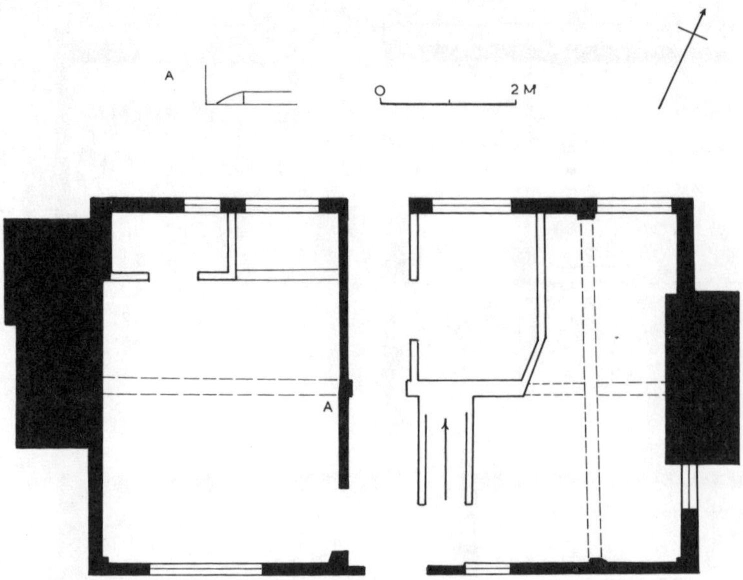

Figure 5.8 No. 32 Pages Lane, Higham: a two-cell 16th-century house without cross-rails; the cross-beams supporting the joists are tenoned into the main posts. Probably a service area to N, below opposed doors, although none of the framing at this point is visible. The main beam in the room to S is only chamfered on the N side; the bay to S of this probably held an internal chimney, probably of brick.

beams and spine beams into the hall to carry the ceiling joists.

Two smaller houses were remarkably constructed without cross-rails in the hall. At The Lodge, Coney Weston, and No. 32 Pages Lane, Higham, the two-bay hall has a cross-beam running across it jointed into two posts with intermediate jowls; both structures are one-and-a-half storeys high. This is an unusual and aesthetically awkward arrangement; no other examples from this period are known, though this arrangement was sometimes used to insert ceilings into open halls and a similar technique also appears in the mid to later 17th century. The more usual arrangement, however, in both new and altered houses was the use of cross-rails and spine beam running along the axis of the house. Cross-rails themselves can be argued to be the product of the evolution of storied ends within open houses, their purpose being to carry the joists of the parlour and service ceilings. So as Hubka asserts, the innovation here is a reordering of older elements into the new.

Innovation was also required in the stack's insertion into the existing frame. At Riverside, Chelsworth, the stack is simply added to the rear wall of the hall. This pattern in itself involves no alteration to the craft tradition and is

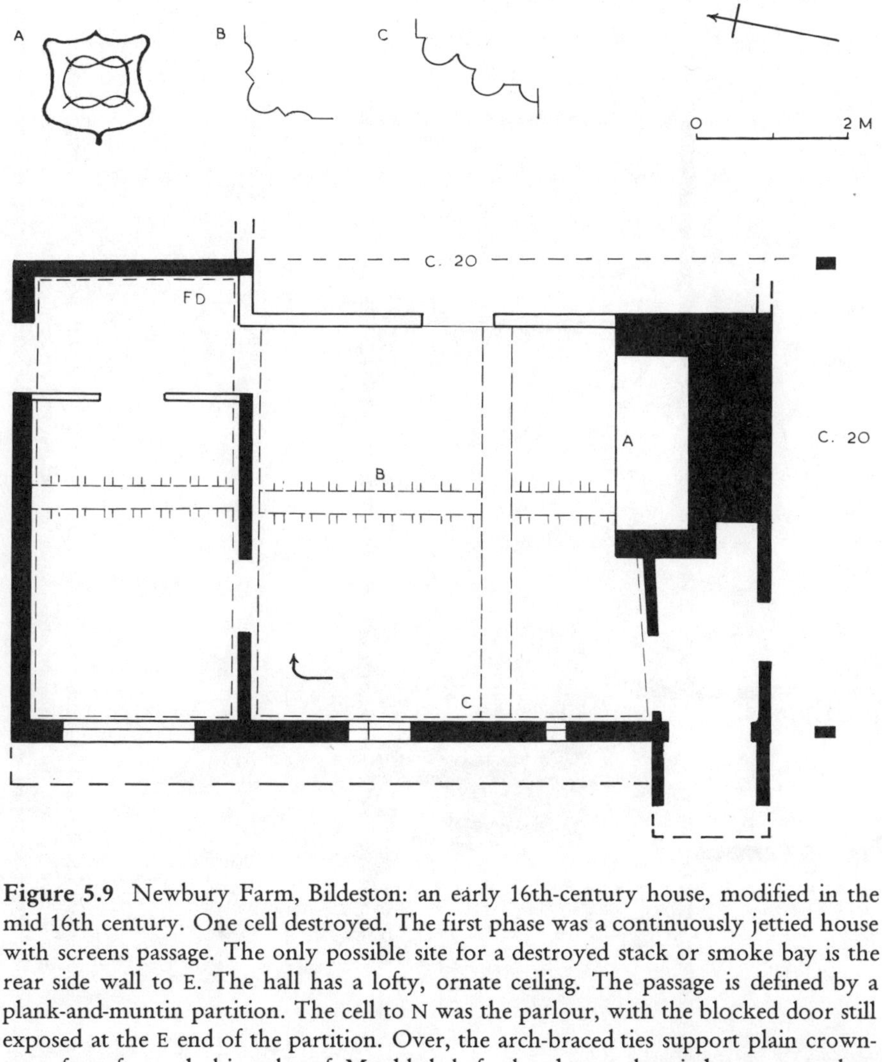

Figure 5.9 Newbury Farm, Bildeston: an early 16th-century house, modified in the mid 16th century. One cell destroyed. The first phase was a continuously jettied house with screens passage. The only possible site for a destroyed stack or smoke bay is the rear side wall to E. The hall has a lofty, ornate ceiling. The passage is defined by a plank-and-muntin partition. The cell to N was the parlour, with the blocked door still exposed at the E end of the partition. Over, the arch-braced ties support plain crown-posts for a formerly hipped roof. Moulded shafts, brackets and capitals are exposed on the front of the house, with moulded and decorated windows. The door to W is also heavily decorated. Glazed windows on the ground floor; shutter grooves over. This house was modified in the mid-16th century by the addition of stack and porch. The stack is inserted into the screens passage. It has a lintel with oak-leaf moulding and the motif of the Bourchier knot. The porch has a four-centred arch, with the Bourchier knot in the spandrels. In 1541 William Lord Price acquired the manor of Bildeston in right of wife Ann Bourchier, heir of the Earl of Essex (Growse 1892: 14). A tie and partition were inserted between the second and third ties over, probably in the 17th century. The hall has had its wall to E destroyed and a modern partition inserted a little W of the former line.

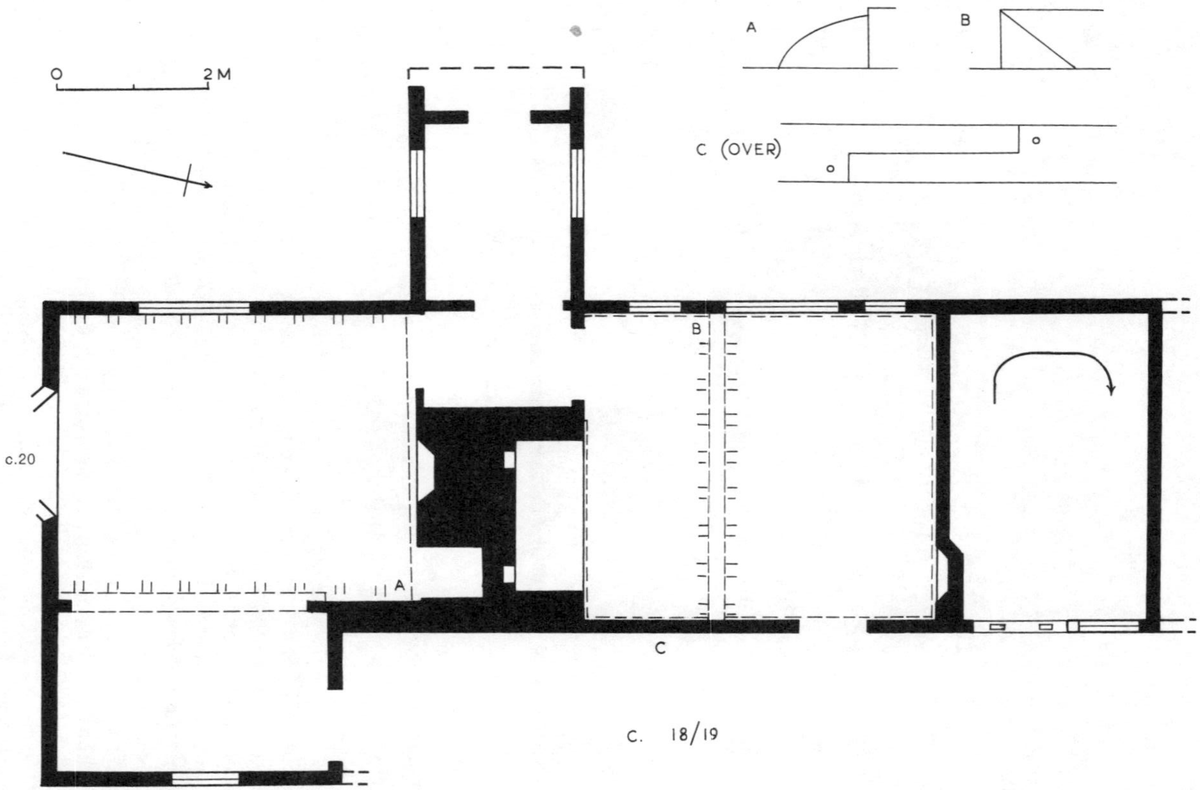

Figure 5.10 Vaiseys, Brent Eleigh: an early/mid-16th-century house with 17th-century additions, in timber framing and brick nogging. Three-cell lobby-entry plan. The first phase has five bays plus chimney bay. Two-bay service cell, much altered. An unusual arrangement in the parlour, with an apparently first-phase annexe. It may be a stair wing to the parlour. The house is fully ceiled. Over, wide arch-braces to central truss and its neighbour to N. The tie on the N side of the stack appears to be reused. A roof with plain crown posts over hall and service. This phase had diamond-mullioned windows and shutters. The porch was added in the 17th century. Jettied front, with carved brackets, plain joist ends and reused bressumer. Fine carved door with vine patterns on posts. Plastered ceiling inside the porch. Part of the main roof was rebuilt in clasped-purlin form at this point. A late 17th- / early 18th-century wing extends to the rear from the N end of the building. At the same time a large stair was inserted into the former service cell and the ceiling removed.

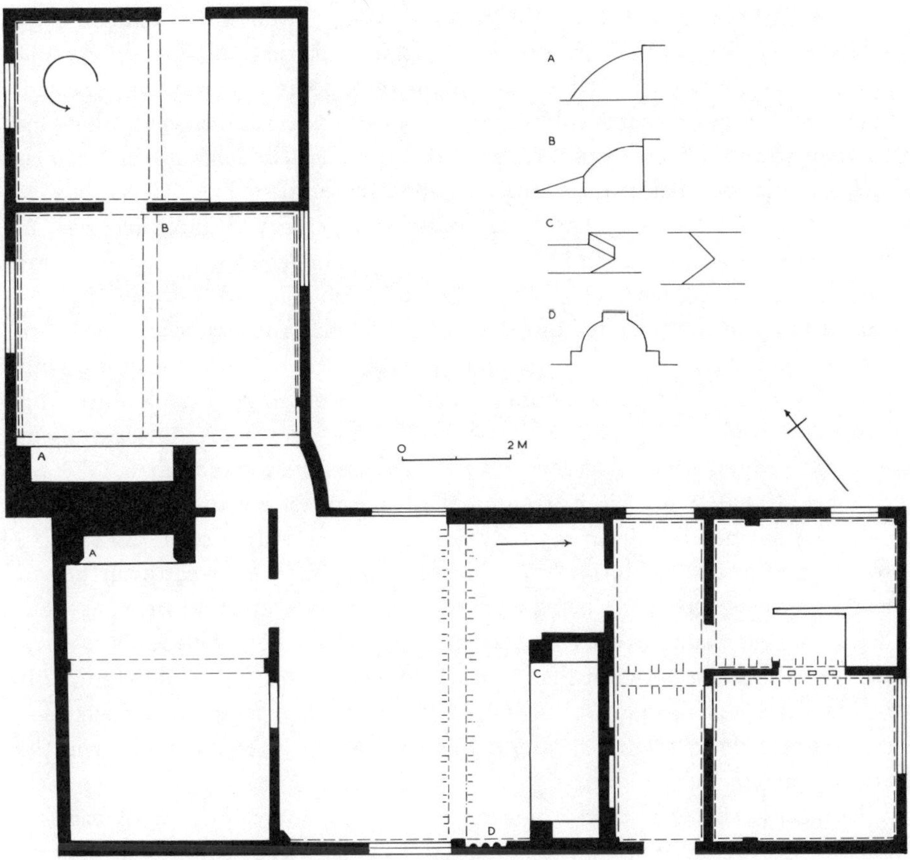

Figure 5.11 Cooks Farm, Hartest: an L-shaped house of 16th-century origins. The two wings are of different phases but uncertain relationship, although the house had assumed its present form by *c.* 1580. The main range is of three cells; submedieval service partition and doors. The stack has two four-centred brick arches in its back and two arched recesses. There is a two-bay hall, with two-bay parlour beyond; the parlour door has been moved twice but was originally to N. Over, there is a plank-and-muntin partition under the central tie. The hipped roof is of wind-braced clasped-purlin form. The wing is of uncertain date, but was probably used as a service range with separate access to the hall. It may be part of an old 15th-century house. There is a baulk stair over; the framing is waney and the scantling poor. Various partitions and stairs were inserted in the 18th/19th centuries.

more frequent in the north and west of England and Wales as well as in larger houses within the sample. Requiring little alteration was the single-fireplace stack backing on to the cross-passage, which could be easily inserted into the lower bay of the hall and again with little violence done to the craft tradition.

The most radical innovation – one that dominated closed houses – was the stack with back-to-back fireplaces in its separate chimney bay flanked by a lobby entry (Fig. 3.4). Seen superficially this broke several rules in the old competence, particularly that of the placing of opposed doorways and the centrality of the open hearth. However, deeper consideration suggests that this element too may have been a recombination of old elements of the competence even if the final, surface structure appeared entirely new.

Consider for a moment the compromise arrangement of the smoke bay, in which the smoke is confined to a smaller space by placing a ceiling over part of the open hall. At Tudor Cottage, Brent Eleigh (Fig. 5.12), for example, a smoke bay was first inserted into the open hall, then the smoke bay itself had a timber stack inserted into it.[2] Finally a brick stack was inserted in the position of the largely destroyed timber stack. A lobby entry was placed in this bay, certainly by the time of the insertion of the brick stack and possibly as part of the smoke bay, as is the pattern with other examples (Harris 1978: 8).

It is difficult to pick out a moment of revolutionary innovation in this sequence of open hall, chimney bay, timber stack and brick stack. Rather, we see the piecemeal "implosion" or "closure" of the space allotted to the hearth and its smoke, each stage being a reordering and continuation of what went before. Other examples offer an analogous sequence where the stack was inserted into the space between the opposed doorways creating a lobby entry. It is, therefore, not too fanciful to suggest that the through passage or space for the opposed doors are the conceptual antecedents for the chimney bay in the competence of the builder.

Ironically, therefore, the arrangement of lobby entry in front of back-to-back fireplaces was both an innovation and an element of continuity. It occupied the same place as the old pair of opposed doors in the open competence but led to a very different circulation pattern within the house.

The competence, however, did not transform itself in isolation: it needed the volition of individuals to carry this process through. This is apparent when we consider why some older elements were retained and others rejected in some houses. Langleys Newhouse and Wolfe Hall (Figs 5.13, 5.14), for example, were laid out with back-to-back fireplaces and separate chimney bay but without lobby entry. Rather the older pattern of opposed doors at the lower end of the hall was retained. It is plausible to argue that such patterns of partial retention and innovation are partly due to an attempt to keep the old referents in the hall to the patriarchal values discussed in Chapter 4, but to introduce new elements of comfort and privacy for the master and mistress of the house: thus innovations relate to the sorts of manipulation of ideas and architectural referents discussed in Chapter 3.

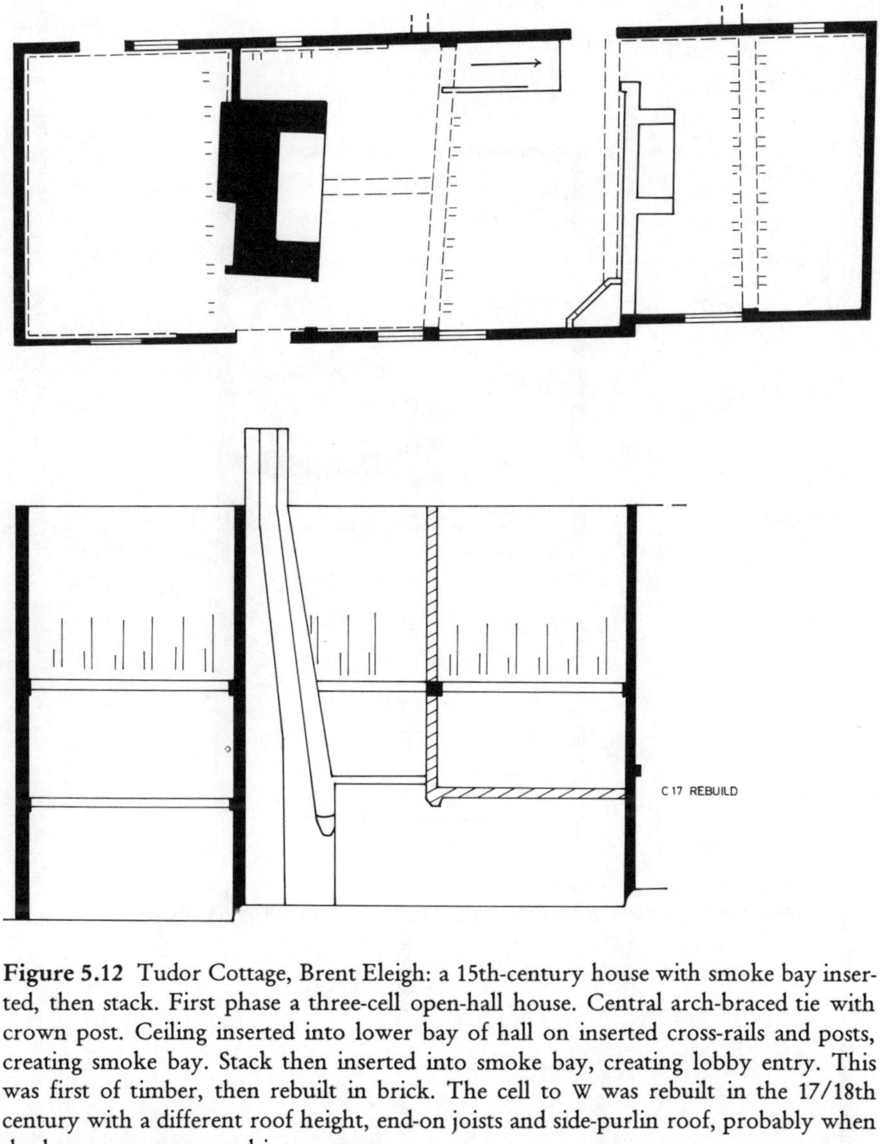

Figure 5.12 Tudor Cottage, Brent Eleigh: a 15th-century house with smoke bay inserted, then stack. First phase a three-cell open-hall house. Central arch-braced tie with crown post. Ceiling inserted into lower bay of hall on inserted cross-rails and posts, creating smoke bay. Stack then inserted into smoke bay, creating lobby entry. This was first of timber, then rebuilt in brick. The cell to W was rebuilt in the 17/18th century with a different roof height, end-on joists and side-purlin roof, probably when the house was converted into cottages.

At Langleys, for example, the ground plan and three-dimensional form is a combination of old and new features. The hall had the open pattern of opposed doors at the lower end, but has ceiling and stack with back-to-back fireplaces. A stair was placed next to the stack. The arrangement of the upper end of the house, in particular the back-to-back fireplaces, the site and form of the stair, and the ceiled hall, were all new features, as was the provision of

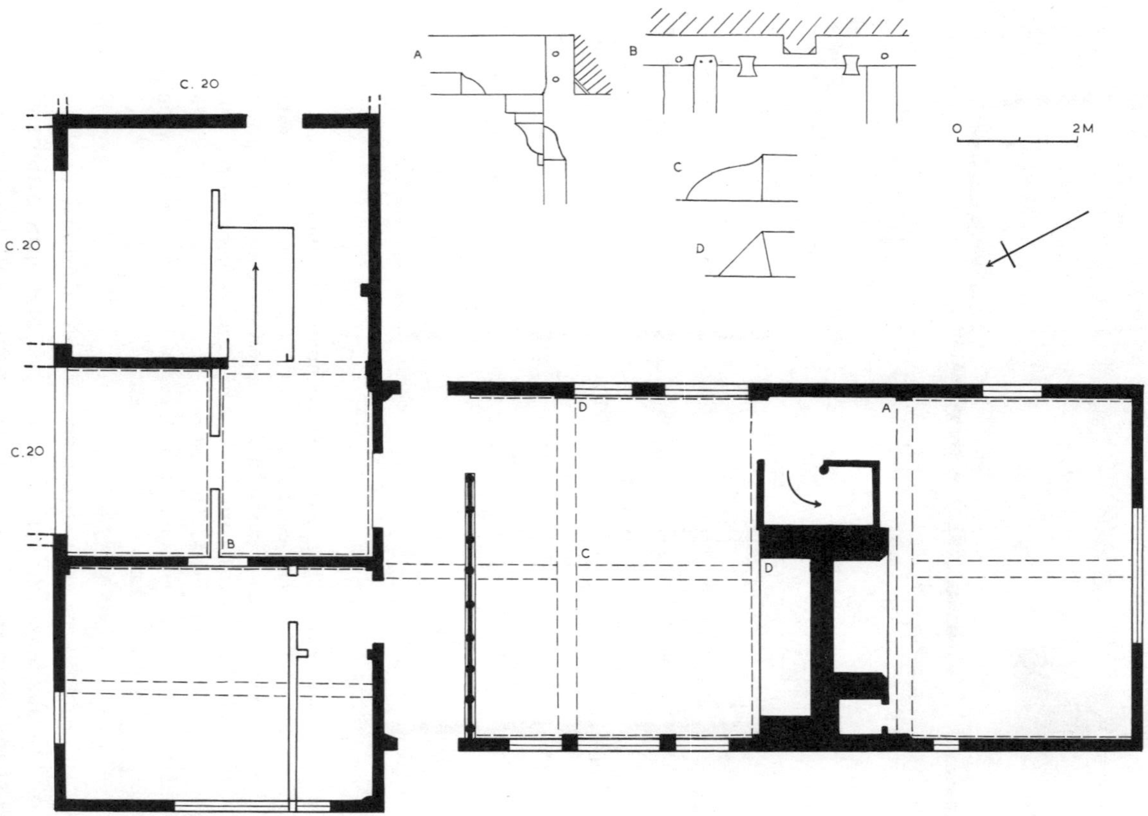

Figure 5.13 Langleys Newhouse, Hawkedon: a 16th-century house with crosswing, altered and extended in *c.* 1600. First phase a two- or three-cell house with back-to-back fireplaces and opposed doors. The stack in the parlour and parlour chamber has depressed brick and plaster arches, with vine/leaf friezes over. The parlour has space to N of the stack, now fitted with 17/18th-century lockable doors. The stack has four cylindrical flues, each with a different moulded brick design. The studding on the front of the range is closer than that on the back. Clasped-purlin roof. This phase coincides with the tenure of John Langley as rector of Hawkedon from 1554 to 1560. The wing was added later in the 16th century; the central partition has a hinged flap of uncertain date and purpose. Five-bay clasped-purlin roof. Plank-and-muntin partition inserted in the hall. Bay added to the wing in the mid- to later 17th century; parlour and lobby-entry doors have been inserted and removed at various points. There is a 16/17th-century five-bay barn to NE.

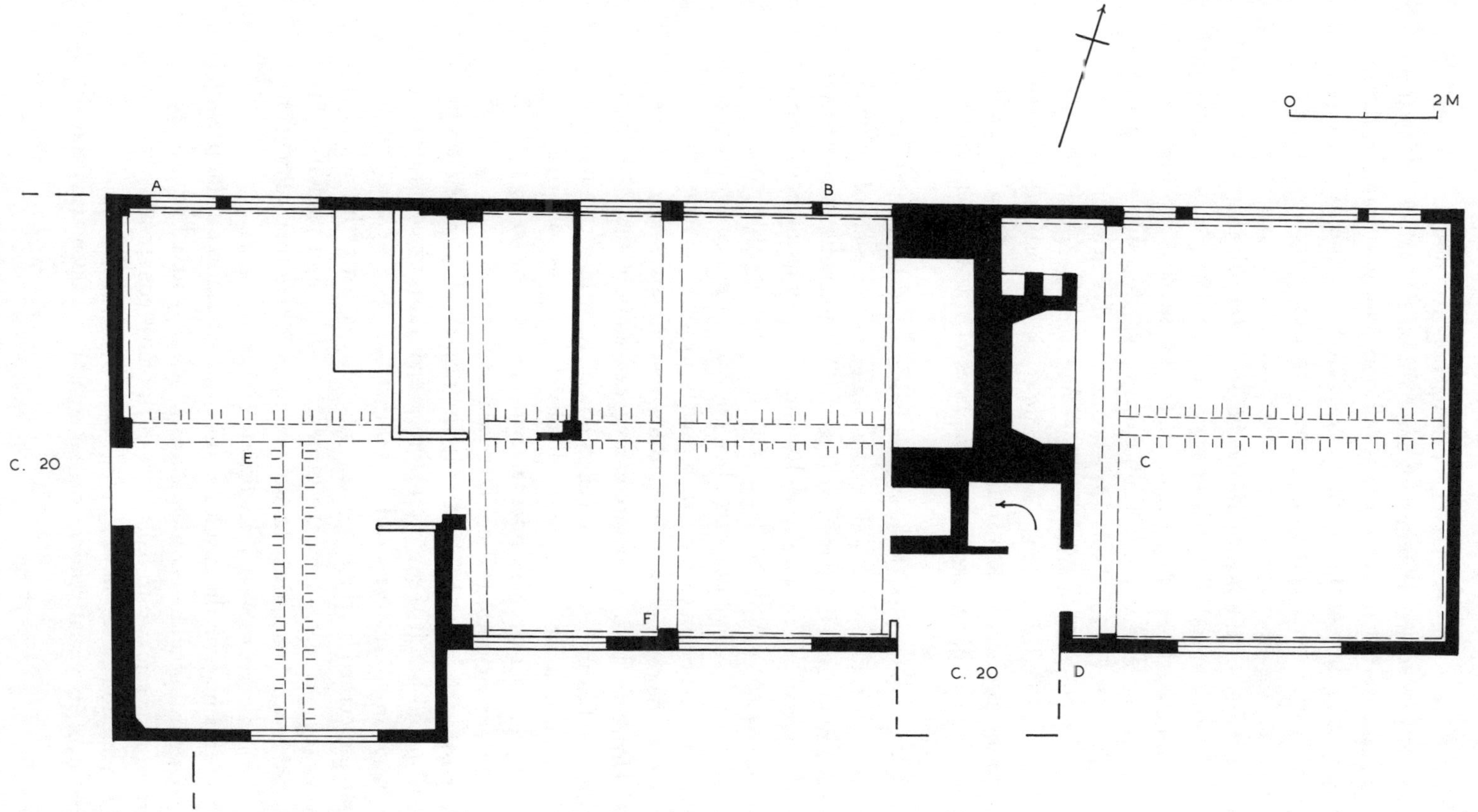

Figure 5.14 Wolfe Hall, Barrow: mid-16th-century house with additions of *c.* 1600. The first phase was a two-cell house with axial stack and continuous jetty to N. Roll-moulded mullioned windows and vertical glazing bars to N on both floors. Opposed doors at the lower end of the hall. The plank-and-muntin screen, however, appears to be inserted into the hall. The partition was probably inserted at the time of the addition of the service wing. The stack has back-to-back fireplaces, both with ashlar posts of reused Norman moulded columns. These are probably from the Abbey of Bury St Edmunds, 9 km away. There is the site of a bread oven to N. Over, the only former partition is that S of the stack. The roof is of wind-braced clasped-purlin type. A map of 1597 shows the house as "Warner's Tenement"; the Warners are mentioned throughout the 16th-century tax records for the parish and by 1611 have reached gentry status (Bury SRO 862/2; FL525: 10; Hervey 1909: 257; Hervey 1910: 340). The service wing was added *c.* 1600. At a later point in the 17th century, the opposed doors were blocked, a lobby entry to S created and the house turned to face S. There is a painted motto above the hall fireplace, probably 18/19th century.

upstairs accommodation; the lower end, with its opposed doors, was old. Some features appear to evoke old values of emphasis on the hall as a central area of social interaction but to use new ways of doing so. For example, the large scantling and moulding of the beams and joists in the ceiling at Langleys and in many other transitional halls replaces the former open roof. Again, the ornamentation round the fireplaces and the large scale of the fireplace in the hall stress the centrality of the hearth area as before, although this hearth is now housed in a brick stack. There is concern for display: although now masked, the studding is closer on the front of the house than on the back. This pattern can also be seen at Wolfe Hall, Barrow, which is similar in plan and shows a similar concern for display in its continuously jettied front with moulded brackets. Again, the interior combines opposed doors at the lower end of the hall and a fine hall ceiling. The ornate stack has posts made of re-used ashlar columns, probably taken from the Abbey of Bury St Edmunds a few kilometres away. It has back-to-back fireplaces and a stair next to the stack (Johnson 1989).

Other houses show more directly how conservatism and innovation interacted within the craft tradition, as well as the strategies and goals of individuals. No. 42 Egremont Street, Glemsford (Fig. 5.15) is puzzling in its transitional phase. It appears to be a fully ceiled three-bay, two-cell house into which the stack has apparently been inserted: not only has the hall spine beam been cut back to receive the stack, but the Roman numerals inscribed by the carpenter on that beam to assist with prefabrication and reconstruction on site indicate that the ceiling was to have run across the space now occupied by that stack. However, if the structure is imagined without the stack there is no provision for heating in a fully ceiled house. A similar case has been noted at Jenkyns Farmhouse, Essex, another fully ceiled house of three bays, where Hewitt observes that "the internal evidence . . . indicates that the builder, the customer, or both, had no fixed ideas as to the ultimate form the house should possess" (Hewitt 1973: 64). Hewitt's observation of the timber frame is not disputed but it seems strange to prefabricate or commission a house in this way; an alternative possibility is that both No. 42 and Jenkyns Farmhouse were specified by the customer to be fully ceiled with stacks, but prefabricated in the old manner by the carpenter, who simply modified his ideas on site. Either way, both these houses present an interesting study of the forces of innovation versus those of tradition.

All these patterns may be the result of conscious intention on the part of the customer/owner, but all had consequences which may have been unintended. The insertion of stacks into halls even in the most conservative manner necessitated a reduction in the floor area of the hall, while the insertion of a ceiling robbed it of its visual referent of the arch-braced open truss and the crown-post: whatever the intentions of the builder or owner, the ceiling-over of the hall radically changed the potential circulation pattern of the house.

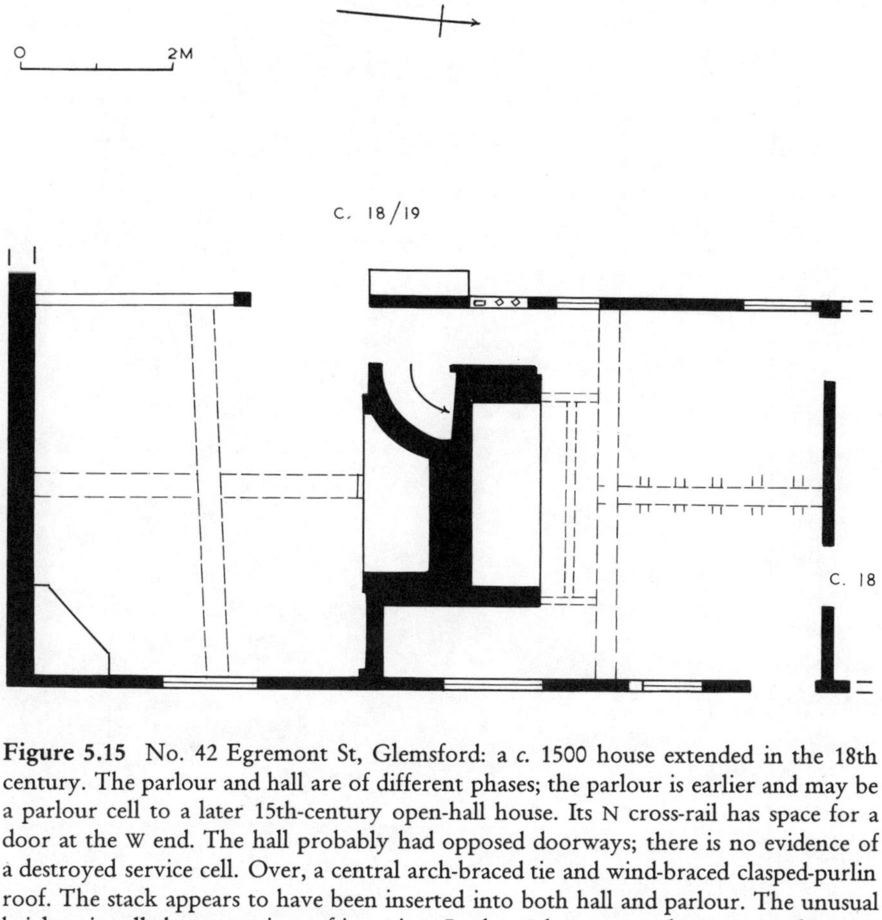

Figure 5.15 No. 42 Egremont St, Glemsford: a *c.* 1500 house extended in the 18th century. The parlour and hall are of different phases; the parlour is earlier and may be a parlour cell to a later 15th-century open-hall house. Its N cross-rail has space for a door at the W end. The hall probably had opposed doorways; there is no evidence of a destroyed service cell. Over, a central arch-braced tie and wind-braced clasped-purlin roof. The stack appears to have been inserted into both hall and parlour. The unusual brick stairwell shows no signs of insertion. In the 18th century a long range of service buildings were added, running N (Plate 5c).

That the potential pattern of circulation and use was not necessarily the actual one at this period is indicated by the evidence of probate inventories. Surviving from the later 16th century onwards, these documents were drawn up on the death of a person, usually the householder. For that person's will to be proved by the ecclesiastical court, an inventory of his or her possessions had to be made up by witnesses. These were often drawn up under subheadings of rooms and thus contain information on room use, values of material objects, and so on. A sample of inventories was transcribed for the years 1576–7 (see Ch. 8 and Table 5.1).

Table 5.1 Room naming and order in inventories (1570s).

Name	Hall	Parlour	Chamber	Solar	Entry	Buttery	Kitchen	Lower C	Shop	Closet	Cellar	Hall C	Parlour C	Buttery C	Kitchen C	Bed C	C over shop	Folks/mans C	Backhouse C	Corn C	Dairy	Pantry	Cheesehouse	Milkhouse	Backhouse	Malthouse	Granary	Barn	Stable	*Other/Comments*
J Norfolk	1	4				2			8				5	6										3	7			9		
A Selfe	1	2						3				4											5							
R Osmonde	1	2	3			6	7													9				8	14			13		Plr 4 Yelding Ho 5 Another Ho 10 Chambers 11-12
J Leesse	1		2			3																						4		
A Webe	1		2				3																							
J Ludbroke	2		1			3																								Chamber 4
T Crowch	1			4			3		5							2														
T Frank	2	1				3						4																6		Cartho 5
J Morlye	1		3				2																						4	
J Corder	1		2	3		6								4										5	7					
R Rastall	2	1	3	5									6											9	8					Chamber 4 Plr Chamber 7
R Pecok			1			2																								only partly room by room (?shared ho)
M Fuller	1	2															3													
J Parman	1	2	4			6							3								9					8				Chamber 5 Working Ho 7
J Hall	1		3			5										2								4				7	8	Chamber over Bed Chamber 6
R Collinson	1	2				4						3																		Outhouse 5
W Stockinge	3					1		2	4																			5		
J Whiters	1	2							6				3		4		5								7					
J Grymes	1		2			3		6						5											4					
W Peeck	1	2				3							4											5	7	8		10	9	Chamber over Milkho 6 Barns 11 and 12
T Hayward	4	1				6	5						2															7		South Chamber 3
L Deathe	1		2				3																							
R Gayfford	1		2						3																					
R Game	1		2				4																		6	5		7		Chamber above 3
A Myles	1		2			3																			6					Chamber 4 Tanho 5
W Nunne	1		2			3																								
W Baker	1		2			3																						4		
J Mauldon	1		2			3			4																					Shop 5
G Hoowe	1		2																											
E Manwood	1		3	5		4										2										6		7		

The picture suggested by the inventories corresponds to that indicated by the architecture. All but one inventory has a room listed as the hall, and in only five cases is this room not listed first in the inventory. In other words those drawing up the inventory felt it natural to start their listing of goods in that room, reflecting its cultural and symbolic primacy. The second room is usually the chamber or parlour.[3] After this comes the service end, with listing of kitchen, buttery, or other service rooms. The existence of wings at one or other end of the house is frequently indicated by the listing of more than one room at ground-floor level at the upper end of the hall or more than two at the service end. In short, the division of space at ground-floor level indicated by the inventory evidence reflects the pattern indicated in the architecture.

The problems in resolving the two classes of evidence begin when we move to the first floor. Only 3 out of the 33 inventories mention a "chamber over the hall" or "hall chamber". However, most inventories also list a trammel, which requires a stack for support; and one, that of T. Crowch, mentions "hale in chimney" without also listing a hall chamber. It is possible that some of these houses had stacks without ceilings, but only one example of separate stack and chimney insertion was noted in the architectural analysis. It is therefore most probable that hall chambers are simply not being mentioned in the inventories. This may be because they are empty, or because there are no partitions, or only one partition, at first-floor level.

The lack of mention of upper chambers as a whole is clearly anomalous, since even late medieval houses had parlour and service chambers. Of the 33 room-by-room inventories only 15 mention any upper chamber at all, though some of the rest may list first-floor rooms under the catch-all title of "chamber". Of these 15 only 7 list more than one upper chamber. As demonstrated above, these chambers exist physically. They may not appear in the inventories because they were empty, or had goods within that were not worth valuing. Alternatively they may have been occupied by servants with their own possessions, which are consequently not listed as the owner's property. (This second option is unlikely since it is generally recognized that servants in husbandry travelled with few possessions of their own, particularly during this early period (Kussmaul 1981: 31–42).) These chambers may also have contained stored crops and other goods, which only show up on the inventories under general farm headings. Of the 44 inventories from this period 8 have clear evidence of one form or another of storage of food upstairs. (This is more properly 8 out of 32 since such storage will rarely show up if the inventory is not room-by-room.)

The ceiling-over of the hall gave the first floor the potential to be developed as a sphere of interaction in its own right, it being possible now to move across the upper chambers; something which is clearly seen in the later inventories. But to some extent the 1576–7 inventories indicate that houses were being built in a new way but were still thought and used at least partly in the old way. Thus, we see the elements of a new physical and conceptual structure to the house being laid out in this period. Their unfolding and full impact, however, did not occur till the closed period. It is to that period that we must now turn.

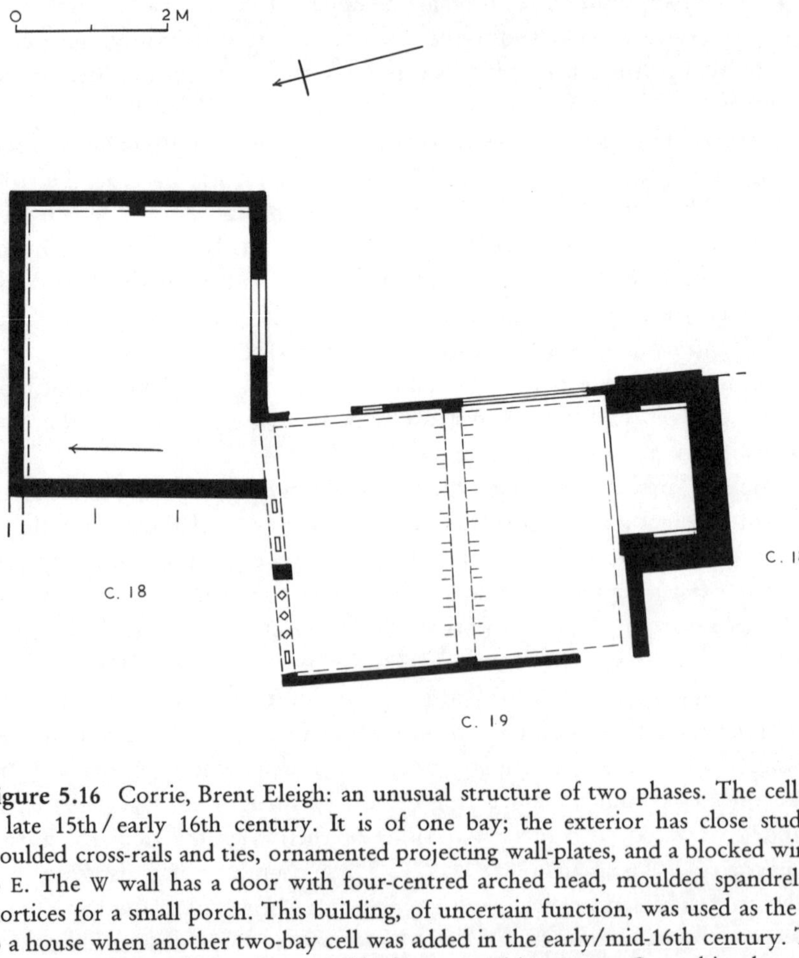

Figure 5.16 Corrie, Brent Eleigh: an unusual structure of two phases. The cell to N is late 15th/early 16th century. It is of one bay; the exterior has close studding, moulded cross-rails and ties, ornamented projecting wall-plates, and a blocked window to E. The W wall has a door with four-centred arched head, moulded spandrels and mortices for a small porch. This building, of uncertain function, was used as the wing to a house when another two-bay cell was added in the early/mid-16th century. There is a large stack, with door in probable former position to W. Over this, the central posts have no tie. Roof with two crown-posts in the gable ends, both with arch-brace to collar purlin. No traces of sooting. The ceiling was inserted into cell to N in 17/18th century. The end-on joists are carried on inserted cross-rails. The roof of this cell was heightened and rebuilt in 18th century. In the 18/19th century the building was converted to the appearance of an L-shaped farmhouse.

Notes

1. Dating is again problematic, although there is much more rapid stylistic change in this period, plus a few firm historical dates. Several very early examples of conversion and fully ceiled plans can be closely dated. As noted in the previous chapter, a few 15th-century chimney stacks were known at least at the supra-vernacular level. There are also unpublished reports of late 15th century- stacks found in neighbouring Essex and in urban areas, as well as in other areas of Britain (cf. Smith 1992). However, there is only one possible example of this practice in the sample. This is Mill House, Alpheton, where a large decorated stack of *c.* 1500 was inserted into an early or mid 15th-century hall. Newbury Farm, Bildeston, is a new house; its first phase is fully ceiled, and has a stack and porch have been added in the 1540s. Again, a date around *c.* 1500 for the first phase is likely. There are other houses that are probably of *c.* 1500–30 but with less firm dating evidence. Examples of very late conversion include Ark Farm, Whepstead, dated to 1612, and 31 Egremont St, Glemsford. Church Farm, Brettenham, formerly an open-hall and cross-wing house, has its main range completely rebuilt, the rebuilding being dated 1587. Early maps of both Norfolk (1550) and the Weald (various of the mid and late 16th century) indicate that many if not most houses in these areas had stacks by the later 16th century (Yates 1982: 219–24), though other areas of Britain have much later dates for the ceiling-over of halls.

Within this period, various dating criteria can be used as rules of thumb. "Plank and muntin" work is classically found forming the screens passages of open halls although the majority of known examples in the sample are from 16th-century contexts and other partitions also use it. At Wolfe Hall, Barrow, and Langleys, Hawkedon, plank and muntin work is stratified later than the mid 16th century. Roll-moulded styles on chamfers, mullions and other features may end a little earlier than plank-and-muntin work, around the mid to late 16th century. Similarly, the use of diamond-mullioned windows, usually with wooden shutters rather than glazing, is a medieval technique but for which no definite examples can be found in the sample after *c.* 1550 (as in Essex; Scott 1984a): there are no examples known nationally from documentary evidence after this date (Salzman 1952, 198). The stepped chamfer stop probably runs on, though in decreasing numbers, to the late 16th century. McCann feels its demise in neighbouring Essex must be *c.* 1570–80 (McCann 1985: 2–3).

Crown-post roofs are clearly found in 16th-century contexts. The known examples are: Hawkedon Hall, Hawkedon, Vaiseys and Corrie Farms, Brent Eleigh (Fig. 5.16), and Newbury Farm, Bildeston. All these houses are suspected to be early 16th century in date on other grounds, though some crown-posts from the 1560s are claimed in Essex (McCann 1984: 4). The tradition of four-centred arched heads to doors may also disappear early in the 16th century. The technique of stud-bracing can also be dated to the earlier 16th century (Scott 1984b), but is unknown from late 16th-century contexts.

Criteria known from 17th-century contexts and having origins in the later 16th century are more difficult to define. The lambs' tongue chamfer-stop is known from a house in Essex dated 1564 (McCann 1985: 3) and rapidly becomes standard. Equally ubiquitous is the clasped-purlin form of roof (Plate 2b), and again this is of little use in dating. Many probable mid 16th-century houses have clasped-purlin roofs. Windows with glazing bars and ovolo-moulded mullions are not known from any definite context before *c.* 1570. Depressed or square heads to doors appear early, as at Newbury Farm, Bildeston.

It is interesting to note a large number and variety of decorative features unique to and diagnostic of this period, including leaf-stops, double-ogee chamfers, serpentine-braces, and schematic vine and hop designs. None of these rules of thumb, however, has any secure or absolute value.

2. Timber stacks are more common in mid-Suffolk and examples are known also from Essex (McCann 1984, Padfield 1985a). This is the only example of a house with positive evidence for a timber stack from the sample: the survival rate of this particular practice must be very small for obvious reasons.

3. The term "parlour" has been used for the sake of consistency throughout the text although the contemporary 15th- and 16th-century term may well have been "solar" or "chamber", and these rooms are listed as such in Table 5.1.

CHAPTER 6
CLOSED HOUSES

If transitional houses were diverse in form and lavish in decoration, closed houses were uniform and plain in both plan and detail. The period from the late 16th century onwards is dominated by one type of house: the two- or more usually three-cell lobby-entry form, with internal, axial chimney stack and back-to-back fireplaces (Figs 3.4, 6.1–3; Plate 4c). This type of house is one of several found in the transitional period, as observed in Chapter 5, and builders and owners were certainly familiar with its logic and arrangement from an early date. A building contract of 1577 gives a detailed specification for this type of house (Johnson 1981: 53). So just as the open period saw a general type in the open-hall house, so the closed period had the three-cell lobby-entry house.

W. G. Hoskins suggested that the first part of this period witnessed a major phase of rebuilding (Hoskins 1953: 48). If anything, however, the reverse is the case. Of the 25 houses surveyed, 13 are mid- or late 17th-century as opposed to only 5 which are definitely early. It is interesting that this indicates a positive acceleration of the rate of building through the 17th century.[1] This was not expected, but on reflection this is perhaps because previous fieldwork has concentrated on the more exposed and impressive frames of the early 17th century rather than on those of the later period. Just as with the absence of wings from many late medieval houses discussed in Chapter 4, the lack of true randomness in previous work has perhaps blurred the picture of surviving houses. From the evidence of western Suffolk, Barley (1985: 653) is therefore correct to suggest that "the concept of a Great Rebuilding has outlived its usefulness, and to retain it risks hindering further understanding".

Such a suggested rate of activity can be readily related to the rise and fall of economic forces, such as the history of the textile industry. Decline in the later 16th century was followed by the temporary flourishing of the "new draperies" after 1660, as well as the expansion of arable and dairy farming at the social level of the yeoman and husbandman (Dymond & Betterton 1982:

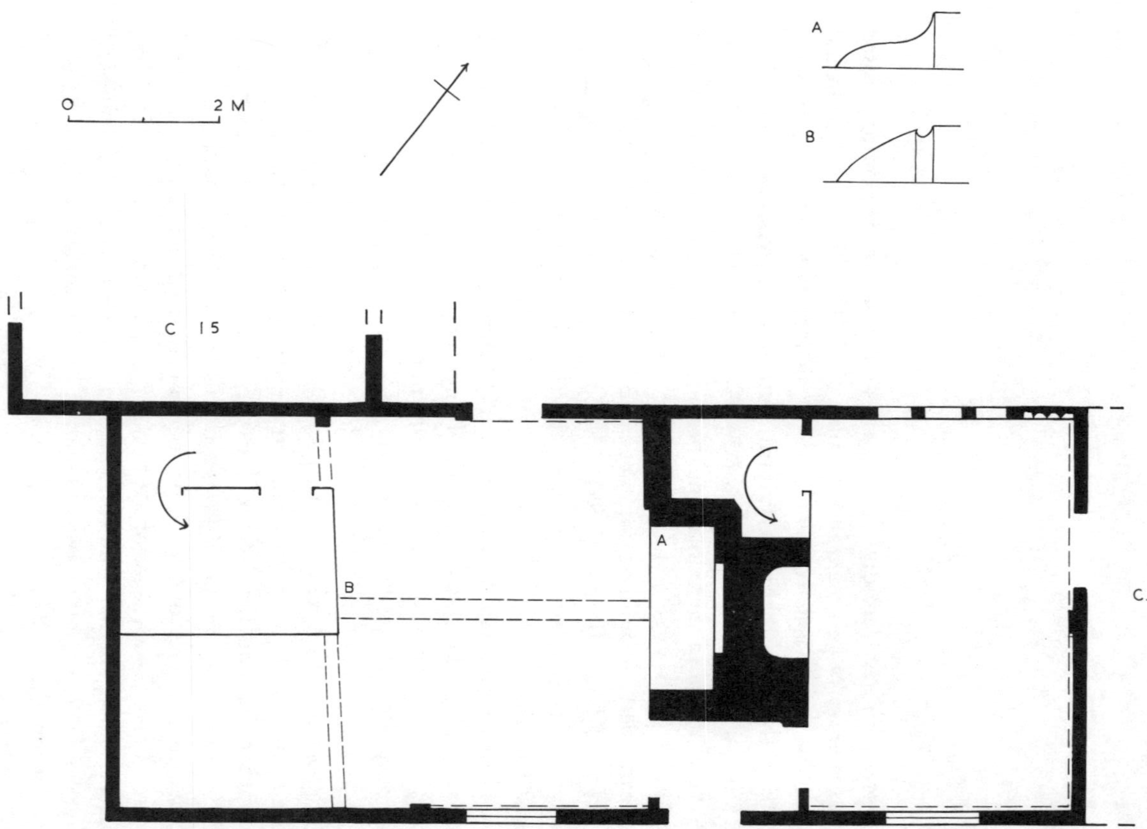

Figure 6.1 Old House, Hitcham: an L-shaped building of two phases. The second phase only is illustrated: it is of typical three-cell lobby-entry form. The first phase is the later 15th century/early 16th-century Guildhall, which was reused as a service wing to the later house.

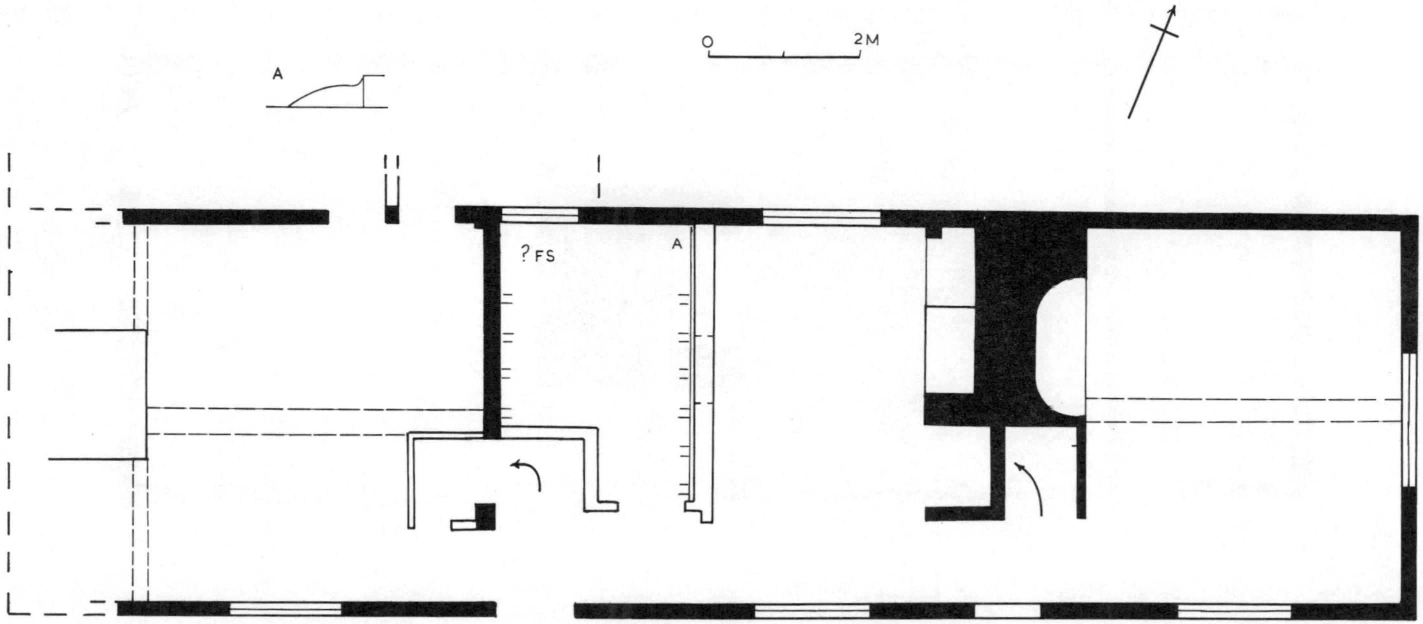

Figure 6.2 Bryers, Hawstead: a typical three-cell lobby-entry house, *c.* 1600. Blocked lobby entry. E end wall has straight tension-braces above the cross-rail and a blocked window over. Old, thatched roof destroyed by fire; photo in possession of owners indicates a former clasped-purlin roof. The house is mentioned as "lately built" in 1611 (Cullum 1913: 171). The hall was reduced in size by a flint-and-brick wall creating a pantry in the late 17th century or 18th century. The framing was exposed externally after 1930, and the date of 1593 placed there in recent years.

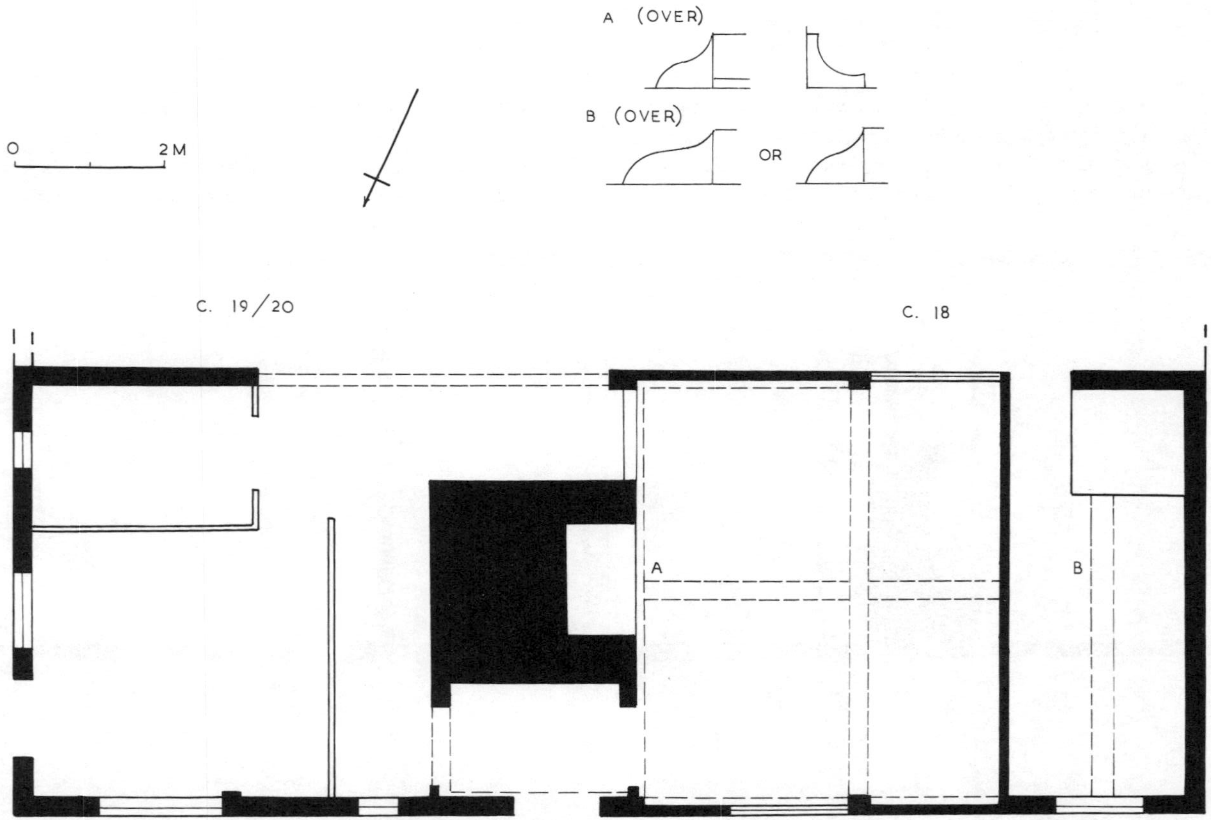

Figure 6.3 Wattisham Hall, Wattisham: a later 16th / early 17th-century three-cell lobby-entry house, standing within a complex of moats. Two-bay parlour. Stack has room for a stair to rear; over, the stair to attic rises over the lobby entry. The arrangement has been altered at the service end of the building. Stack has four brick shafts, now encased in concrete. Partitions inserted into hall and parlour and a rear range added in the 18/19th century, since rebuilt. Three large barns nearby of the 16th century and 17th century.

32–6). It is tempting to go further and to note the lack of definite mid-16th century examples such as Church Farm, Great Waldingfield, and suggest that the bulk of the "mid or late" building took place after the economic depression of the English Revolution, as well as a series of poor corn harvests in the 1630s and late 1640s after a pattern of "no discoverable rhythm" in harvests earlier (Hoskins 1964: 1968).

Grammar

As we have seen was the case with the competence underlying open houses, a limited set of grammatical rules gives rise to a limited set of final forms. Unlike the grammar for open houses, however, it does not matter in which order the first three rules for closed houses are placed.

1. A chimney bay of unique dimensions is laid out, with stack, back-to-back fireplaces, stair, and a lobby entry on one side. The stair may be next to the lobby entry or on the other side of the stack. This last detail is obviously important for the circulation pattern of the house, although it is not clear how that choice related to type or date of house.

I suggested in Chapter 5 that, in terms of the grammar, the chimney bay formally took the place of the opposed doors or through-passage. It retained the entry, although now shortened to a small lobby, and was once again a narrow element at one end of the hall. However, this suggestion needs qualification. First, the through-passage or space for opposed doors in open houses was often housed within the lower bay of the hall, whereas the chimney bay is a separate, distinctive element of its own. Secondly, the chimney bay is placed in a different relative position, usually at the upper end of the hall, and we have seen how socially and symbolically important the relation of doors to lower end is in the open plan. The chimney bay should therefore be seen as a new element although with older antecedents. The central point to be made here is that, in its new form, it was capable of taking on very new meanings.

2. The hall is laid out on one side of the stack. This is usually of two bays, as with open halls. Closed halls, however, are clearly smaller than open halls, and the bay division is not necessarily visible or of aesthetic importance within the hall.
3. The parlour is laid out on the other side of the stack from the hall. It is usually of one bay.

At this point the ground plan of the two-cell lobby-entry house is complete (cf. Fig. 6.4).

4. The service consists of a single cell. It is added to the other side of the hall.

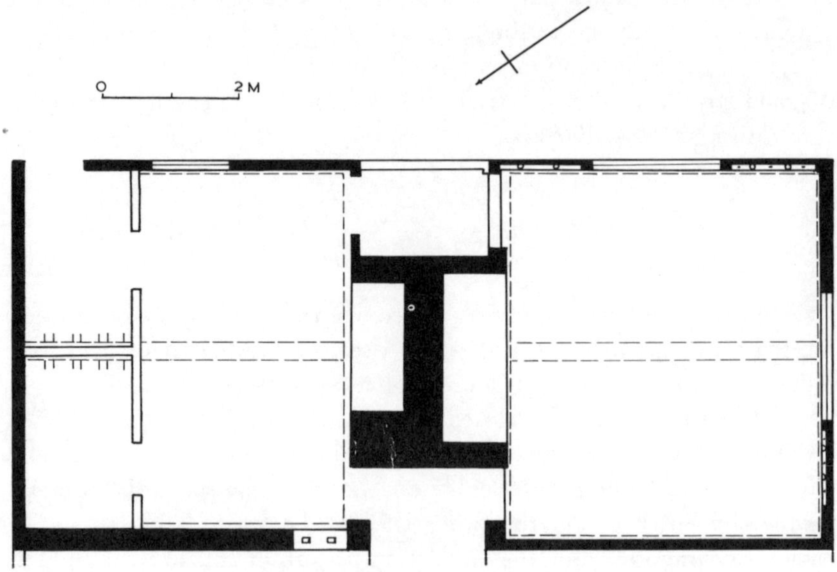

Figure 6.4 Powers Farm, Great Waldingfield: a two-cell lobby-entry house of *c.* 1600. It is unclear which cell is the hall and which the parlour. Three-window ranges to S and W, and similar sets of blocked windows in the end walls over. Blocked lobby entry to E of stack and former stair to W. The stack top has four octagonal shafts. Over, a partition round the stack includes a door frame. Roof of wind-braced clasped-purlin type; six collars. Later 17th-century panelling inserted into hall. Range of farm buildings to W including a 16/17th-century barn.

No examples of "submedieval" service ends were found from this period. It is possible that many if not most services were divided internally in some way: this is certainly indicated by the inventory evidence (Table 6.1). However, there are no cases of definite observations of partitions within a single cell in the field, probably because such partitions are not properly jointed to the wall frame at this period (see Ch. 7). This is of course not the case with service wings. Both closed parlour and service wings are known, but only as additions or modifications to existing structures.

5. The house is fully ceiled. Jetties are forbidden.
6. The roof is gabled. Again, no contrary examples are known.

The three-cell lobby-entry plan clearly dominates over all other forms, in parallel with the dominance of the three-cell open-hall plan of open houses. This is a strikingly uniform pattern. Uniformity is similarly seen in closed alterations to earlier houses. Ten of the transitional houses discussed in Chapter 5 were converted to a lobby-entry form in this period. This was done

Table 6.1 Room naming and order in inventories (1680s).

Name	Hall	Parlour	Chamber	Solar	Entry	Buttery	Kitchen	Lower C	Shop	Closet	Cellar	Hall C	Parlour C	Buttery C	Kitchen C	Bed C	C over shop	Folks/mans C	Backhouse C	Corn C	Dairy	Pantry	Cheesehouse	Milkhouse	Backhouse	Malthouse	Granary	Barn	Stable	*Other/Comments*
T Stewart	1	2				3						7		6					10		4		8		9					Parlour 5
W Frysan	1	2	6			4															3		9		8					Buttery 7
A Wright	1	2	6			4		2	7	5											3	5								Upper Chamber 8
R Poulter	1	2										4	3							9	7		5			8				Meal Chamber 6
H Bradford	2	1	5			3															4								6	
J Parkin	1	2				3						4																		
B Robinson	1					6		5													4									
R Brett	1		3			2																								
R Lettelpr'd	2					3										1		4												
A Payne	1	2				7	6				5		3					4			8				9					
D Steden	2																								3					Lodging Room 1
T Holmes	1		4			3																								Buttery 3 Chamber 4
J Cole	1	4	7			2						6	5																	
S Beachcroft	2	4	13		3	5				20	4	12	16						10		9					6	21	11		Fire Rm 1 Flesh Ho 7 Meal Ho 8 Entry Ch 18
B Smyth	1		3			5		2	6					4																[Yellow Ch 15 Blue Ch 17 Garrets 18 19
J Chilver	1	2				4	3			6		8			7					5	10									Over Gatehouse 9
R Nobes	1	2			7	6			9	8		5	3	4											10					Wool Chamber 11
J Sturgeon	1	2	10			4	3				5				7						6		9							Cellar Chamber 8
M Jowers	1	2	10		15	4			17			16	14		5				12		8		11		6			18		Lodging Rm 3 Lit Rm by Hall 7 Swilho 9 Strs Hd 13
W Muskett	1	2				4	10						3	9		6					7		8					11		Buttery 5
J Johnson	2	1				8							3					11			4		5		7		10			Buttery 9
H Hill	6	5			3	8	9					2	1		4						7							10		Granary 11
J Nelsegood	4					3	1		9	7		6				5					2									Dairy Chamber 8
G Gardner	1		9			7			8	3	6	2				5	4								10		11		12	
H Tillney	1					2						5		6							4									Buttery 3 Vaunce Roof 7
J Kerington	3	4	9			2	1			5				7	6		12	10								8			13	Hayhouse 11
R Park	4	3				7			8			2	1									5				6				Little Hall 3 Beer House 8
J Mynnes	2	1	9		6		12				10	5	4							14	7	3				13	16		18	C over Hall C 8 Dairy C 11 Cart Lodge 15 Malthouse Ch 16 17
W Grant	1	2	3			6								4													9			Buttery 7 Dairy Chamber 8 Hay House 11
T Brincklie	1		3			5										2														
J Boggas	2	1										4	3	6												5				
F French	2	1										5	4							3				7					6	
E Campian		1														2		6		10	4		7							Fire Room 3 Passage Rm 5 Spare Rm 8 C over Lodging Rm 9
J Challes	1	2	4			3																								Wool C 5
E Pleasans	1	2										4	3								5								7	Rm next Dairy 6
A Smith	1	2				7			6		4		3												5					
J Debenham	2	1				4						7	5								3									Dairy Chamber 6
J How	1	2										4	5								6	3								
E Grouse	1	4				3						6	7	5							2									J Dobadoes House 9
J How	1	2	3			5						4									7				6				10	Dairy Chamber 8 Milho 9
B Knockes	2	1	3			6							4							9	8		5		7					

in a variety of ways. Those houses already equipped with back-to-back fireplaces needed only the position of the door to be shifted, as at Denham Priory and Black Horse Farm, Wickhambrook (Figs 6.5, 6.6), although at Wolfe Hall, Barrow, this was accompanied by a change in orientation of the front of the house from north to south. At Clockhouse Farm, Shimpling, a wing and stack with back-to-back fireplaces was added to the existing house, again causing a 90-degree change in orientation.

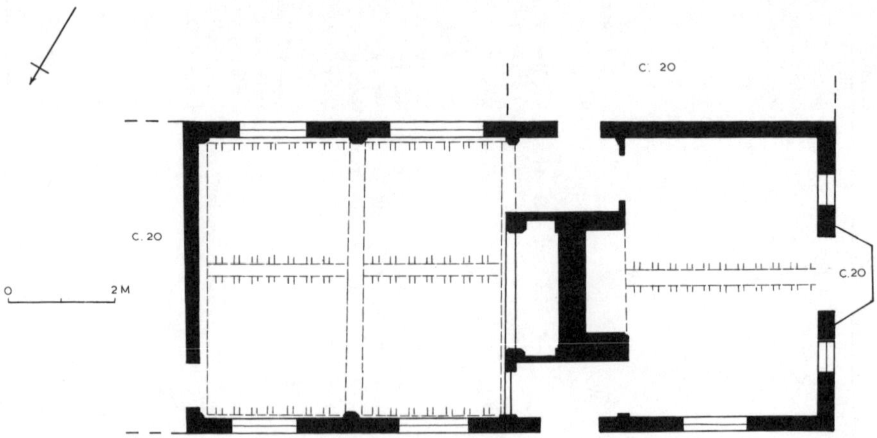

Figure 6.5 Denham Priory, Denham: the hall and parlour of a mid-16th-century continuous-jetty house, now of two-cell lobby-entry form. The 16th-century opposed doors at the lower end of the hall were replaced by the present lobby entry in the 17th century. There may have been a destroyed cell to E. Arch-braced ties over and a clasped-purlin roof. A roll-moulded mullioned window lights the hall chamber. The bressumer has leaf ornament. A photo of 1904 identifies the house without evidence as The Old Parsonage.

In terms of the surviving houses, then, this form is dominant. The plans of the houses listed in a sample of "late" probate inventories taken from the 1680s are more problematic, however (Table 6.1). The average number of rooms mentioned per house rises markedly: from an average of over six for the early sample to over nine for the later sample. Many more upstairs rooms are mentioned; in particular the hall chamber is found in 21 of the 39 room-by-room inventories of this period. Many more different kinds of room name are found, and many rooms in the later inventories are designated by their spatial position or other properties rather than function.

As noted in Chapter 5, the earlier inventories reflected a basic three-cell plan. The greater number of rooms in the later sample of inventories makes their relative location more difficult to infer. If we assume that the officials moved from one room to the next in a logical fashion, the most common plan still seems to be a three-cell one, although often with a wing or at least further rooms at parlour, service, or even at both ends. Again it is difficult to draw a clear boundary between service rooms within the house and ancillary buildings. Here, some are clearly within the building; J. Chilver of Denham, for example, lists the kitchen, buttery and "corn chamber" between the hall and parlour and the upper chambers, but the dairy and cheesehouse at the end of the inventory are probably ancillary buildings.

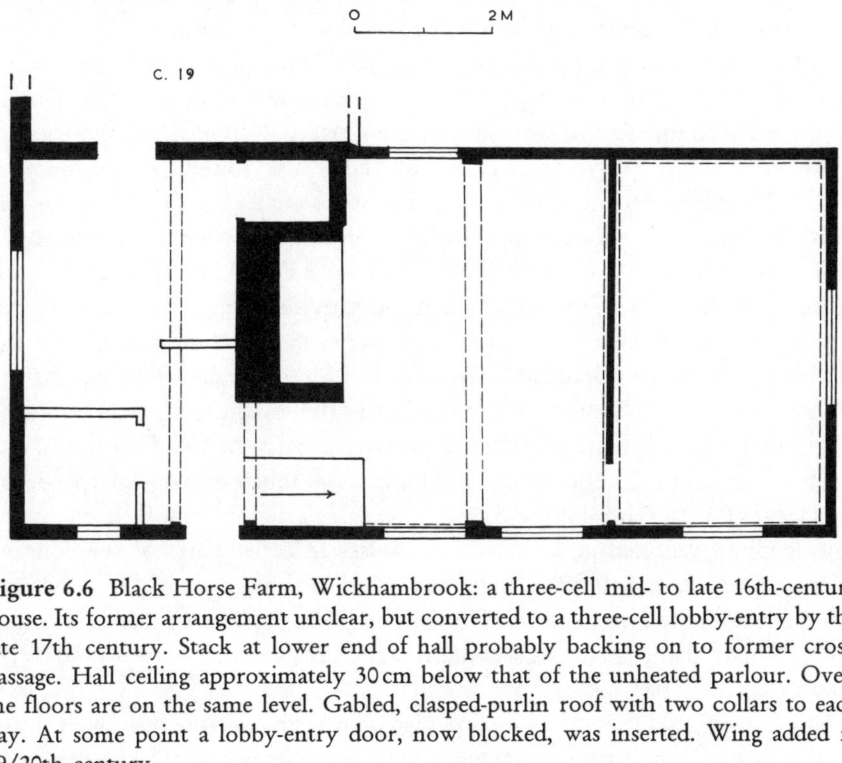

Figure 6.6 Black Horse Farm, Wickhambrook: a three-cell mid- to late 16th-century house. Its former arrangement unclear, but converted to a three-cell lobby-entry by the late 17th century. Stack at lower end of hall probably backing on to former cross-passage. Hall ceiling approximately 30 cm below that of the unheated parlour. Over, the floors are on the same level. Gabled, clasped-purlin roof with two collars to each bay. At some point a lobby-entry door, now blocked, was inserted. Wing added in 19/20th century.

One area of direct conflict between architectural and probate evidence is over heating. Most lobby-entry houses appear to have stacks heating the parlour and hall. The inventories, however, indicate that the kitchen is usually the second room to be heated. It is possible that some of the rooms on the other side of the stack were kitchens rather than parlours, although this is unlikely given problems of circulation between the kitchen and hall, two busy areas. It is more probable that by the 1680s most formerly unheated service ends had a stack of their own. The parlour fireplace, on the other hand, may well not be indicated in many inventories since it lacks extensive hearth furniture compared to that in the hall.[2]

The three-cell lobby-entry plan, then, is the dominant form of the closed period. Yet it was only one of a number of different house forms in the transitional period. Why did it subsequently become so commonplace at the vernacular level?

As with the interpretation of open halls, "commonsensical" or functional arguments prove unconvincing. It could be argued that the through-passage is simply inconvenient or surplus to the requirements of the home, and further that it acts as an unpleasant "wind tunnel" running through the house. Again one must ask "inconvenient to whom?" or, more specifically, "what household form is it that prefers a lobby entry to a through passage?" The lobby entry itself has its disadvantages. It is often narrow and constricted. It may have been accompanied in some cases by an external door at the service end; while no definite physical evidence of these was found, a rear door is repeatedly mentioned in Suffolk folk beliefs (Ewart Evans 1966), and by the mid-17th century the nature and quality of framing is such as to render the detection of former doorways problematic (see Ch. 7, n. 1). The through passage may have been draughty, but it did provide a separation between the service and upper ends of the house, or between the "house part" and the working farm in the Highland Zone household in other areas of England and Wales. In any case, Chapter 4 discussed how the cross-passage was part of a wider architectural frame carrying important social values and messages.

The question of the popularity of the three-cell lobby-entry is sharpened by the fact that as the through-passage was being rejected in Suffolk it was being quite happily retained in 17th-century houses in other parts of the country (Mercer 1975: 50–60). It was also being carried to those parts of the American colonies dominated by Highland Zone immigrants (Neiman 1986, Cummings 1979). What, then, was the household structure which the 16th- and 17th-century through-passage plan represented?

Neiman suggests that "the cross-passage plan seems to have been well suited to social situations in which the relations between its users could be described as "knyt with a knot of collateral amytie", in which masters and men [sic] saw themselves as part of the same corporate community, a society characterized by coherently defined social rôles upheld by mutually felt rights and responsibilities" (Neiman 1986: 307). It was this form, both of community and architecture, that persisted through the 17th century in areas of northern and western England (James 1986); it was this form that underlay the layout of the open houses; and it was this social and architectural form that individual builders and owners at the traditional level apparently rejected in increasing numbers from the mid 16th century onwards in western Suffolk.

If the rejection of elements of the open plan paralleled rejection of the social meanings it carried and the social form to which it related, then the layout of the lobby-entry plan should imply acceptance of a new social form, a new set of cultural meanings. It did so not through outright innovation, but through renegotiation of elements of the old order to be refashioned into the new. This new order will be explored in Chapter 8. Here it is simply necessary to point out the underlying social logic of this process as well as its economic and environmental aspects, and indicate that this logic is related to that of segregation and closure.

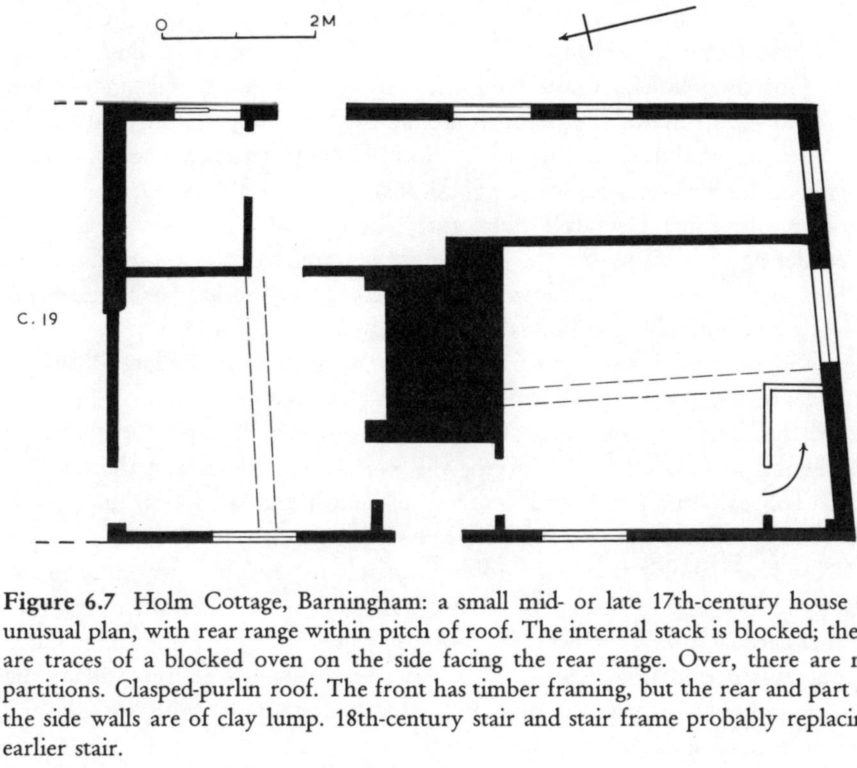

Figure 6.7 Holm Cottage, Barningham: a small mid- or late 17th-century house of unusual plan, with rear range within pitch of roof. The internal stack is blocked; there are traces of a blocked oven on the side facing the rear range. Over, there are no partitions. Clasped-purlin roof. The front has timber framing, but the rear and part of the side walls are of clay lump. 18th-century stair and stair frame probably replacing earlier stair.

Within this apparently stable and uniform pattern further changes did unfold in the course of the mid- and late 17th century. In particular, we see the development of "double-pile" houses and the central passage. The term "double-pile" refers to a plan two rooms deep. S. Beachcroft, clerk, had a house of this form in the 1680s according to the inventory evidence. Plans with a rear range of rooms occur in two forms: in the culmination of piecemeal "encroachment" round the rear of earlier large houses, and surprisingly in two smaller houses in the north-east of the sample area. Holm Cottage, Barningham (Fig. 6.7), appears from external inspection to be a standard two-cell lobby-entry house, but internally it is partitioned with a narrow corridor-like rear range. This range has no clear function although the entrance to the oven in the stack is from this side: it is probably a service range. There is no corresponding partition on the floor above. The Cottage next to Bell House, Pakenham, has a symmetrical front with rooms of equal size, lobby entry, and again a narrow rear range under the same roof, although here a stair runs up behind the rear of the stack.

In both these cases the service functions, already marginalized, have been at least partly relegated to the rear of the house. Both examples contradict the theory of social diffusion: neither is a tiny cottage, but both are smaller than most and neither sits within a farmstead; they are possibly of husbandman level. The two houses again hold interesting implications for innovation within the competence. The competence allows internal partitions within the service area (see above). In the case of Holm Cottage, this rule was simply extended in the form of a partition right across the house after the laying-out of the form of a typical two-cell lobby entry. Innovation was achieved again by a reordering of ideas within the antecedent hierarchy of the competence.

This reordering of old ideas in a form two rooms deep has been argued for the origins of "double-pile" houses in general (Barley 1979: 163). It is interesting to note the popularity of this form in New England in the later 17th and 18th centuries, where it is termed the "salt-box" house. St George has suggested that its popularity arose from its expression of competition between households and class relations during this period. He argues that the salt-box house concealed its productive centre (the hearth and service) from outside gaze and combined segregation with centralization (St George 1986).

Closed households faced two different problems. The first was how to lay out an ideal house, whereas the second was how to adapt an older structure to new needs. Older structures, then, often had service or parlour wings added during this period (Fig. 6.8). In both cases we can see a desire to place the service and parlour ends of the houses ever further apart, both socially and architecturally, although this has architectural results.

A further development was the use of a central hallway or passage, with a room on either side. This produced the house form classified by Eden as "Class T" (1968; known in North America as the "I" house), usually with chimney stacks in the end walls. Sparrows Hall, Stanstead (Fig. 6.9), is a typical example of the type, probably late 17th century in date. It is a middling sized house although the framing is of narrow scantling and, unusually, of elm. The stair position is unclear but was probably in the central room, while the rooms to either side probably acted as hall/service and parlour. Block Farm, Bradfield Combust (Fig. 6.10), was converted to this form at some point in the early to mid 17th century as part of an unusual and complex rebuild. This rebuilding involved addition to an unclear three-room plan of

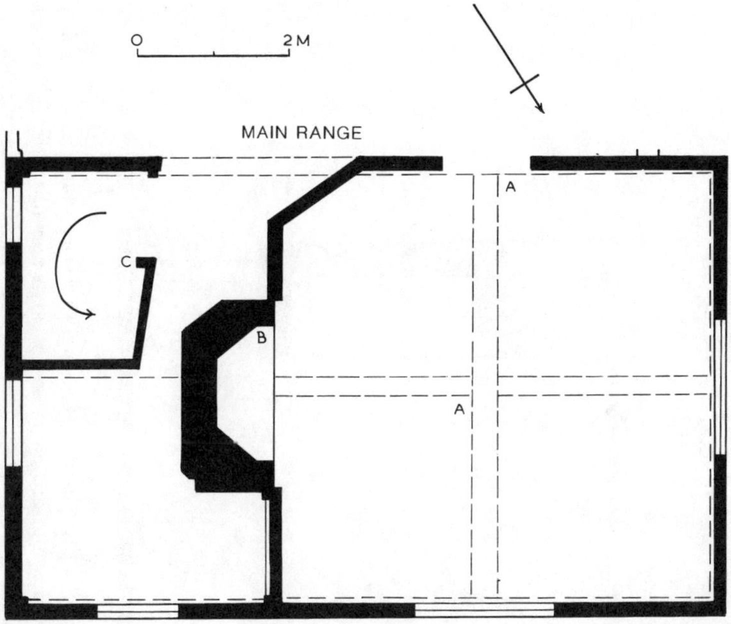

Figure 6.8 Church Farm, Great Waldingfield: crosswing to a main range now destroyed. The wing is of two cells and three bays, with a stack within the rear cell. A framed stair in the SW corner runs up to the attics. The wing is unjettied, but has a projecting tie with the date 1670 and initials D. C. on it. There is a vine/hop design either side and on the bargeboards to the gable.

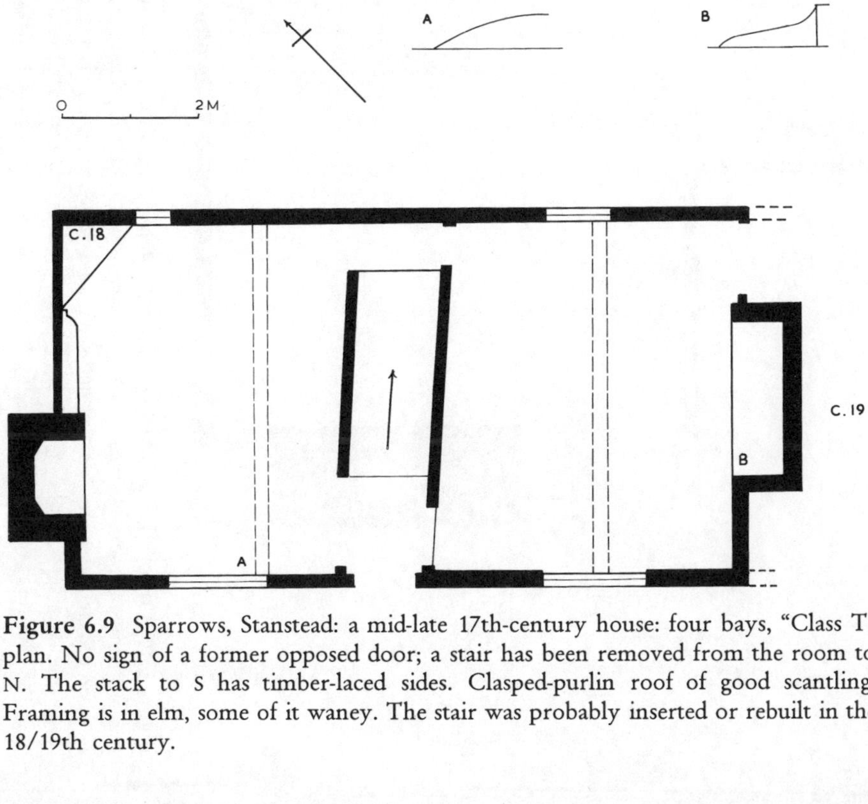

Figure 6.9 Sparrows, Stanstead: a mid-late 17th-century house: four bays, "Class T" plan. No sign of a former opposed door; a stair has been removed from the room to N. The stack to S has timber-laced sides. Clasped-purlin roof of good scantling. Framing is in elm, some of it waney. The stair was probably inserted or rebuilt in the 18/19th century.

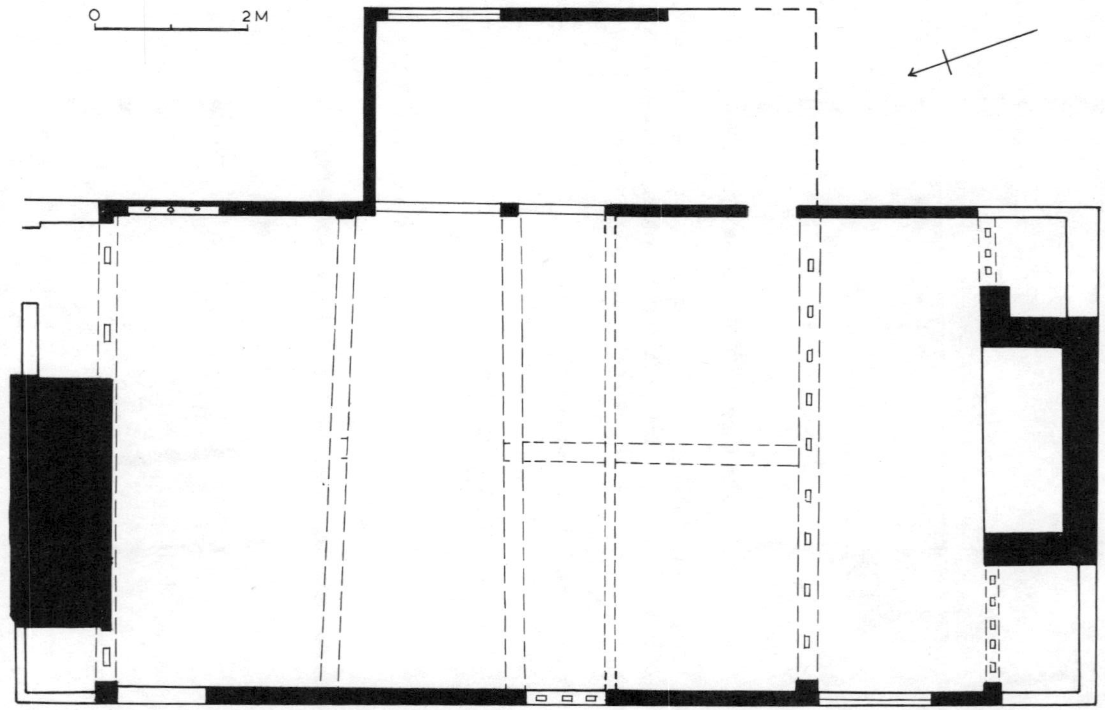

Figure 6.10 Block Farm, Bradfield Combust: a 16th-century house of complex development. The first phase is a five-bay, three-cell house: the central bay was probably a chimney bay for a stack, now removed. There is a break in the plates at all levels within this phase, so this phase may be subdivided in two. Arch-braced ties; mortices for diamond-mullioned windows. There is a four-centred arch in the N end wall over, but this may have been rescued from an earlier building. In the mid- to late 16th century stacks were inserted into the gable ends along with a series of roll-moulded mullioned windows. At this stage the ties were rearranged, probably to assist circulation over. A staircase wing was added in the 17th century, giving a T-shaped plan with two end-wall stacks. There is a complex of 17th- to 19th-century farm buildings to S.

a large stairwing at the rear of the house and probable removal of an axial stack, the rearrangement of the ties above and the addition of two end wall stacks.

The so-called Class T house provides one extreme form of polarization within the household, with a central room dividing the two ends of the house and central access to the upper floor. In terms of circulation pattern it is similar to the two-cell lobby-entry form, but in symbolic terms it must mean more than this: the central unifying symbol of the hearth, once a central open feature, then divided in two but under a common stack, is finally torn apart to opposite ends of the house.

These new forms went alongside steady alterations to the form of older houses and less radical innovations in the new. These included the provision of separate stacks at the service end of the house and the increasing height of houses to allow freer circulation and accommodation at first-floor level. Both these features can be observed in a few 16th-century houses: Wolfe Hall, Barrow, and Newbury Farm, Bildeston, for example, have two full storeys, both fully ceiled and well provided with glazed windows. But the practice of ceiling upper floors and making more provision for first-floor and attic accommodation and circulation generally became more dominant by the later 17th century. Where houses were one-and-a-half storeys high, dormer windows, ceilings set into the roof space at collar level and gabled roofs could be added. These additions transformed previously murky space reserved for storage into a well lit and possibly heated chamber. In a few houses, a tie-beam could be omitted as a hindrance to movement at the upper level. This is first known in the 16th century at Shrub End, Great Barton, and is a common 17th-century technique.

All these changes can be seen in terms of centralization of both the circulation pattern and social meanings of the enclosed house. In addition, they can all be seen, as Mercer points out, as regional variants on a single national theme (Mercer 1975; Smith 1985: 738, 774; Harrison & Hutton 1984: 74; Pearson 1985: 69). The activities within the house were drawn in, rationalized and divided according to criteria of function. The end result of this process was the fully "Georgian" layout characteristic of socially middling and upper-class houses of the 18th century. These houses, with segmented, segregated, symmetrical double-pile plans, three or four storeys high, can be found in great numbers in the villages of Suffolk. The town of Bury St Edmunds, as a market and emergent social centre for the county gentry, is still full of these Georgian structures and facades, which cast their refined gaze over an increasingly segmented, segregated world.

Georgian architecture at the local level is generally seen as a result of the imposition or grafting of pattern-books and national architectural ideas onto the regional vernacular; even Glassie reverts to such a model for his forgotten corner of Virginia when he suggests that "a local builder may have travelled to the East . . . possibly an Easterner or a new arrival from England requested that an alien house be built. A book carrying plans and elevations may have been bartered for some barrels of Indian weed" (Glassie 1975: 88). Such was the immediate, proximal cause. I suggest, however, that in order to make imposition successful, for it to be a fatal blow to traditional forms of architecture rather than a shallow gloss over it, the craft tradition itself had to be ready to accept such an imposition. The plant had to be a close enough form for the graft to take. But to explore this tradition in more detail, and to suggest how it reached this weakened state, some consideration of the technical system that went with it must be made. This is the subject of Chapter 7.

Notes

1. The removal of the judgemental component of the sample scarcely alters the relative proportions, since of this component three houses are late, one is early and two are mid-17th-century.

Very few of the houses in western Suffolk have dates inscribed on their fabric compared to other areas of England. Of 17 dated houses within the area the majority of dates given were discovered on inspection to be modern while the remainder of those visited turned out to be extensions or rebuilds of earlier houses. Again, therefore, dates are suggested for each house on an inductive basis, based on the following criteria.

The dominant trend during this period is the steady diminution in scantling and overall quality of the framing, along with a general decrease in the quality of carpentry. Around *c.* 1600 many houses are still close studded with tension-braces. The wing at Church Farm, Great Waldingfield, has scantling of middling quality, although ornamented and carefully put together, dated 1670. The vast majority of the houses listed as mid- or late 17th century have poorer frames with much re-used timber and crude methods of dealing with ceiling beams and joists that often resemble insertions (discussed in Ch. 7). An interesting house in this context is Bryers Farm, Hawstead, which is referred to as "lately built" in a document of 1611 and is therefore probably *c.* 1600 in date (see Cullum 1813: 171). The frame of this house already has narrow studs and straight braces, usually plastered over but exposed here by the present occupant; such a house might be considered to be mid-17th-century archaeologically. It suggests that scantling is partly a function of social status rather than of date, and that therefore many of these houses might be earlier than we think.

There is a relative paucity of decoration or other datable features of the frame during this period, as there is of exposed framing generally. The lamb's tongue chamfer-stop is almost universal. Simple run-out stops are also unhelpful since this style also runs all the way through the period and is often a consequence of the use of waney timber in any case.

Ovolo-moulded mullioned windows, with or without transoms, occur only in early contexts and not in late: early examples include Church Farm, Brettenham, dated 1587, and the facade of Monks Hall, Glemsford, dated 1614. Observed examples of late 17th-century windows are rare and not tenoned into the frame, thus leaving little trace when removed. Scarfs do become shorter and also of simpler form. Finally, stacks become smaller and narrower in line with the size of their fireplaces, and the elaborate large shafted tops of the 16th and early 17th centuries give way to smaller plain square tops.

2. This general interpretation of the inventories is at variance with that given by Silvia Colman (1979). Colman infers a range of plans from the 1665 inventories, and specifically indicates the retention of many more submedieval service ends and through-passages than suggested here. Service arrangements are difficult to infer from the probates, given that, as we have seen, it is generally difficult to draw a definite line between rooms inside and outside the house. In addition, there is a lack of specific reference to through-passages and opposed doors; although these were probably largely bare of items to record the archaeological evidence as argued suggests that only a few were still extant. Some were retained, but hardly in the numbers suggested by Colman.

CHAPTER 7
THE TRANSFORMATION OF THE TECHNICAL SYSTEM

I have now looked at houses between 1400 and 1700. I have tried to relate the forms of houses observed to stability and innovation within the competence governing the craft tradition. I related this competence in turn to the structure and changing form of the household, the social unit within the house. The closure of the open hall and emergence of the lobby-entry plan were understood in terms of changes in cultural values and meanings, values and meanings expressed and played out at an everyday level within and around the house. This long-term process was called "closure".

The use of the term "closure" is a deliberately new one. Part of its meaning relates to the rise of privacy, segregation and symmetry in the early modern period. However, architectural change is more complex than this. In Chapter 4 I showed that symmetry and segregation are far from absent from the open house. I suggested that a more complex pattern of symbolic space, of the differential and selective use of segregation and symmetry, must be explored.

The question of privacy itself is a complex one. The need for privacy is not "natural" or invariate. Paradoxically, it is social in nature. Privacy is something which an individual demands or requires; it is an expression of his or her autonomy. Some people need privacy more than others, and some cultures stress privacy and the individual more than others. Therefore, the strength of the whole concept of privacy is one that depends upon deeper and underlying theoretical questions of the relationship between the individual and society, and the difficult question of "the category of the person" (Carrithers et al. 1985). If privacy is one way in which the notion of the individual is developed and given expression, then it is necessary to look at other aspects of individualism and ask how, culturally and materially, the individual came to be emphasized in everyday life and in domestic architecture in particular.

I suggest that the rise of privacy is one aspect of a much wider social change expressed and played out through architectural change: from a community based on face-to-face relations and governed by conceptions of authority, custom and status (*Gemeinschaft*) to a society based on less personal relations of class and capitalistic economic relations (*Gesellschaft*).

These are very broad shifts occurring over the very long term; they are manifested materially in the closure of the houses in many different ways. We have seen the closure of the house in terms of its layout. Such closure involves, essentially, a move away from references to status within a large body of open space towards a closure of that space into discrete segments. In other words, the architectural referents of the open hall became lost and replaced by different rooms, different classes within the household occupying different spaces. This is the central idea behind the use of the term. This central idea manifests itself in various ways through the organization of space and the divisions between it.

Relations of status depend on everyday interaction; they depend on being played out within an open architectural frame. Master and servant, husband and wife, have to be able to see each other if everyday expressions of authority and deference are to have meaning. The social actors also have to have some common frame of meaning in order to communicate, although that frame may be read, like a text, in different ways (cf. Moore 1985). If a wall is placed between upper and lower ends of the hall, or if upper and lower ends withdraw from the hall to the ends or back of the house, then there is a loss of the old status-based customary rules and a growth in social distance. Relations of class, on the other hand, depend on a different ethic and attitude to work conditioned by that class's structurally distinct part in the relations of production. They therefore depend on the very extent to which that class is divided off from the rest of society and is consequently able to develop its own consciousness, to become a class "for itself" as well as "in itself" (Marx 1977: 228).

The transition from status to class can also be seen in the use of moveable goods rather than architecture to indicate social position. Many of the status indicators within open halls were fixed, such as the benches along the side of the hall in larger houses, as well as the architectural referents already discussed. The shift to moveable goods seen in the inventory evidence (see Ch. 8) indicates growing concern with material wealth as indicator of social position (Ch. 9) as well as growing perception of fluidity of social relations. So the frame of the house itself began to lose some of its social meaning to the objects within it.

The changes in grammar observed across Chapters 4–6 can be seen in terms of transition between a unitary and a fragmented competence. The open competence depended strongly on the relationship and order between the various rules, and stressed the centrality of the open hall. The closed competence did not place the first few, key rules in any particular order. So the centrality of the open hall and the social meanings it signified were encoded deep within the open competence. The closed competence, however, could be manipulated independently of the social meanings the closed house bore. This point will be returned to below.

The final form of the house changed from having cells or rooms in a line, one room deep, to a more compact, organic, centralized, "rational" plan. The final form, the symmetrical Georgian house, lies outside the scope of this study, but the antecedents of the Georgian plan were traced in Chapter 6. Within the Georgian house, the central principle of layout shifted from having reference to social status to functional differentiation. As noted, the later inventories show far more stress on specialized service rooms than do the earlier ones. The hall itself became less of a general activity area, its functions becoming restricted to cooking and eating.

The term "closure" expresses this matrix of changes through its reference to the closure of the open hall and hearth area by the use of ceiling and stack, and more subtly in terms of its reference to demarcation; delimiting; physical boundary formation; physical segregation; lack of visibility and contact between physical and social spaces, and thus between human groups. Closure is an infectious, emergent process; it divides space and human groups, and through its division it creates a series of new divides: between work and leisure, between public and private. Many of these divides existed before, but in a very different form: the upper/lower divide was a boundary within the open hall, not between two rooms. Closure is equally structured and structuring; it both expresses and enforces new patterns of everyday thinking.

The process of closure suggests that the social divides it indicates existed before, but also in a very different form. We have already mentioned the parameters of these: age, gender, master/servant. It is these specific relationships whose transformation is echoed in the architectural changes: it is social and cultural closure that architectural closure is mapping out.

The process of closure can be seen as providing the antecedent conditions for "panoptic society", a phrase used by Foucault (1979) to describe certain forms of modernity. In particular, panoptic society involves mass observation and labour discipline. This involves a paradox. The retreat into upper and lower ends of the house made observation of the subordinate members of the household less possible in a superficial sense: but the very distinction between observer and observed, the mental image of such a process, depended historically on that social and physical distance being developed in the first place. The process of closure is therefore a much wider and deeper constellation of changing forms and social attitudes than the so-called "rise of privacy" or "comfort"; these changes are in fact rather superficial manifestations of it.

Closure is thus much more difficult to grasp theoretically and explore through the evidence.

One implication of the process of closure is that it is not simply about layout of houses. It also penetrates and underlies the changing technical system of the timber-framed house. It was stated in Chapter 3 that in pre-industrial societies it is impossible to separate technical system and social meaning (Lemmonier 1986, Ingold 1990, Pfaffenberger 1988). That is, the way a house is put together – its framing, technique of decoration and details – is as expressive of the system of ideas to which it relates as the final form of the house itself. It is time to explore these aspects.

I suggest that the framing, roof form, treatment of functional and decorative details and so on relate ultimately to three long-term movements within the folk tradition: first, from the formal congruence of spatial form, technical system and the social ideas that form both and that both carry, to a divergence of these three elements and thus a closure of the connections between them; secondly, a movement away from openness towards closure in terms of architectural form; thirdly, a movement from the unifying, centralizing house to the segregating, dispersing house. These three long-term movements, when taken together with the analysis offered in Chapters 4–6, can ultimately be related to a shift from a view of the house and household as community (*Gemeinschaft*), as outlined in Chapter 4 to a view of the house and household as society (*Gesellschaft*: Fig. 7.1).

I shall pursue this argument by means of a structural analysis loosely inspired by Glassie's analysis of the construction and decorative details of Virginian house forms (Glassie 1975: 114–61), although the specific changes involved and the structure and implications of the links made are very different. For example, the culture/nature divide is not an appropriate starting point for analysis. It is difficult to argue that the processing of the framing members (in terms of how the tree is transformed into the building) passes from "cultural" to "natural" forms or in the other direction through time. There is, throughout the period 1400–1700, a relentless, merciless imposition of culture on nature: the tree is felled, squared, adzed into shape and rendered as un-treelike as possible. We pass through time, however, from the use of curved wind- and tension-braces to the use of straight braces, and from the use of straight, good timber of large scantling to curved, waney timber of narrow scantling. The tie of the open truss in medieval houses is often cambered and braced with curved, cusped arch-braces; the straight collar of post-medieval clasped-purlin roofs has nevertheless a concave soffit or underside. At all times the use of curved "natural" forms is far less than that in other parts of England: wind-bracing is never popular, only few houses having this feature, while the tension-braces used characteristically in "Kentish"

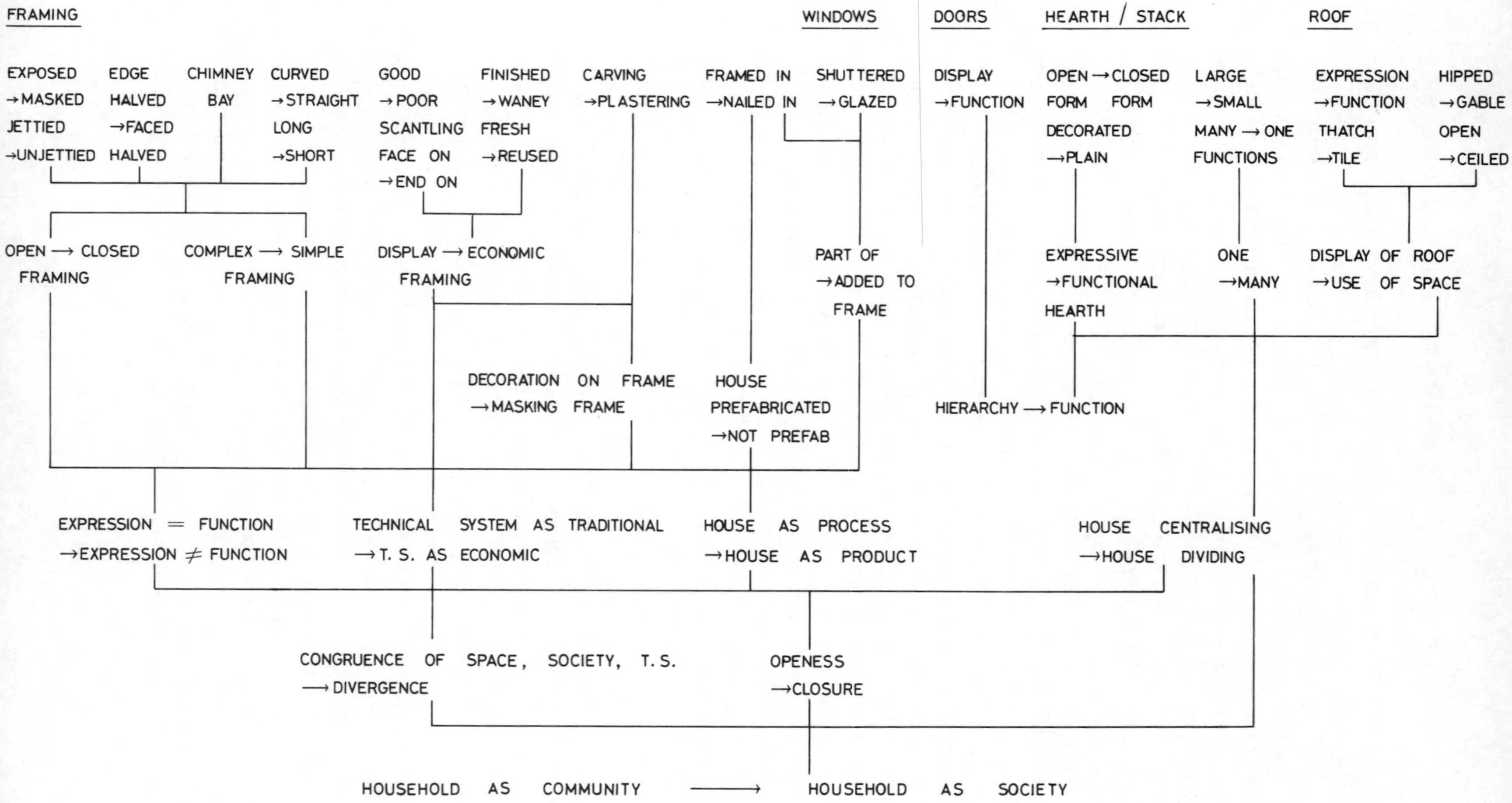

Figure 7.1 Diagram of structural analysis.

framing and stud-bracing are often almost straight and often masked behind plaster in any case.

What can be noted is a general preference throughout the period for straight pieces of timber and rectilinear patterns, in contrast with the exuberant treatment of curved framing in Cheshire, the Welsh Border, the West Country of England, and also in contrast to the general pattern in Suffolk in the 13th and 14th centuries. There are isolated exceptions, such as those of decorative purpose at Church Farm, Brettenham (Fig. 5.2). There is also a general preference in Suffolk for lighter scantling compared with the West Country. This contrast is not dictated purely by relative shortage of timber since this contrast recurs between communities from East Anglia and the West Country in New England where there was no such shortage (St George 1986). In any case, the mapping of woodland available in western Suffolk from the late medieval period onwards shows continual shortage rather than an increase in scarcity through time (Dymond & Northeast 1988: 50).

It is more useful, therefore, to put the nature/culture divide to one side and to think rather in terms of a transition from "open", exposed forms of framing to "closed", masked forms. This can be seen most clearly in the exposure or masking of the timber frame. Open and transitional houses usually had their frame exposed externally or internally, with panels of plaster rendering applied over only one or neither of the sides of the posts and studs (Plates 2a, 3b). The timber skeleton, the way the house is put together, is thus overt, exposed, open for all to see. The frame of a typical closed house has no such exposure (Plate 4c). It is unlikely that this pattern has been unduly distorted by later replastering; few framing members from the open period are keyed for plaster whereas the one externally visible closed frame, that at Bryers, Hawstead (Fig. 6.2), was uncovered by a recent occupant. Closed fireplace lintels are frequently keyed for plaster; the practice of plastering over the fireplace is an ornamental technique of *c.* 1530–1650 (Easton 1986).

Such a perspective on the open/closed distinction may help us to understand the rise and fall of the practice of jettying (Fig. 7.2). Jettying is present on many open and transitional houses, and is virtually the rule for parlour crosswings. It declined in the later 16th century, and the few examples from *c.* 1600 onwards show a different technique, where the joists are tenoned into the bressumer, which thus masks them, rather than directly supporting the bressumer and having their ends exposed. None of the closed houses in the sample has jettying, and few examples of this practice are known in East Anglia after the early 17th century.

The debate over the origins of jettying is a classic case of the sorts of approach discussed in Chapter 1. Jettying does have a structural use; the counterthrust from the upper wall reduces the sag on the joists and rails supporting the jetty. However, as Harris (1978: 56) points out, it is not clear that medieval carpenters were aware of this. It also increases the floor area of the upper floor. Again, however, this does not explain its presence in rural areas where, in general, space is not at a premium. I suggest that we have to look at what the jetty *means*. It indicates the existence and dimensions of an upper floor room, usually of some size, to the outside world, at a time in the open period when such rooms were often unused. It also provides a display feature that could be decorated with a moulding or repeated motifs, although the bressumer and the joist ends were often left plain. So again, the loss of the jetty meant the withdrawal of the cross-rail and the floor division behind the rendering, a masking and enclosing movement, as well as a triumph for the "economical" use of timber over that of "display".

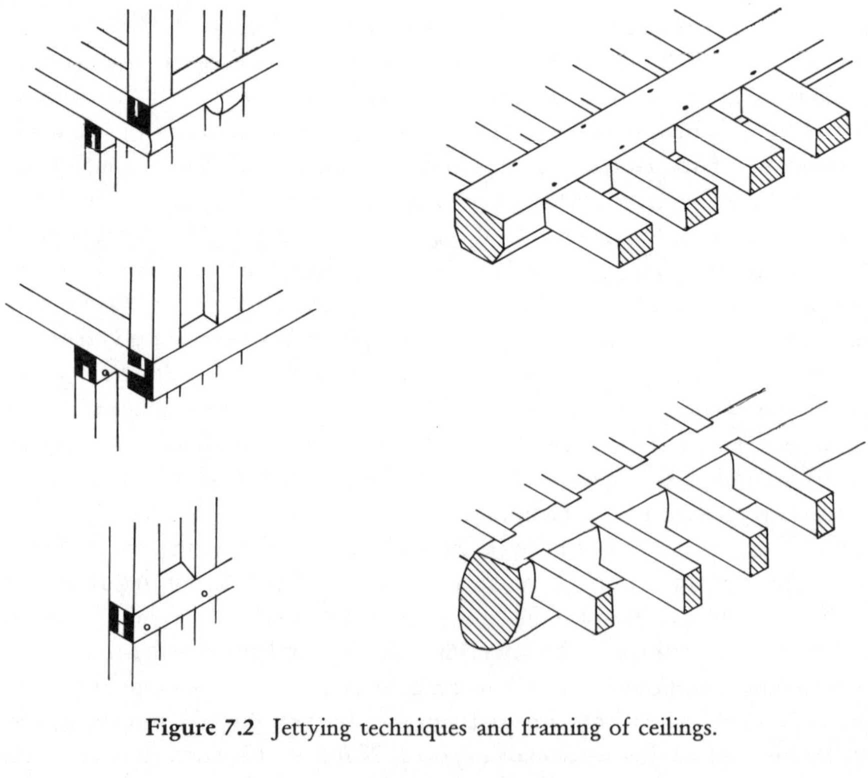

Figure 7.2 Jettying techniques and framing of ceilings.

We can also understand the origins of the chimney stack at the traditional level in these terms. The replacement of the open hearth by the stack is, fundamentally, a stage-by-stage process of closure (Fig. 5.12). There is no direct evidence for the placing of open hearths within the sample, but on the assumption that they were in the centre of the open hall they were not even

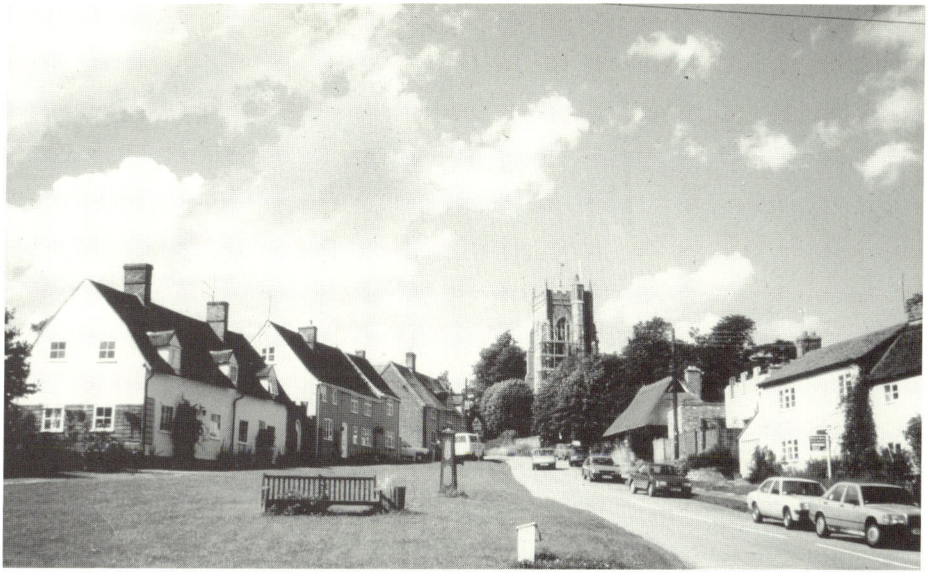

Plate 1a A Suffolk village: Monks Eleigh, near Lavenham.

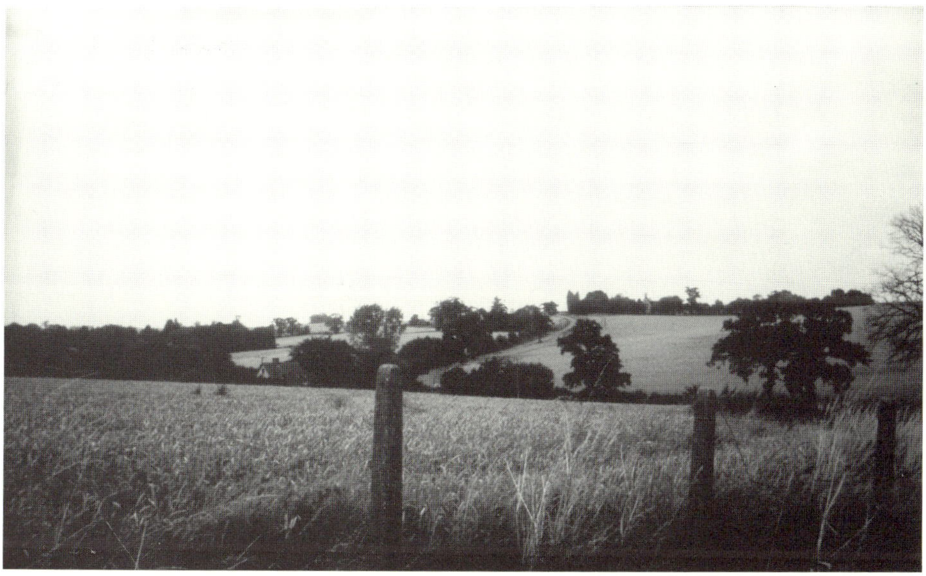

Plate 1b Wood-pasture countryside in Hawkedon parish.

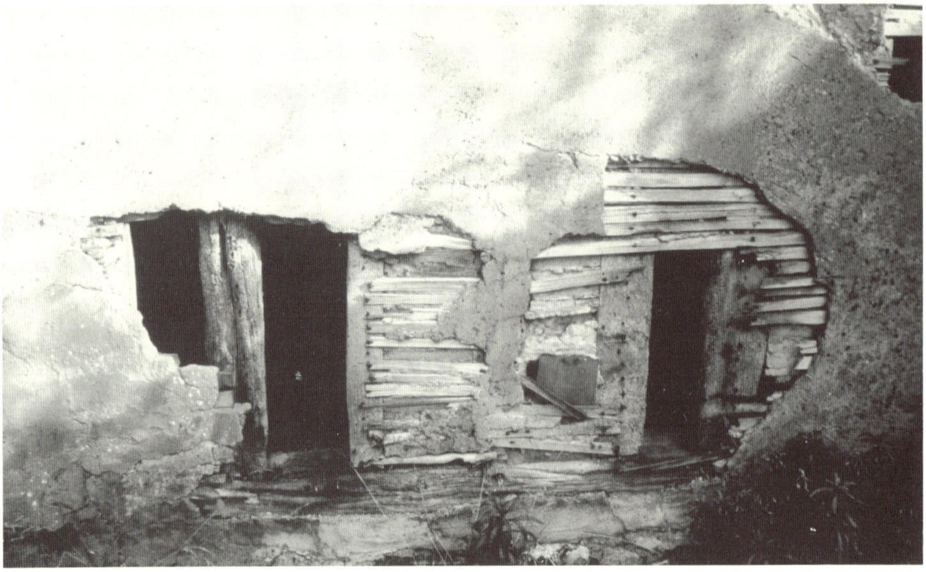

Plate 2a A decayed barn at Lower Farm, Risby, showing laths and plastering over the timber studding.

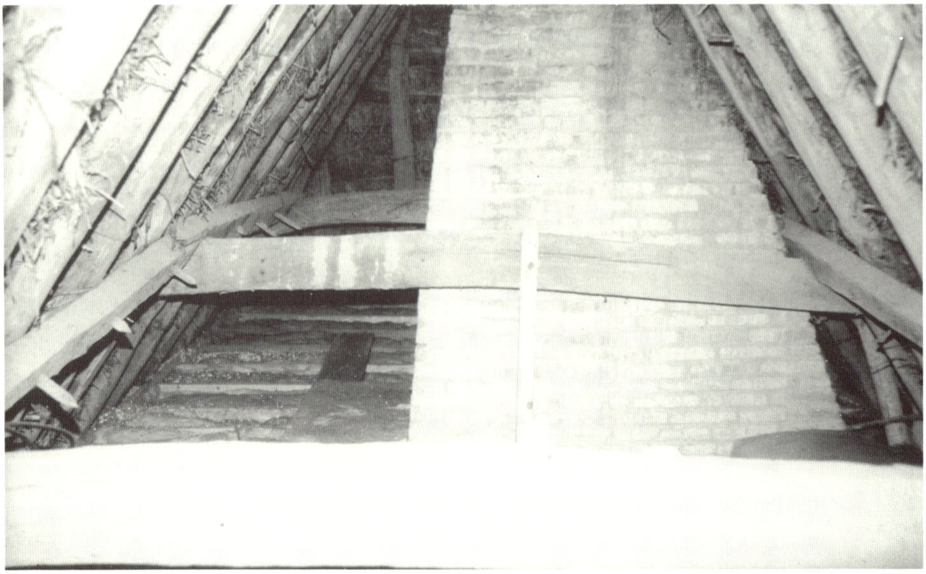

Plate 2b A clasped-purlin roof at Mill Post Farm, Hawstead.

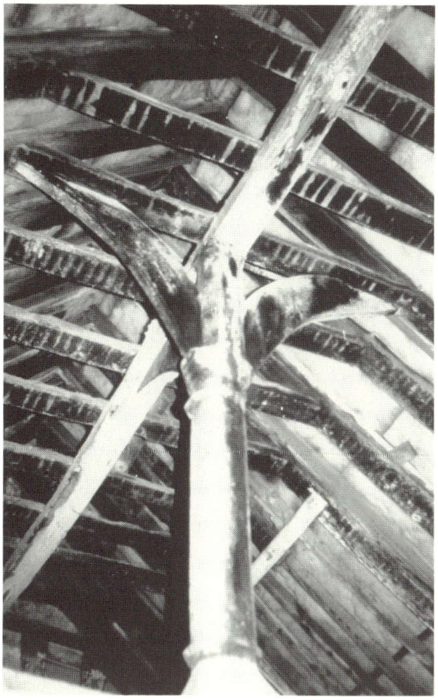

Plate 3a A crown-post roof with sooted timbers at Layers Breck, Rougham.

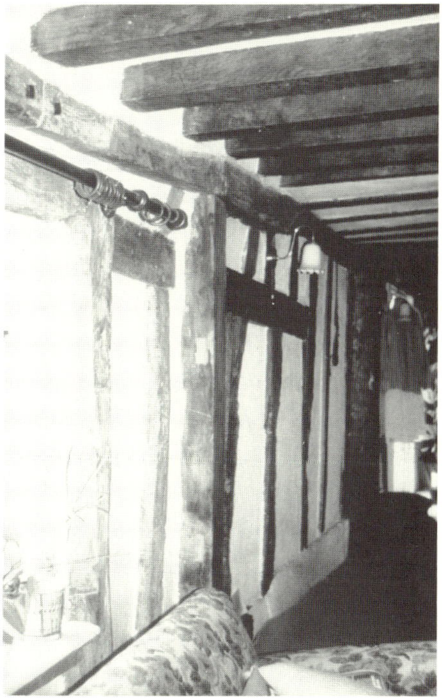

Plate 3b A medieval hall with inserted post and ceiling at Oaklands, Stanstead.

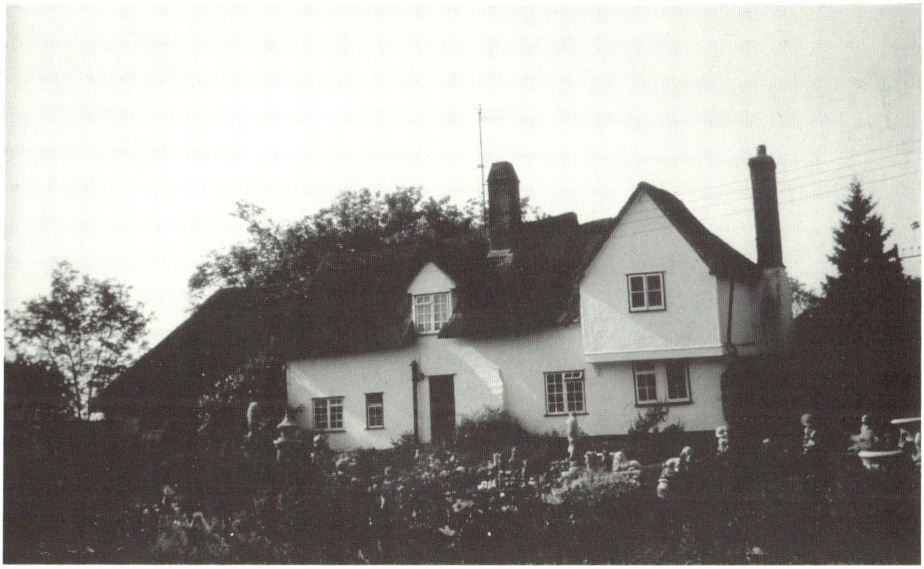

Plate 3c Highbank, Brent Eleigh: an open house with jettied wing.

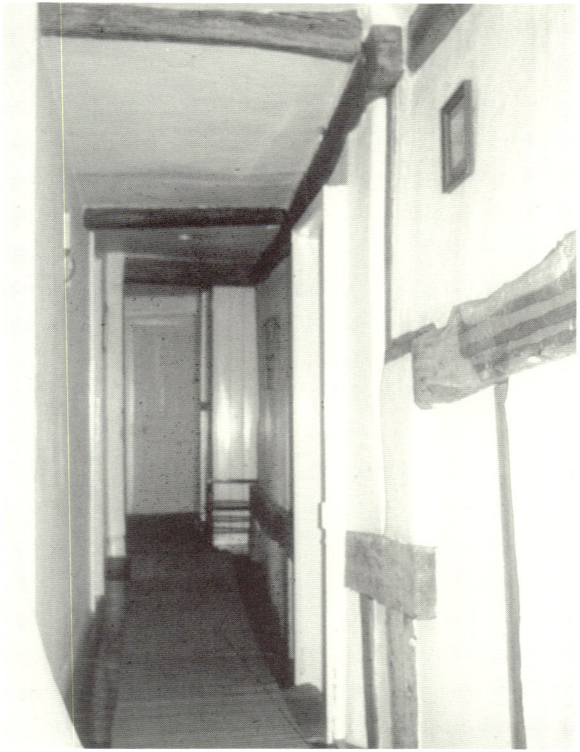

Plate 4a Lodge Farm, Coney Weston: the wall plates indicate an initial build and two successive heightenings of the building within a century.

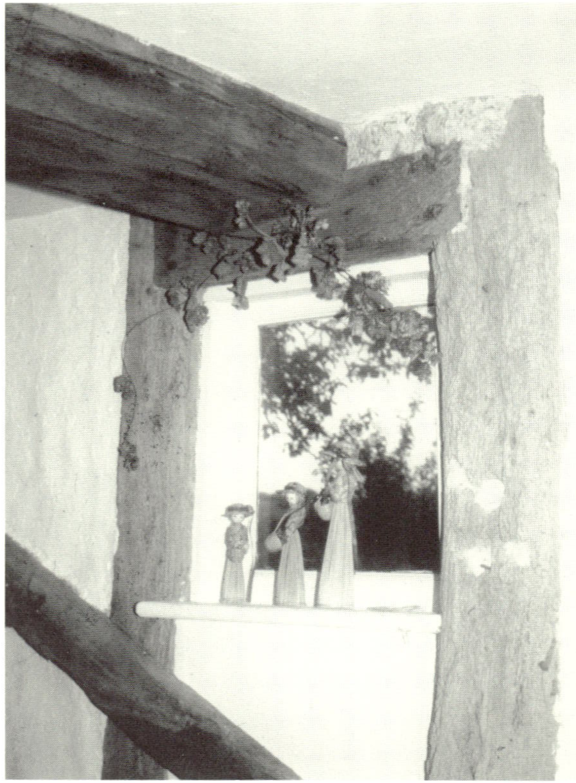

Plate 4b Ferncroft, Glemsford: re-used and waney timber in a late 17th-century smaller house.

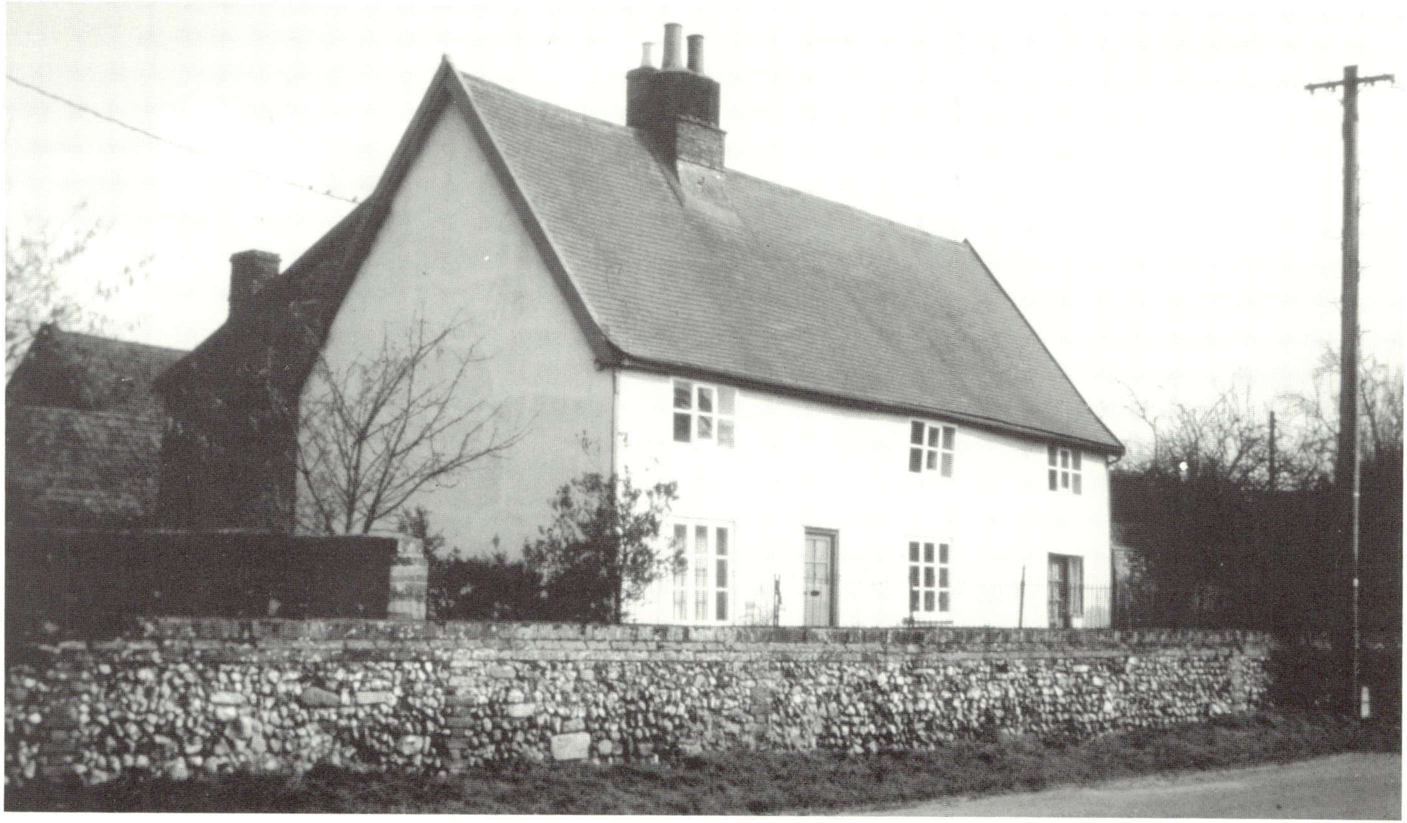

Plate 4c Street Farm, Troston: a typical three-cell lobby-entry house.

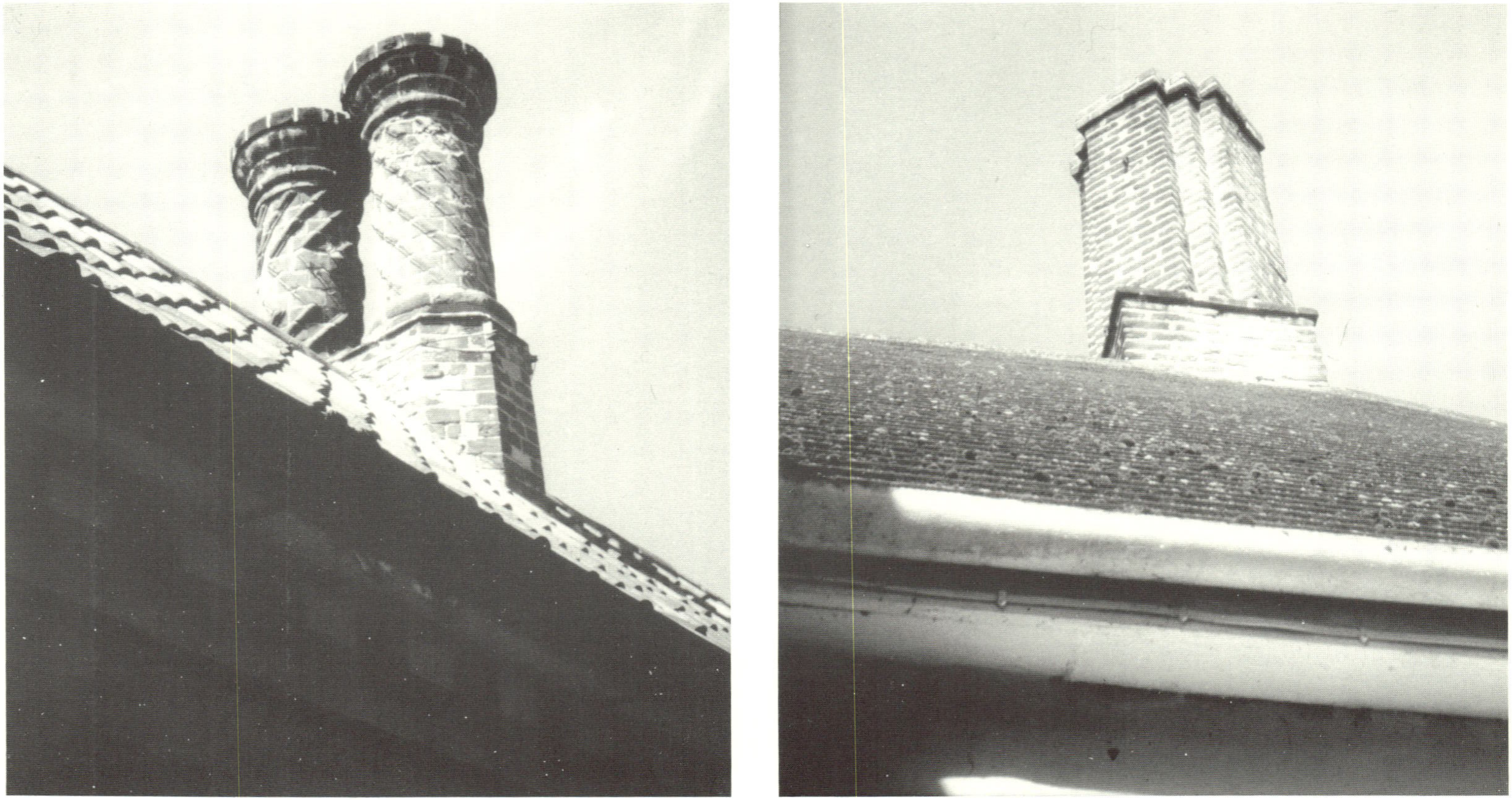

Plate 5 Different styles of post-medieval chimney stack: (a) left, almshouses, Ampton; (b) right, Virginia House, Cavendish.

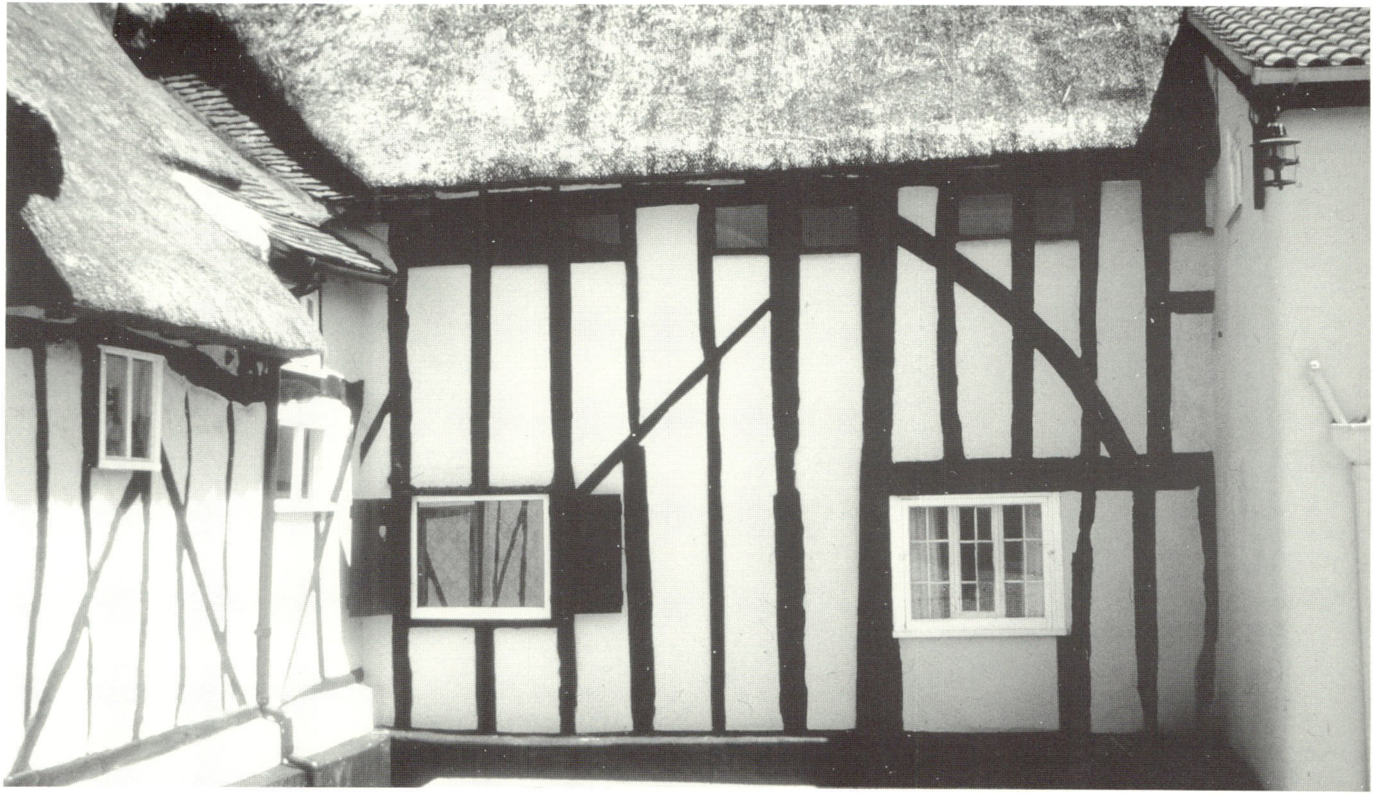

Plate 5c 42 Egremont St, Glemsford: contrast between 16th-century and later framing.

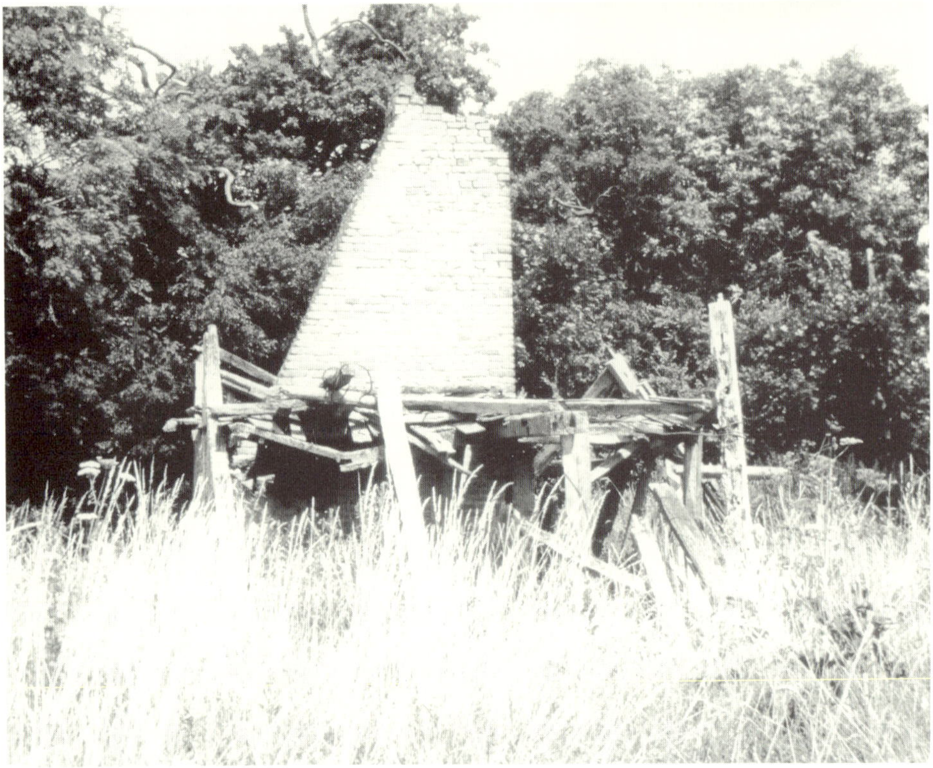

Plate 6a The collapsed frame of cottages near Manor Farm, Monks Eleigh.

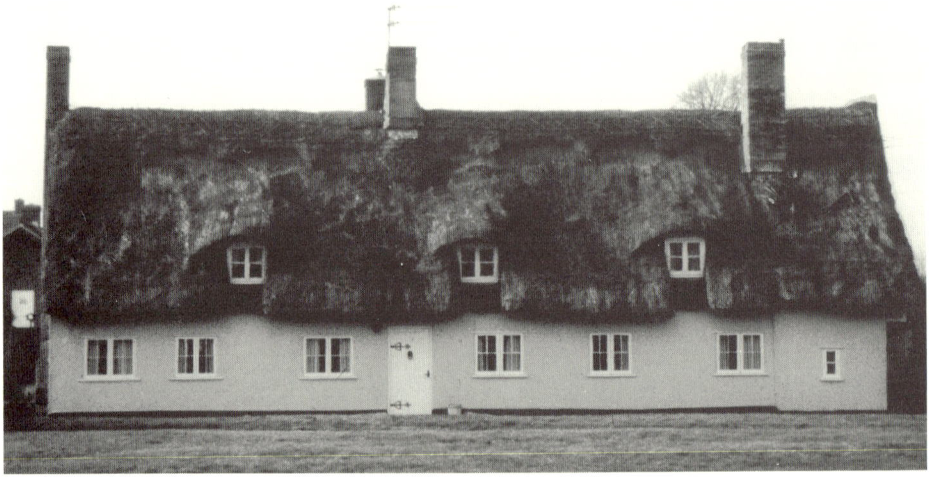

Plate 6b The Green, Fornham All Saints: a row of cottages, now one house.

confined to one particular bay. The smoke bay, seen in the service wings of Layers Breck, Rougham, and Mill House, Alpheton, and in the hall of Tudor Cottage, Brent Eleigh, is a closure of the space available for the hearth and its smoke, and the early, large stack a further closure. The closed plan of back-to-back fireplaces and separate, narrow chimney bay confined the symbol of the soul of the house (Ewart Evans 1966: 74–81), and the household's productive centre (St George 1986), as closely as possible. Finally, the mid- to late 17th century saw a steady diminution in the size of fireplaces. This is unlikely to relate to the replacement of wood fuel with coal since many later probate inventories mention wood for firing and none lists coal in any case.

Related to the closure of the frame was closure of the opportunity for display through it. The patterns made by arch- and tension-braces were now masked behind the rendering, so those features declined in terms of their width and the attention paid to their joints. They were eventually replaced by the straight passing-braces, not halved into the studs, of the later 17th century. The use of timber of good scantling for display purposes was also obviated, so waney and re-used timber, and timber of poor scantling, was increasingly used.

Joists and rafters, as well as having their scantling reduced, were turned end-on by the late 17th century (Fig. 7.2). This is a more structurally sound position than the former face-on rule in the craft tradition. The face-on rule has been explained by other scholars by reference to the ease with which waney timbers could be translated into use as rafters if laid face-on (Harris 1978: 18). However, this is hardly applicable to a period in which many houses were closely studded for display purposes, and it cannot explain the shift from face-on to end-on joists in a period of constant shortage of timber. Rather we see again the use of open forms of framing, in which the broad face of the timber should, logically, be the visible one.

The turning of the joist or rafter by 90 degrees thus represented two things: the preference for closure over openness and the preference for "economical" methods of framing over "display" methods. The argument that good quality timber was increasingly hard to find, and that increasing shortage forced this shift, is difficult to prove or disprove. Reyce, writing in 1618 on Suffolk building practices, commented that "the careless wast of this age of our wonted plenty of timber, and other building stuffe, hath enforced the witt of this latter age to devise a new kind of compacting, uniting, coupling, framing, and building, with almost half the timber which was wont to be used, and far stronger as the workmen stick nott to affirme, butt the truth thereof is nott yett found out soe" (Hervey 1902: 51). Rackham, however, has pointed out that there is no necessary reason to believe in the link between shortage of timber and reduced scantling used in construction (Rackham 1986: 89–91).

The continued wave of rebuilding through the 17th century shows that there were wealthy people building at the vernacular level. They simply did not choose to display that wealth through the timber frame.

We have seen that one way of displaying wealth in the closed house was through moveable goods rather than the frame of the house; another way was through decoration masking the frame rather than upon the frame itself. Open and transitional houses often have their frames elaborately incised and moulded, the crown-post, bressumer over the jetty, parlour ceiling and so on bearing the bulk of this carving. Forms of display range from the elaborate mouldings on beams found in the early transitional period to the crown-posts of the open period (Plate 3a).

Decoration on closed houses is, overall, not so popular, and when it occurs it frequently masks rather than forms part of the frame. The obvious example is pargeting, or moulded or incised patterns in the plaster rendering. Pargeting is nearly impossible to date: this technique has little application on a close studded wall, since it has to be used on large rendered panels for effect. This is particularly true of the most common form of pargeting, namely an incised herringbone pattern. Other examples are plastering and painting generally, although this was present in the open and transitional periods (Carrick 1985, Easton 1986).

Within the house, common joists were increasingly masked behind a covering of plaster and boards. This not only related to closure of the frame, but to the increased perception of the need for privacy, sound travelling through a floor with exposed joists more easily. Closed ceilings were often packed with walnut shells or other materials for the purposes of insulation and reduction of noise (Ewart Evans 1966: 43–5).

One possible objection to such a view of the closure of framing is that since we have more houses from the later period from the middling and lower classes such a decline in quality of frame and degree of decoration is more apparent than real, being a function of status rather than of date. But we have seen that the open period has a large number of small or medium-sized houses of probable yeoman or even husbandman status. A comparison of, say, Poplars Farm, Brettenham, tension-braced and close-studded despite its small size, and comparable although larger closed houses with much smaller scantling and poorer framing such as Sparrows, Stanstead, and Street Farm, Troston, makes the point eloquently.

The frame was losing its expressive functions and its openness in other ways. Open windows are generally diamond-mullioned, with the mullions tenoned straight into the cross-rail or wall-plate in a diamond-shaped mortice. In only one house in the sample have the shutter slides been preserved, at Malting Barn, Great Waldingfield, although another example is known from

Essex (Scott 1984a).

Again, a stage-by-stage transformation may be observed, with the mullions of transitional windows often having a simple rectangular tenon, while 16th- and early 17th-century mullioned-and-transomed windows have mullions tenoned into the window frame which is then tenoned in turn into the wall frame. The final end point of this sequence is marked by negative evidence: no mortices for the mullions of closed windows were observed, although the position of the windows could frequently be inferred. In other words, late 17th-century windows do not appear to have been framed in at all. Doors were similarly treated: the four-centred arched heads of early doors were tenoned into the frame, whereas the doors from the closed period have no evidence of such treatment. Joists and rafters were also less frequently tenoned in and instead simply rested on the spine or cross-beam or were supported in other ways: in late 17th-century houses the spine beam loses its direct relationship with its post, being carried instead on a small sill resting on two posts (Plate 4b).

If open fittings such as doors, windows, joists and rafters were tenoned directly into the principal elements of the frame, then the whole frame of the building down to the last detail had to be prefabricated. That is, it had to be thought out with care in the builder's yard and put together on site with reference to modified systems of Roman numerals (Corner Thatch, Honington; No. 42, Glemsford and others). Such a building may be picked up and moved, or taken apart and reassembled elsewhere (see for example Ewart Evans 1966: 33; Padfield 1985b, Woodward 1985: 180). The control of the system of ideas articulated by the craft tradition over the final form and details of such a house is strong.

The control of the craft tradition weakens with the literal weakening of the links between window, door and frame, in the sense of the loss of the mortice-and-tenon link between these elements and the close relationship between post and plate. At Abbey Farm, Cockfield, and Seven The Green, Fornham, both mid- to late 17th century in date, we see areas which must have had partitions that were not tenoned into the frame. At Fornham and also at Ferncroft, Glemsford (Plate 4b), the jointed relationship between the spine beam and the post is destroyed. So it became more possible to construct a building on site and less essential to think out the building beforehand. A shift is seen away from careful prefabrication of all elements of the house to a more differentiated and less unitary building process.

At this shallow, early stage of the structural analysis it is possible to discern a shift from the house and its fittings away from overt expression of a social hierarchy towards the house as a mere functional unit. The design of doors is a good example of this. Houses in the open sample show decoration and display around the door, in the arches, spandrels and mortices for porches found. This tendency towards decorative and symbolic elaboration of the threshold is continued through the transitional period, but ends abruptly with the dominance of the lobby entry. With this plan, the front door is reduced in importance, and no examples of decoration or elaboration can be found in the sample taken. The shift in the nature of the door and of the threshold is more complex than this. Open doors in small-scale traditional communities are traditionally exactly that: a threshold through which visitors were encouraged to pass (Glassie 1982). By the mid-17th century, folk concerns about the threshold became more defensive in nature, focusing on the need to safeguard the threshold against penetration of evil influence (Ewart Evans 1966: 61–5).

One feature elaborated in the mid- to late 17th century is that of internal circulation in the form of the stair. Simple "baulk" stairs are known from open houses such as the Old House, Hitcham, Hawkins Farm, Monks Eleigh (Fig. 7.3), and Balsdon Hall Farm, Acton, while other houses may have had no more than ladders. By contrast, the stairs at Church Farm, Great Waldingfield and Dover House, Ixworth (Fig. 7.4) are both spacious and well decorated. What decoration there was therefore shifted away from rooms towards those spaces segregating and marking boundaries between them.

The fire also moved away from expression and towards function. The open hearth was traditionally a centre of folk sentiment (Glassie 1982); transitional stacks are again often the centre of decoration of various kinds (Plate 5a,b). The earliest stack known, that at Mill House, Alpheton, *c.* 1500, has an arcade with probable castellated top. Later stacks are smaller, plain, and with fewer peg holes indicating former functions such as spit-turning (Ewart Evans 1966: 36). The stack top also becomes smaller and plainer, decorated brick shafts being replaced with a plain square top.

Finally, the roof structure epitomizes this shift. Open crown-post roofs (Plate 3a) are clearly designed to be seen, with the central ornate post braced four ways forming a central focus. This focus is lost with the ceiling-over of the hall, although a few roofs with plain crown-posts were built over ceiled houses (Newbury Farm, Bildeston; Vaiseys Farm and Corrie, Brent Eleigh; Hawkedon Hall). It is interesting that crown-posts do appear to become less ornate during the 15th century and that therefore it is possible to identify the origins of this particular transformation back into the earlier open period. The closed clasped-purlin roof (Plate 2a) is much less structurally complex or aesthetically attractive; it also lacks the particular focus of a uniquely ornamented truss marking the division between upper and lower ends. It performs its structural function competently, however, and also leaves the space below the collars free for passage. The shift from hipped to gabled roofs creates further space for living and storage. So we move from a roof structure,

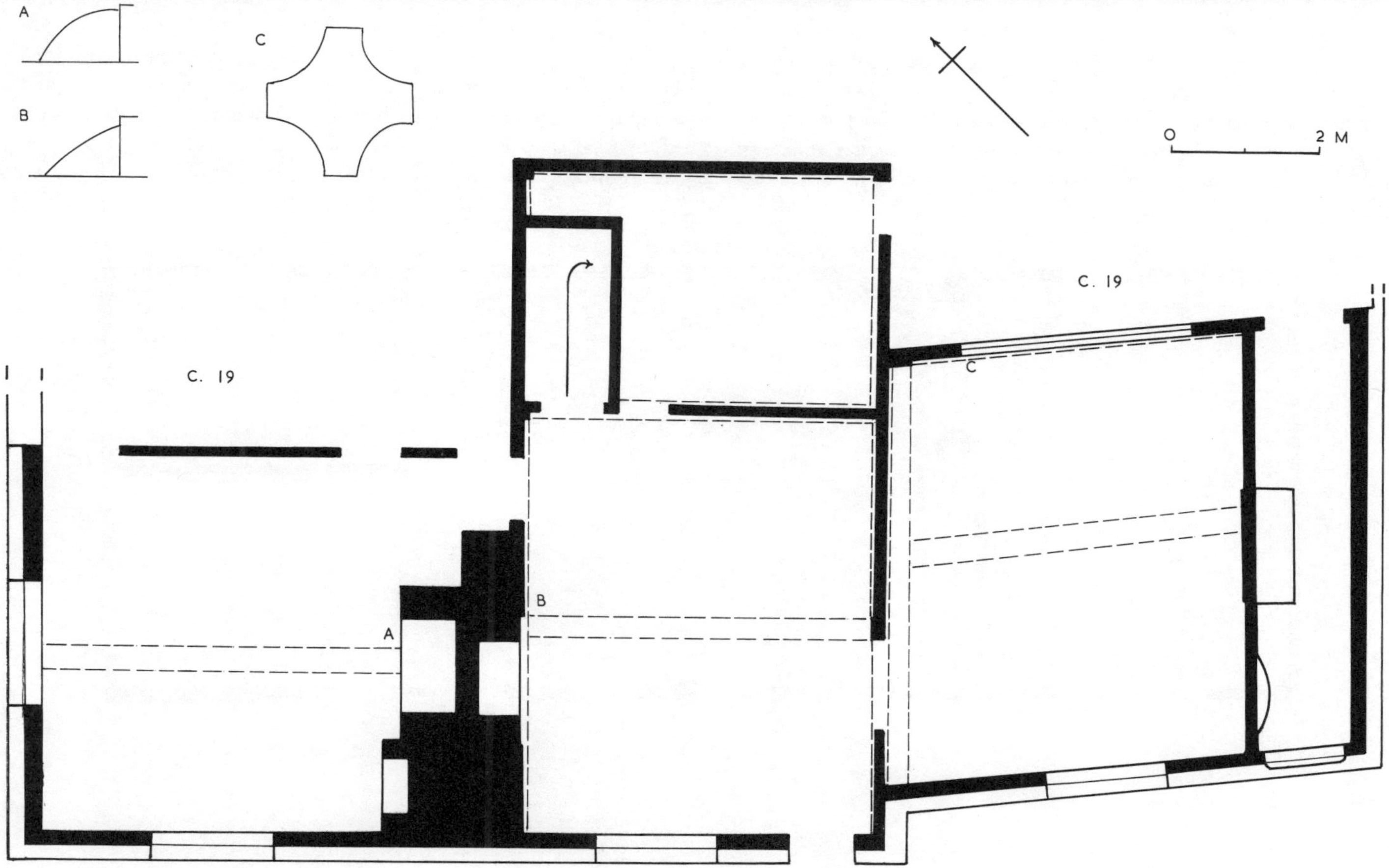

Figure 7.3 Hawkins Farm, Monks Eleigh: a house of 15th century origins, unusual plan and development. The first phase was probably a hall and cross-wing house, of which the three-bay crosswing remains, including the site of a baulk stair in one corner. This has a blocked four-centred arched door to E, probably opening into former hall. The present door to S of this is inserted. There is space in the pegging for a stack to W on the position of the present fireplace; similar indications of a stack over. The two-bay cell and crosswing to E of this is an addition/rebuild of the early or mid-16th century. It has a cross-passage with mortices for doors at either end. A large window with ten moulded mullions survives. There is no sign of any stack. The cell on the other side of the 15th-century wing is a later 16th-century addition. The house was refronted and reroofed in the 19th century.

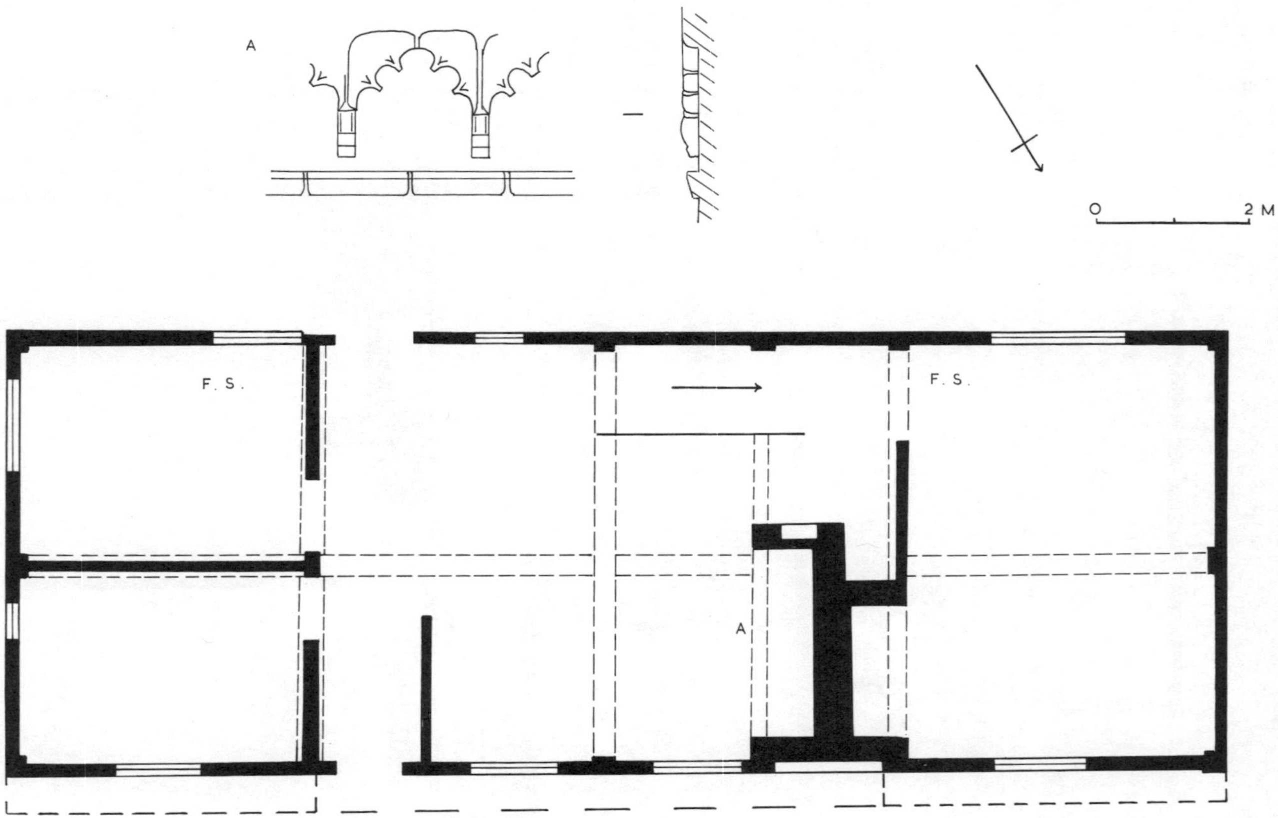

Figure 7.4 Dover House, Ixworth: a Wealden house previously surveyed during renovation (Colman 1962). First phase 15th century, with jettied and storeyed wings, and a half-hipped crown-post roof. Sites of former stairs are preserved on the S sides of parlour and service. The hall had two equal bays, one of which contained the cross-passage. The hall was impressively ceiled in the early to mid-16th century. The stack has back-to-back fireplaces and decoration including folded-leaf carving and quatrefoils in circles on the parlour fireplace lintel. The hall fireplace lintel is also carved and there is arcading over it. The cross-passage was retained. A fine stair with barley-sugar twists was inserted in the late 17th or early 18th century into the hall.

that is open visible and expressive to one closed, masked and functional.

The transition from thatched to tiled roofs is difficult to date; the thatched tradition obviously continues to the present. Tiled roofs have obvious practical advantages: they are less susceptible to fire, and need less sharp roof pitch. Again, however, at a deeper level this transition has social and symbolic meanings. The need for less sharp pitch is another aspect of structural closure, of masking part of the frame of the building rather than openly displaying it. It has also been suggested (St George nd) that while tiling a roof requires a larger initial outlay in the early modern period, its lack of any need for regular repair by a fellow villager skilled in thatching freed its owner from another of the ties binding him to the traditional community.

The diminution of stack and fireplace size has already been accounted for in terms of the shift from open to closed forms of framing. It also plays its part in a shift from a house in which one large hearth bears all the functions of the household to one which has several separate hearths doing this. With the splitting of the functions of the hearth, as we have seen, the functions of the house and the everyday lives of its members were split: the house moved from *centralizing* to *dividing*.

The opposition between centralizing and dividing space is by now familiar. Some of the other oppositions which this analysis is moving towards are less familiar but go hand in hand with this one. The first to be discussed is the opposition between *identity of expression and function* on the one hand and *lack of identity* on the other. The frames of open houses are both expressive and functional. In open framing, in the translation of trees into houses, in the "facing-in" of members, in making the principal elements of the frame the bearers of social messages and displays of wealth and status, in the identity of bay and cell units, in the prefabrication of the house, we see the structural necessities of sound framing. These necessities are difficult – in fact impossible – to disentangle from the way in which that frame relates to the layout of the house and expresses social meaning. At what precise point are braces redundant or is close studding too close? Is the crown-post roof an answer to structural problems posed by antecedent forms of roof or is it decorative/symbolic in nature? These questions cannot be answered in an either/or fashion: structural factors go hand in hand with social and symbolic ones. Put another way, the very frame, the structure and body of the house, is itself the surface, the display, part of the system of social meaning. This *unity of structure and meaning* is lost in closed houses. No longer do bay divisions necessarily mark cell divisions, for partitions are no longer necessarily framed into the main posts. The frame is no longer an object of display: rather the moveable goods within and pargeting and other details without bear much of this function.

So along with this loss of identity between expression and function goes a loss of identity between the *surface* of the house, what it appears to be, and the *essence* of the house, the way it is constructed. With this divorce, it becomes possible for the builder or owner to apply criteria of formal economy to the building of a house. It is difficult to see how, within the open craft tradition, an opposition or "trade-off" between cost effectiveness and sound framing could come about or even be conceived of in the mind of the builder. The craft tradition in this sense provides a useful demonstration of the substantivist school of economic theory (Dalton 1971). With the separation of expressive and functional aspects of house construction, it becomes possible to conceive of the most economical way of putting a building together in a different way from doing this according to the craft tradition. It is more economical in terms of time to assemble a house roughly on site; it is cost-effective to use waney and re-used timber; and so on.

The expression/function divorce and the tradition/economic divorce go hand in hand with a separation between *house as process* and *house as product*. The way in which an open house is put together is part of its social meaning as much as its final form, as we have seen: it was "natural" for the carpenter to translate trees into frames with the social meanings of that frame in mind. It could be argued that the system of social meanings that is the house is already latent within the living tree in this scheme of thought, just as Thomas (1983: 41–50) has argued that the natural world was traditionally modelled on the social world. The very processes by which the house was raised, such as the tradition of "rearing" and other ceremonies associated with house-building, themselves symbolized the values expressed by the final form of the house (Ewart Evans 1966: 30–31). As elements of the house bearing social meaning moved away from the frame to mask the frame, so the final form of the house became more and more divorced from the way it was put together. What is manifested here is a shift from the house as process to the house as product or, more accurately and profoundly, a transition from identity of the process of house-building and the end product of house form and meaning to lack of identity between these two elements.

The shift from openness to closure in framing, decoration, stack and roof design has been outlined. We can see this transformation at this deeper level in terms of a general move from identity to lack of identity, from unity to segregation, of the various elements of the craft tradition. Underlying this still we see a shift away from the idea of house and household as *community* towards the house and household as *society*, in terms of its move towards segregation of social elements rather than unity and its stress on functional differentiation rather than social status. Thus the structural analysis outlined here provides contextual support for the analysis of change offered at the beginning of this chapter.

Of course, elements of the closed house lie latent within those of the open house. I tried to demonstrate this by an examination of the origins of the chimney bay and the ceiling of the open hall in earlier chapters. It is also latent in terms of the separation already existing structurally between the timber frame and its plaster infill. Some elements of open framing such as tension-braces in close studded walls were always masked in the open tradition. At the other end of the process, the final closure of the house was not given concrete form till after 1700, by the death of the craft tradition and by the appearance of Georgian and Victorian forms of house. So the pattern is not as simple as it has necessarily been portrayed above.

Despite this partial picture, we have seen how this process of closure works. This chapter has tried to deepen understanding of the nature of this process by considering how the changing technical system fits into the picture. Such a picture is now, I hope, very detailed in purely archaeological terms. Chapter 8 will attempt to fill in some of the cultural and social details, by looking at the evidence we have of everyday life on the early modern farmstead.

CHAPTER 8
ORDER AND MEANING IN THE CLOSED HOUSEHOLD

The rest of this book will move outwards; it will look more widely at the social and cultural context of closure. I have already discussed much of this context. I have referred to wider social structures and changes, including the structure of late medieval society at the level of the upper peasant household, as well as the forces of change at work within and transforming this structure.

Such an ascription of architectural to wider social changes is limited in two ways. First, it gives little hint of the local and regional characteristics of households and communities. These characteristics varied from place to place and structured life within the household as much as within the parish. Secondly, we must explore the question of how the wider changes discussed were actually negotiated at an everyday level. We must ask how specific cultural linkages were made between house form and social structure.

I discussed in Chapter 4 how the symbolic meanings expressed by the open house played their part within a social matrix and I suggested a series of linkages. For the later, closed period, we have still more detailed evidence of social context, and this chapter will use such evidence to draw a picture of the closed house and household. It will do so first by considering the inventory evidence for both the 1570s and 1680s and will go on to consider the house as a centre of a working farm. Finally, the static, synchronic analysis thus presented will be related to the wider, dynamic picture of change in the family and household presented by many social historians.[1]

Household goods in the 1570s

To our eyes, the Suffolk house of the 1570s would have appeared relatively bare, with few apparently non-functional items; the furniture would be solid, plain and sparse. This perception may be due to a lack of detail in some of the inventories, but in others this is not the case. L. Deathe, for example, had only three chairs, a form and a table in his hall, whereas a detailed list of cooking and eating implements was given by the assessors for his kitchen.

The main room, the hall, may have had the only hearth; the contents of this room usually included hearth furniture of various forms (trammels, pothooks, firepans and so on), including cooking implements and vessels. In addition most halls had a table, seating and "cupboard". The table often had a stained cloth or carpet upon it. The cooking and eating implements stood upon the cupboard; these included pewter and wooden dishes and salts. The seating consisted of stools, benches and chairs.

Much has been made of the social distinctions between chairs and other furniture, it being claimed that the head of the household sat in the chair at mealtimes while other members had stools and forms (Garrard 1982). These were frequently accompanied by cushions. Chests and coffers were sometimes kept in the hall (R. Gayfford, J. Hall), although not in such frequency as indicated in the later sample (Table 8.1).

The hall was an area serving many functions, as I argued in previous chapters; several inventories list beds in the hall. Spinning wheels and other cloth-processing implements are often mentioned, as are farm tools. Other, more rarely stored items kept in the hall included cradles, bibles, a brass bell, a barrel and weapons.

The room listed second or third in the inventory is that referred to in previous chapters as the "parlour", although inventories often term this the "chamber" or "bed chamber". The differences in naming pattern do not have any obvious reason in terms of room content or function. Beds and bed furniture dominated these rooms: the bed was often the most expensive item in the house and was frequently of four-poster type. These included bedsteads with or without curtains/hangings round the bed bolsters, and furniture of blankets, pillows, and so on. There was usually more than one bed in the room. "Cloths" are frequently mentioned. Sometimes they are referred to as "over the bed" (i.e. round a four-poster) or "about the Chamber" (i.e. around the walls).

The parlour contained more personal objects than the hall. These may well have been kept in the hutches, coffers, presses and chests also more frequently mentioned here than in the hall, with as many as five hutches appearing in one room (A. Myles). Other personal items included a silver spoon, ring and "two pairs of eyes" (J. Mauldon; the last are presumably glasses). A few chairs, stools, forms and tables were sometimes present.

There are a few mentions of food being stored in these rooms, but this was usually a rare practice. New cloth was also stored here. R. Rastall had a "chamber adjoining the hall" with the usual bedding and, unusually, a "cham-

Table 8.1 1570s inventories.

	Hall						Chamber/Parlour							Service												Shop	Chambers over						Farm					
																														Food								
Name	Hearth	Table	Seat	Cook	Hutch	Cloth	Misc.	Bed	Hutch	Hth	Seat	Table	Cloth	Misc.	Kettle	Pot	Cook	Brew	Milk	Hutch	Food	Utensils	Shelves	Wheel	Misc.		Bed	Seat	Hutch	Proc.	Raw	Misc.	Grain/Pea	Animals	Wood	Cart	Plough	Misc.
J Norfolk	X		X		X			X	X		X		X	curtn	X	X	X		X			X	X	X	seat	looms	X	X			X	cradle	X	X	X			
A Selfe	X		X					X	X		X				X			X	X			X					X	X	X		X			X				
R Osmonde	X		X				weapons	X	X	X	X	X	X	cradle	X	X	X	X	X	X	X						X						X	X	X	X		
J Leesse			X	X		X		X					X	ladder					X														X	X	X	X		
A Webe			X			X		X							X	X	X			X		X		X									X	X		X	X	
J Ludbroke			X			X	bed	X										X	X		X	X			seat								X	X				
T Crowch	X		X		X		wheel	X					X		X		X	X								shoes	X								X			
T Frank	X		X			X																						X		X		cloth						
J Morlyle	X		X	X				X									X														X			X			X	
J Corder	X		X				barrel	X		X					X	X	X	X	X		X	X			seat		X	X	X		X	gun	X	X		X	X	
R Rastall							bed	X	X		X						X		X								X						X	X		X	X	
R Pecok	X						linen	X	X		X		X		X	X		X			X	X											X	X	X	X	X	
M Fuller		X						X	X		X		X			X	X		X								X				X							
J Parman	X	X	X			X	carpet	X	X		X	X	X			X	X	X	X								X		X			table		X				
J Hall	X	X	X	X		X	pewter	X			X		X		X	X	X		X			X				boards	X		X			wheel	X	X		X	X	
R Collinson	X	X	X			X		X	X		X	X			X	X	X		X	X	X	X			chair		X			X			X	X				
W Stockinge		X	X	X		X	pewter	X			X		X												bed	iron								X				
J Whiters		X						X	X		X					X	X	X								looms	X		X	X		wool	X	X		X	X	
J Grymes		X	X			X	cushion	X	X		X					X	X	X				X					X						X		X			
W Peeck	X	X	X	X	X	X		X	X	X	X	X	X	ch. pot	X	X	X	X	X			X		X			X		X				X	X	X	X		timber
T Hayward		X	X			X									"divers and sundry implements"																		X			X	X	
L Deathe		X	X					X								X	X																	X				
R Gayfford	X	X	X		X		pewter	X					X													iron							X	X		X		
R Game		X	X			X									X	X	X	X	X	X							X				X		X	X		X	X	
A Myles	X	X	X			X	cushion	X	X		X		X				X					X				hides									X			
W Nunne	X		X	X	X	X	shelf	X							X	X							X									cradle	X					
W Baker	X	X	X	X			wheel	X			X		X		X	X	X																					timber
J Mauldon	X	X	X			X	bed	X	X		X		X	books	X	X	X	X								w'ving												timber
G Hoowe		X	X	X	X			X						quern																				X		X		
E Manwood	X	X	X	X	X	X	cradle	X			X		X				X	X	X											X	X		X	X		X	X	

ber adjoining that" containing tubs and firkins. Pewter tableware and candlesticks were occasionally kept in the parlour as were spare tablecloths, a quern and grindstone, weapons, a basket and a ladder.

At the other end of the hall, the service rooms were mostly full of food preparation equipment and hearth furniture of various forms, such as kettles, brass and earthenware pots and pans, hearth furniture, wooden and pewter dishes and platters, querns, mortars, cauldrons and brewing equipment. It is unclear whether these items were being used in the kitchen and buttery or merely stored there and brought out to stand over the hall fireplace; the latter arrangement is more likely. The rarity of stools or other seats in the buttery at this period suggests that these rooms were no more than work and storage areas.

The milkhouse usually contained churns, bowls, and other cheesemaking equipment, while the backhouse had tubs, farm tools, and kneading troughs. Surprisingly little food was stored in service rooms, an exception being the cheese and bacon found in the buttery of R. Pecok and the barley in the backhouse of J. Grymes. Other rare items include a bed and furniture (W. Stockinge), cloth processing items and four "flower pots" (W. Peeck; this may refer to jars full of flour, although flowerpots are known from this period (Jennings 1981: 118)), planks and shelves (W. Nunne), and a "barbers pot" (J. Mauldon).

The chambers over the ground floor mainly contained either or both bedding and stored goods. Some of the rooms with beds were similar in appearance to the parlour below, with cloths hanging about the chamber, hutches and tables. These were generally above the parlour/bedchamber. Others had beds amidst stored goods, or beds only. Stored goods kept in upstairs rooms include cloth, scales, farm tools, cloth production tools (J. Hall), cheeses and cheese vessels (J. Whiters; E. Manwood), malt, rye, hops, corn, peas and bullimong. Conversely to chambers containing beds these goods tend to be stored above the service end of the house. J. Norfolk kept peas, malt, a "stockerd frame", hops and other goods above his buttery.

It has been noted that hall chambers were generally not mentioned in the inventories from the 1570s. One exception is that of T. Frank, whose presumably cramped hall chamber included among other things: nine beds of various types plus their furniture, three pairs of shoes, twelve yards of cloth, two baskets, a chair, six shelves, six honey pots, various farm tools, thirty-two cheeses, butter, fourteen bushels of various crops, six bacon flitches and "diverse pieces of iron". It is difficult to see this number of goods in one room; perhaps the hall chamber extended without partitions over service and/or parlour end of the house.

Some rooms are listed as shops; these usually contained trade, cloth-related and/or farm tools. There is an absence of other items. It is interesting to note the provision of specialist work space at this time in a rural area: the number of weaving shops again indicates the importance of the cloth industry.

Household goods in the 1680s

Late 17th-century households, although still bare by modern or even 18th-century standards, contained on average many more goods than households a century earlier. The rooms themselves, however, often exhibited a similar range of functions (Table 8.2). For example, in the hall, the same range of seating and table furniture was still present, as was hearth furniture, cooking implements and pots and pans. The major change was an increased degree of material comfort: some chairs, for example, now had leather backs. Again, more pewter vessels were kept: the wooden vessels of a century earlier had gone.

Storage items did appear more frequently in the hall. In particular "keeps" were now listed, often of glass. It is not known precisely what form this item took. Cupboards were in one case specified "with drawers" (J. Kerington). Again, a few halls still contained beds (R. Brett, a labourer whose house does not have a parlour; J. Sturgeon), spinning wheels, farm tools and weapons.

The parlour, however, was a much changed room. Three houses had no ground-floor room listed as a parlour at all. These had instead a hall chamber or other first-floor room with beds and furniture. Eleven further houses had parlours with no bed, a radical departure from the 16th-century pattern. These contained tables, stools and chairs, as well as cupboards, hutches and presses, and also a range of new items: a "green couch" and desk (H. Hill), a brush (J. Kerington), a "sword belt" (M. Jowers), and an "old bible" (B. Smyth). However, a majority of inventories still indicate traditional parlours with beds present. Some of these continued the former practice of naming the parlour as "bed chamber" or "lodging room". One such parlour even had eight cheeses stored there (R. Brett). Even in these traditional parlours, increased standards of material comfort are indicated in the new items such as looking glasses, a pudding pan, a pair of virginals, an old clock and books.

Service rooms became functionally differentiated: that is, there were more of them by the 1680s, and they were devoted to different specific purposes. This profusion of and differentiation between service rooms is echoed in the architectural evidence. Mill House, Alpheton, for example, has two or three phases of 17th-century outshuts at the service end.

Many more rooms over the ground floor were listed in the later inventories, although the space given by them was available in the 1570s houses;

Table 8.2 Inventory evidence for room function (1680s).

	Hall							Chamber/Parlour						
	Hearth	Table	Seat	Cook	Hutch	Cloth	Misc.	Bed	Hutch	Hth	Seat	Table	Cloth	Misc.
T Stewart		X			X			X	(not detailed)					
W Frysan	X	X	X	X	X									
A Wright	X		X	X			tools	X			X	X		
R Poulter	X	X	X				gun	X	X		X	X	X	l.glass
H Bradford	X	X	X					X	X		X			
J Parkin	X	X	X	X	X		pewter	X			X	X		l.glass
B Robinson	X	X	X	X			wheel	X	X		X	X		
R Brett	X	X	X	X	X		bed	X						
R Lettelpr'd		X	X		X		bed	X	X		X			
A Payne	X	X	X	X			h.glass	X			X	X	X	l.glass
D Steden		X	X				pewter	X			X	X		
T Holmes	X	X	X					X			X	X		
J Cole	X	X	X	X				X			X	X		
S Beachcroft	X	X	X	X	X		maps		X	X		X	X	viol
B Smyth	X	X	X	X	X		h.glass		X	X	X			bibles
J Chilver		X	X		X				X		X	X	X	
R Nobes		X	X						X			X		
J Sturgeon		X	X		X		bed		X	X	X	X		
M Jowers	X	X	X	X	X		books	X	X		X	X		
W Muskett	X	X	X	X	X				X	X		X		
J Johnson	X	X	X		X				X		X	X		
H Hill									X		X	X		desk
J Nelsegood	X	X	X											
G Gardner	X	X	X	X	X									
H Tillney	X	X	X	X	X		gun							
J Kerington	X	X			X				X	X				brush
R Park	X	X	X	X			books	X	X		X			
J Mynnes	X	X	X		X		clock	X	X	X	X	X	X	
W Grant	X	X	X	X	X			X	X		X	X		books
T Brincklie								X	(not detailed)					
J Boggas	X	X	X	X	X			X		X	X	X		
F French	X	X	X	X				X	X	X		X		clock
E Campian			X	X				X	X	X		X		
J Challes	X		X	X	X			X				X	X	
E Pleasans	X	X	X	X			books	X				X		
A Smith	X	X	X	X				X	X		X		X	l.glass
J Debenham	X	X	X					X	X		X			
J How	X	X	X	X	X			X	X	X	X	X		
E Grouse		X	X		X		silver	X						
J How		X	X	X	X		weapons	X			X			
B Knockes	X	X	X				pewter	X						

	Service											Shop	Chambers over			Food			Farm					
	Kettle	Pot	Cook	Brew	Milk	Hutch	Food	Utensils	Shelves	Wheel	Misc.		Bed	Seat	Hutch	Proc.	Raw	Misc.	Grain/Pea	Animals	Wood	Cart	Plough	Misc.
T Stewart		X		X	X	X												scales						
W Frysan	X	X		X	X		X						X						X	X		X		
A Wright	X		X		X		X				seat		X	X	X		X	scales	X	X				
R Poulter	X	X			X		X		X		table		X					hearth	X	X				
H Bradford					X		X						X	X						X		X	X	
J Parkin		X		X		X							X	X	X						X			
B Robinson		X	X	X	X		X		X							X				X				
R Brett	X	X									p'ter										X			
R Lettelpr'd					X															X				
A Payne			X	X	X		X		X										X	X				
D Steden																			X		X			
T Holmes		X											X				X	hearth	X		X			
J Cole	X			X	X				X		seat		X					curtns		X				
S Beachcroft	X	X		X	X	X	X				table		X	X	X	X	X	hearth	X	X	X	X	X	
B Smyth	X	X	X	X								grain	X	X				table		X	X			
J Chilver	X	X	X								seat		X	X	X		X	desk						
R Nobes		X		X								yarn	X	X						X				
J Sturgeon	X	X	X		X	X	X				seat		X		X			hearth		X		X	X	
M Jowers	X	X	X	X	X		X				seat		X	X	X			table	X	X	X			
W Muskett					X	X	X				table		X	X	X			hearth	X	X	X	X	X	
J Johnson	X	X		X	X	X	X						X	X	X					X	X	X	X	
H Hill		X		X	X						p'ter		X	X	X			hearth	X	X	X	X	X	
J Nelsegood		X	X	X	X								X		X			table	X	X	X	X		
G Gardner		X		X			X					goods	X	X	X			hearth	X	X	X			
H Tillney	X	X	X		X		X				table		X	X	X			hearth	X	X	X	X	X	
J Kerington	X	X	X	X	X						table		X	X			X			X	X	X	X	
R Park	X	X	X	X	X						p'ter		X	X	X			hearth		X	X			
J Mynnes	X	X	X	X	X	X			X		seat		X	X	X				X	X	X	X	X	
W Grant				X	X		X		X	X									X	X		X	X	
T Brincklie																								
J Boggas	X			X									X	X	X					X	X	X		
F French	X	X			X								X		X									
E Campian	X	X			X		X		X		table		X	X	X	X	X		X	X		X		
J Challes												scales	X		X					X	X			
E Pleasans	X	X	X	X	X				X				X	X						X	X			muck
A Smith	X	X	X			X			X		p'ter	tools	X	X	X		X				X	X		
J Debenham	X	X			X						p'ter					X	X		X	X			X	loom
J How	X	X		X	X				X				X							X				
E Grouse	X					X							X	X	X					X				
J How	X	X	X	X	X								X		X		X		X	X		X		
B Knockes					X	X		X			table		X		X		X		X	X			X	wool

and they had many more beds, furniture and stored goods. Many had stools, desks, tables and other items which suggest that they were not used simply for sleeping. Many also had beds and other items found in the parlour in other houses. R. Poulter, yeoman, had such a room, above a parlour without a bed. Downstairs he presumably entertained his guests, where they could sit on five leather-backed chairs and admire themselves in a looking-glass; upstairs in a room with no other obvious display items he kept his bible. Only one chamber over seems to have been used for reception/display purposes: that of Mr R. Park, who in addition to various beds and furniture kept seven leather-backed chairs, his linen in a chest of drawers, various gold and silver items, a looking-glass and two swords.

With this partial separation of the old parlour and sleeping functions went a separation between space used for sleeping and that used for storage. Rooms with both beds and stored goods were rare; separate servants' rooms are also rare, although these were entirely absent from the earlier sample. There are two references to "Mans" or "Folks" chambers, in other words rooms for servants; these contained simply beds and "other things".

There were more rooms used specifically for storage than in the earlier sample. Stored goods included wheat, bullimong and rye under a general heading of "Chambers" (J. Sturgeon) and bullimong in the hall chamber and wheat in the parlour chamber (J. Debenham). There are a few references to work upstairs: five bays in the hall chamber (R. Nobes, a bay maker). A wheel and reel in A. Smith's house presumably represent his wife's activities, since he was a blacksmith.

The closed house of the 1680s thus showed both continuity and change from its transitional 1570s counterpart. The hall and service, generally speaking, do not seem to have changed their character although their relation with other rooms does change. The major changes were:

(a) the development of the parlour, as seen in the wider range of items found there and the much larger minority of later parlours with no bed;
(b) the shift of much activity, in particular sleeping, to the parlour and to the chambers over;
(c) the overall rise in quantity of moveable material culture within the house;
(d) the rise both of stored goods and items such as hutches and chests specifically designed for storage;
(e) the rise of unifunctional rooms at the expense of multifunctional space.

The closed farmstead

The inventories also indicate that most houses in rural Suffolk were also the centres of working farms. Virtually all the inventories indicate some form of farming activity undertaken by the household, even where some other title is given to the occupation of the deceased: many inventories specifically refer to a barn, or note the presence of farm animals (Table 8.2). The activities that went on in and around the farmstead were closely related to what went on inside the house. We have seen the practical difficulty of drawing a line in the inventories between service rooms inside and outside the house.

If, then, the farm layout is related to that of the house, then the critique in Chapter 1 of approaches to traditional houses is equally applicable to the construction of farm buildings and agricultural life in general. To repeat, activities within houses cannot be seen as commonsensical or purely economic in nature. It follows that activities within the farmstead, including "subsistence" activities, are as much a system of cultural expression as any other aspect of household life. As with traditional architecture in general, this topic has not been treated in detail by most scholars. What follows, therefore, will be an attempt to sketch the layout of the farm as expressed architecturally and through the probates in terms of contemporary cultural meanings.

The major farm building, mentioned in a large number of inventories, was the barn. Barns were as much objects of display as houses: barns were often constructed of re-used and waney timber but a large minority are very well built and their external appearance is usually respectable, with weather-boarding or rendering, and even pargeting, masking the frame. They are rarely placed to the rear of the building and are often well in front (Figs 8.1, 8.2).

Other farm buildings did not share the same investment of effort as the barn; few survive, which is probably an indication of their relatively poor construction. However, barn and other farm buildings were often clustered together in an area spatially distinct from the house. Some have a central yard between house and farm buildings, such as Vaiseys and Hill Farm, Brent Eleigh, and Powers, Great Waldingfield; other, larger houses may have the farm buildings in a separate quadrangle, as at Thurston End, Hawkedon, and Wood Hall, Little Waldingfield (Fig. 8.3).

However, in none of these cases are the farm buildings "tucked away" out of sight to the rear, and in most cases the farm buildings are nearer the service end of the house. Where the farm buildings face the house they are often placed slightly to the service side.

A spatial link was therefore set up between the service end of the house and the farm buildings, a link also seen in the inventory evidence. But distance between the elements in this chain is also stressed. In no case is the prac-

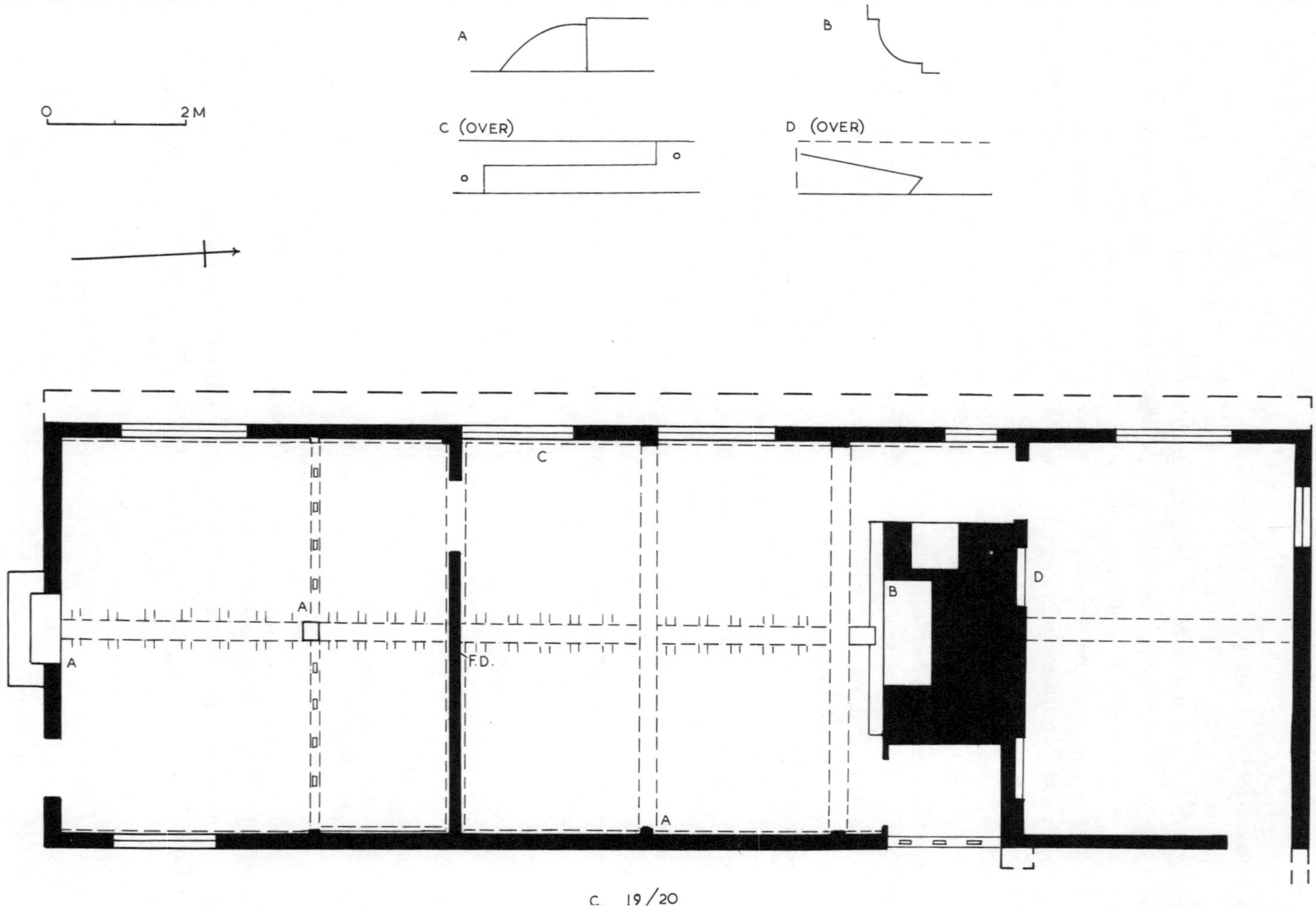

Figure 8.1 Hill Farm, Brent Eleigh: a 16th-century continuous-jetty house with service crosswing, with the parlour end remodelled later. A probable third bay at the E end of the wing has been destroyed. Screens-passage area to N of this. The central tie is arch-braced, with peg-hole for a crown-post. No evidence for a lobby entry. The wing to E was probably added around *c.* 1600. It may have extended to S. The W wall-plate has a partly obscured splayed scarf of medieval type; probably re-used. The wing has a jetty and close studding, tension-braces above and below the cross-rails, and a clasped-purlin roof. There are three large 16/17th-century barns to W of property. Rears of wings destroyed when large front range added in the 20th century.

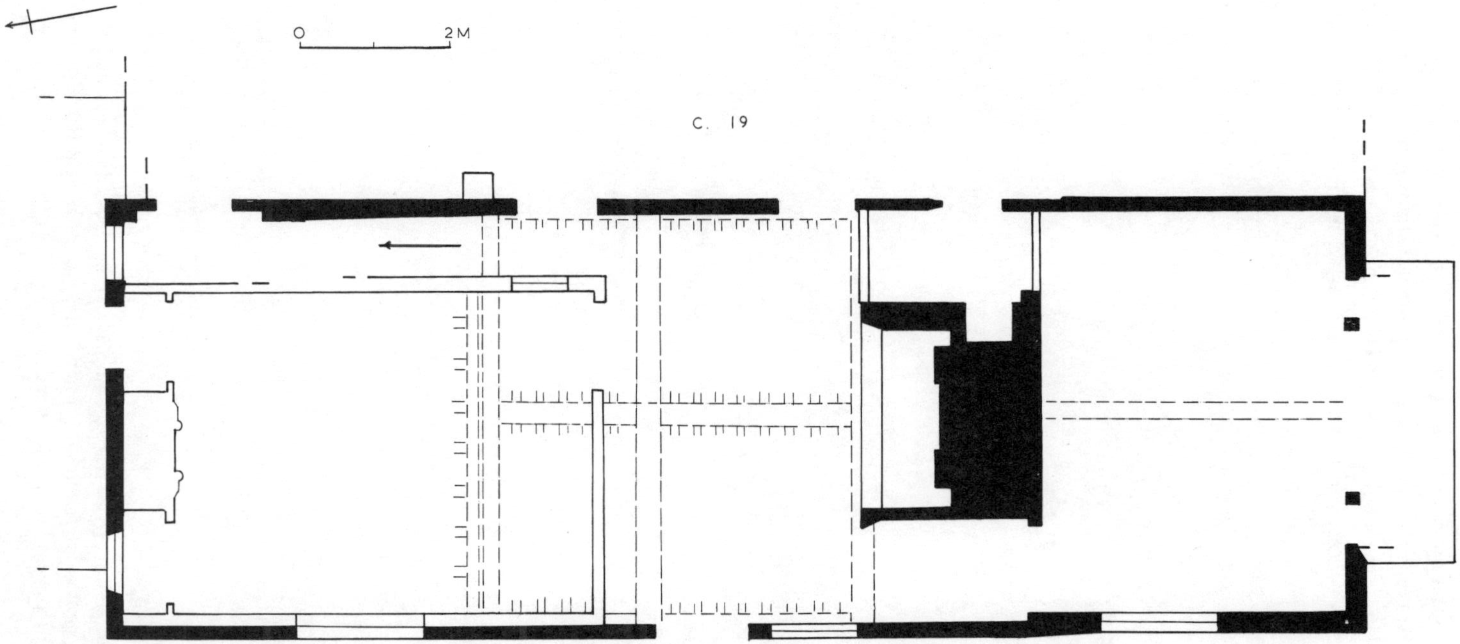

Figure 8.2 The Old House, Great Barton: a mid-16th-century house with later 17th-century alterations. The first phase is a fully ceiled three-cell house with probable opposed doors and a submedieval service end. High, fine hall ceiling. House possibly converted to a lobby entry in the 17th century. In the later 17th / early 18th century the end of the house was altered: a new ceiling with end-on joists was inserted into the 16th-century frame and the previous service partitions removed. The joists run into the end-wall stack, which was added at the same date, and the partitions and stair inserted, reducing the size of the hall. A large 16/17th-century barn to N of the house, and a small 17th-century cottage. The house was heavily altered and the roof rebuilt in the 19th century.

tice characteristic of many areas of the Highland Zone of England, of placing farm buildings against or even immediately adjacent to the house, repeated. In most cases some distance is usually placed between house and farm buildings; only at Langley's, Hawkedon, and Lower Farm, Risby, is there less than 20 m between house and farm building.

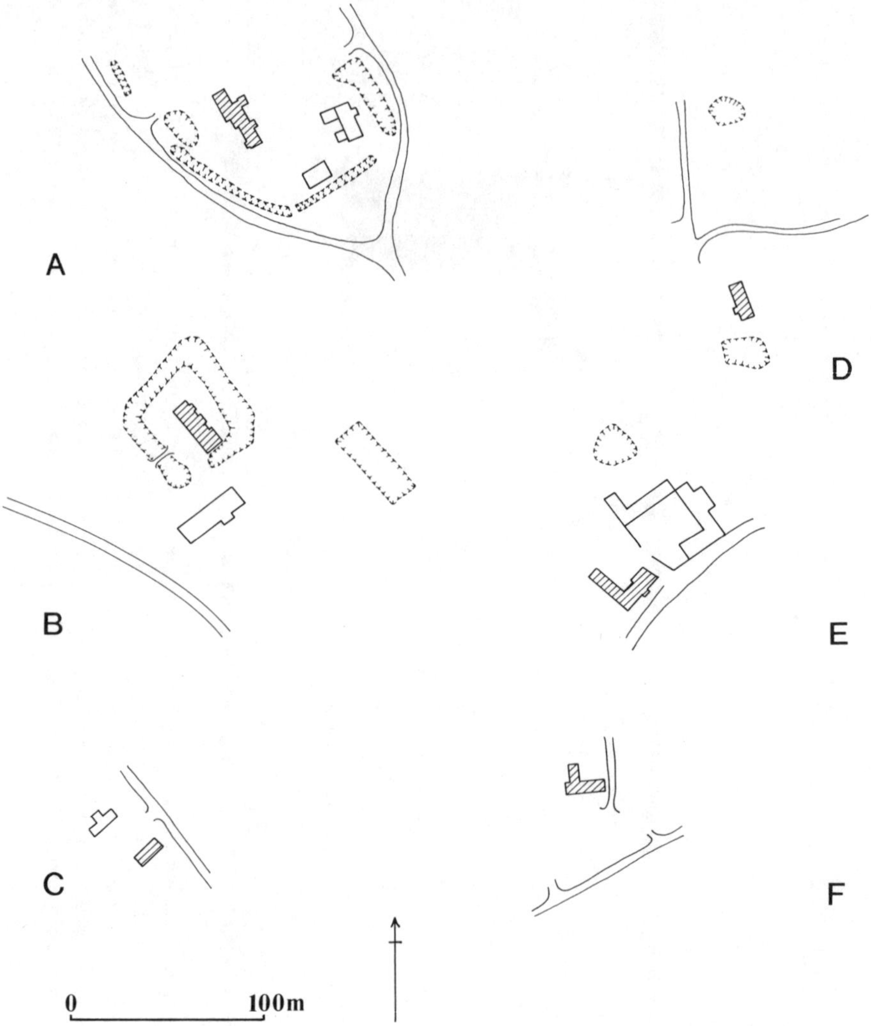

Figure 8.3 Farmstead layout. (A) Thurston End Hall, (B) Wells Hall, Brent Eleigh, (C) Powers Farm, Great Waldingfield, (D) Vaiseys Farm, Brent Eleigh, (E) Wood Hall, Great Waldingfield, (F) Bryers Farm, Hawstead.

Finally, there is other evidence of the layout of farmsteads in the form of moats and walls. Moats usually date from the 12th and 13th centuries in Suffolk. They are, therefore, usually two or three centuries older than the standing house and are indicative of an older habitation on the site. Standing houses and farm buildings were often placed adjacent to or outside moats rather than within them, or were placed on the fourth side of a three-sided moat. It is uncertain what the moat and moat area were used for by the closed period. Moats apart, walls and earthworks enclosing or subdividing the tenement were noted in a few cases, but there are too few examples to generalize.

Within the farmstead the different elements of the household found their place within an orderly layout. This layout in turn referred to a system of ideas about the human and natural worlds.[2]

Farmsteads make clear a separation between the human and natural worlds. Farm buildings were placed away from the house, keeping live animals away from the human world. This was not a matter of attempting to mask the function of the house as a working farm; this was made clear by the location and visibility of the farm buildings. It should be noted that this was a concentric distance rather than one of orientation: there is no clear pattern to the physical orientation of houses in the sample.

Such distance was important in an age when the human and animal worlds were seen as links in the Great Chain of Being (Tillyard 1972: 33–45). It was necessary to keep distance between these links to preserve their identity as it was nevertheless to unite them in coherent order. The links between these elements were explicitly exploitative ones; the natural world was classified according to its uses for Man. (Note that the term "Man" is used here and below in its 17th-century sense, its ambiguity denoting patriarchal values then as now.) Nature was a hostile, intractable wilderness that could only be made beautiful if tamed (Thomas 1983: 29, 254). This model of the world was adopted at both gentry and yeoman levels. The task of the yeoman farmer was to engage in a "productive wrestling with Nature" (Roberts 1985: 133); to do this, nature in all its forms had to be disciplined, segregated, controlled, tamed, brought into order.

The principles governing the house/farmstead division operated in microcosm within the house just as such a view operated in macrocosm within broader categories of the natural world. Such a hierarchical classification had spatial elements in a Man-centred universe with natural disorder on its margins. The house thus became the ordered cultural centre of a world that was increasingly disordered, hostile and "natural" the further away one moved from the house. Thomas Tusser, writing at the end of the 16th century, advised that its doors be locked at night for cultural as well as practical security (Hartley 1931: 177).

It followed that natural things from that outside world should be drawn into the house in stages, with the farm buildings and immediate context of the house acting as an area to mediate this transition. The most obvious example of such a classification played out spatially is food, a natural product that had to be transformed into a cultural one (Levi-Strauss 1970). Raw, unprocessed food (grain, peas) was harvested on the margins of the farmstead, in the fields; it was stored in the barn, well away from the house. Its processing from a raw to prepared state took place in the barn (threshing) and in the service area adjacent to and in the service part of the house (brewing and dairying in detached structures, or food preparation within the service end). Finally, the cooking and eating of that food took place within what was still the centre of the house, the hall.

Animals were treated similarly. Domesticated animals were kept in buildings outside the house and their transformation into cooked food accompanied their movement into the centre of the house. The perceived proximity of the horse to the human world (as opposed to that of oxen, swine and sheep) may be seen in the proximity of stables to the house (Mortimers, Preston, is the only example where the stables survive). Pets such as dogs were allowed free rein of the house, although working dogs were again kept outside (Thomas 1983: 120).

Such a model of the relationship between nature and self derived its ideological power from its apparently logical extension onto the social world. Nature became, in the conception outlined above, everything beyond and outside Man's inner soul: thus servants, women and children were worked into this scheme of things by being considered as natural beings, or at least beings whose greater perceived proximity to nature justified the use of discipline in their "taming" and legitimated the exploitation of their services. We can see each of these three groups placed carefully on the margins and the lower end of the closed household.

Servants in husbandry were steadily marginalized to the edges of the closed household as we have seen. Servants' disorderly conduct, away from the eyes of their masters and a "natural" phenomenon, was quite explicitly linked to the "staying out of doors" of servants and young people, particularly on Sundays (Hill 1966: 175; St George 1986). The later inventories show more beds in the chambers over the lower end of the house; these are best interpreted as servants' beds. The overt aim of service in husbandry, of taking young people into one's household, was to discipline them and render them able to go away and head households of their own.

This formal correspondence is supported by a series of specific everyday linkages. Obviously servants in husbandry – raw products being transformed into a cultural state – were the group most intimately involved with agriculture and food processing. They slept in the chambers over the ground floor where semi-processed food and goods were stored. They were expected to wait at table in larger households where such a linkage was explicit (McCracken 1983: 310).

This scheme was not a rigid binary division but rather a series of progressive stages. These stages were cross-cut by the division between the spheres of women and the spheres of men. Male servants in husbandry worked out in the fields, women around the house; although both men and women would work in the fields when necessary (Kussmaul 1981). The wife was responsible for the "inside", for looking after the house, sometimes even taking over the household accounts (Morgan 1944: 43), while the husband was more concerned with the outside world in two senses: in heading the "public face" of the household and in agricultural rather than domestic activities. Women's activities such as brewing, dairying and food preparation nevertheless centred around the lower end of the house.

At the centre of both planes of social and cultural order was the hearth, which corresponded to the soul in contemporary thought just as the house corresponded to the body (St George 1986). Given the rôle of the house as expressing and enforcing natural and cultural boundaries, it is not surprising to find both the hearth and the threshold the centre of ritual precautions of various kinds. Witchcraft precautions in particular centred around the hearth. Witchcraft was a powerful, external force, closely linked with attacks on the independence of the house associated with claims of neighbourliness (Thomas 1971: 560–7). A series of houses in Suffolk has stoneware "witch bottles" buried directly under the hearth area (Merrifield & Smedley 1961). According to Suffolk folklore these could be used to combat witchcraft by placing some urine or hair from the victim in the bottle, together with nails or needles, sealing and placing it in the fire. The bottle would be liable to jolt violently as the witch attempted to escape: hence the need to bury it securely (Ewart Evans 1966). The presence of mummified animals in the service stack at Mill House, Alpheton, is suggestive in this context. Various practices in Suffolk folklore such as the "topping out" ceremony and the placing of ox bones on the chimney stack again point to the centrality of this area to the system of ideas articulating the household, as well as to various rites relating to the threshold and establishing a link between the wellbeing of the house and the physical and moral health of those within it (Ewart Evans 1966: 54–81).

The closed house thus related to an orderly, coherent system of values that gained their ideological power not simply through being expressed but by being played out through everyday activity, the daily, weekly and seasonal rhythms of life on the farmstead: the daily move to and from the fields, the weekly visit to the church, and the seasonal pattern of farming.

Such an analysis, however, does not go far enough. This seemingly coherent system of values manifested itself as a series of tensions and ambiguities in social relations. The most obvious area of tension is that in the relationship between master (or mistress) and servant. The general social and economic nature of service in husbandry as an institution is quite clear and has recently been summarized by Kussmaul (1981). A servant in husbandry was hired by a master for a fixed period of time, usually but not always a year, and in return received board and lodging within the master's household plus a wage.

There are several ambiguities here worth exploring. In the first place, servants were not a fixed order or class within rural society, but rather a stage of transition between childhood and adult life undergone by most of the rural population in adolescence and early adulthood. A male servant could, therefore, expect in time to marry at the end of his service, set up as a householder and even employ servants of his own. Servants cannot, therefore, be regarded as a "class" in any straightforward sense. Secondly, despite being paid a money wage, contemporary texts often refer to servants as part of the "family". Certainly this piece of ideology was accepted and even vigorously upheld by the law courts; there are many cases where local JPs upheld the rights of servants to, for example, food and bedding while sick, against the wishes of the masters (Kussmaul 1981: 32).

Although under the command of the master of the household, servants had ways of fighting back that were socially accepted. Most simply, they had freedom of contract: they could refuse to serve under a master known for his cruelty and miserliness, or refuse to re-engage with a master at the end of the year. As already mentioned, they could – and did – go to the local courts to assert their rights. They could also resist in more minor ways (Morgan 1944: 124; Wrightson 1982: 64). That being said, the whip remained literally as well as metaphorically in the hand of the master, petty physical sanctions being the norm.

Relationships between masters and servants were, therefore, although obviously asymmetrical, open to active renegotiation at both immediate and long-term levels. This occurred in various ways that found expression through the spatial layout of everyday activity. Servants were hired at hiring fairs, usually at the local market town; during the term of their contract they were allowed one day off a week, which would be spent out of the house. St George (1986) cites examples of the barn being considered the appropriate place for servants' disorderly activities in comparable New England communities.

The question of age overlaps with that of servants, adolescent youths often being sent to households as servants or apprentices. The master of the household could coerce his kin, having the ultimate sanction of disinheritance at his disposal; although the power of this sanction decreased with wealth and social status. Thompson has suggested that a distinctive "adolescent culture" did exist in England and New England by the mid 17th century (1984: 131).

Asymmetrical relationships of gender cut across these boundaries also; both the mistress of the house and women servants moved within the "inside", domestic sphere. Although a relatively late age at marriage and childbearing may have afforded women greater freedom than in other contemporary peasant societies, the principle of male dominance was still accepted at this social level. Kussmaul demonstrates that even before marriage female servants were considered of lower status than male, being paid at far lower rates. Servants who became pregnant were frequently dismissed by their masters, and sexual advances on female servants by their masters were common (Kussmaul 1981, Stone 1977, McIntosh 1984: 20). In wood-pasture Suffolk, the status of the mistress of the household may have been higher in line with her greater economic power through involvement in and control over dairying activities (Amussen 1988: 69) just as it was through production in urban contexts (Howell 1986: 181).

The layout of the closed farmhouse expressed the tensions and ambiguities outlined above in a series of ways. Socially as well as spatially, elements from the older order were included, and the key tension between centrifugal and centripetal forces seen in open houses was still there. The hall retained its central place as the probates show, although its centralizing rôle was in decline: the old community withdrew from that space in two directions. First, the parlour was now a heated room; with the bed often now moved upstairs, it was purely a living/display area for the master and wife. Secondly, the increasing provision of cooking facilities in the service end of the house deprived the hall more and more of its service functions.

This shift can be read in two ways: in terms of developing class relations within the household and also of changing gender relations. The open household was not equal; rather, it was a little community dependent on everyday face-to-face contact to perpetuate its asymmetrical relations of status. Class relations depend not only on "objective" economic interests, but as Marx acknowledged and as Thompson (1963: 711) has demonstrated for a later period, on the development of a separate consciousness. This depends in part on the breakdown of day-to-day interdependence of the patriarchal community, an interdependence symbolized by the open hall.

At the same time the distinction between service activities and the upper end of the house was sharpened. Women's rôles in food preparation and other service activities were moved out of the central concourse; they were also moved away from the front door. The symmetrical opposed doors carried with them a minimal separation between the front and back of the house, both symbolically and in terms of circulation pattern. If we are correct in assuming that the front, lobby-entry house also had an entry to the rear, service end, an assumption apparently confirmed by Suffolk folklore (Ewart Evans 1966: 71–3), then this front/back separation became more marked and with it the segregation between men's worlds and women's worlds at the level of both master/mistress and servant.

The early 17th century saw a sharpening of male attitudes towards "unruly women", seen in witchcraft accusations, charivaris and prosecutions of common scolds; women were seen as neglecting their accustomed duties within the traditional conception of the household and as requiring to be put back in their accustomed place (Underdown 1985a). The irony was that this acted in practice for an unprecedented marginalization of women at the middling social level in the later 17th and 18th centuries, in terms of their exclusion from everyday public life and "productive" economic activity (Amussen 1988: 185–9). This can be seen at the everyday level, therefore, through a marginalization of women's work within the layout of the house, away from the centre and towards the back.

It is possible to read this differently, in terms of developing women's consciousness of their position and their "marking out" of areas of female control. Women are known to have pressed for an extra servant (Wrightson 1982: 95) and they may have pressed in the same way for an extra chimney stack at the service end. The ceremony of childbirth was one specific period during which men were excluded from an area of the house (Wilson 1990). Just as the breakdown of the old system may have acted to sharpen class consciousness, so the consciousness of women as a distinct group with interests common to their gender may have actively developed these distinctions. Amussen elegantly outlines evidence for an indistinct although developing women's consciousness in this period in comparable wood-pasture communities in Norfolk, by showing how a small but increasing minority of women left land in their wills to other women rather than to men as was customary (Amussen 1988: 93).

One area in which such marginalization or "marking out" may be seen is in the provision of dairies in the later sample of inventories. Dairying equipment was present in the earlier sample and dairying was an important economic activity, and a women's domain, in wood-pasture areas (Amussen 1988). So the increase in provision of a specialized room in the house for this activity, as with the increase in provision of service rooms in general, is another aspect of withdrawal of activities from the general concourse, another aspect of closure.

At the same time the hall retained centripetal functions: many contemporary writers were careful to emphasize the importance of the household as "little commonwealth" and the hall as centre of that commonwealth. Households were still microcosms of the state (Greaves 1981: 292). The hall portrayed by the 1680s probates is by no means an unimportant room.

I have looked at the closed house and farmstead as a synchronic picture, a snapshot taken at a particular moment. It stands in the middle of the social changes under discussion, in the sense that the growing distance between masters and servants and the marginalization of women within the household were processes not completed until the later 18th century. The power of the ideological picture outlined in this chapter depended on this conjuncture. The legitimation of the process of closure depended at least partly on concepts and images derived from traditional ideas of patriarchy, which still held power and meaning over the minds of men and women at this particular point in time.

It is therefore necessary to situate this system of values in its wider social and historical context. It is necessary to understand, first, how the middling farmsteads related to their larger and smaller counterparts and, secondly, how these linkages worked across the social and physical landscape as a whole. These will be the respective subjects of Chapters 9 and 10.

Notes

1. The sample of inventories taken for this analysis comes from two sources: those proved at the Norwich Consistory Court (NCC) and from the Archdeaconry of Sudbury at Bury St Edmunds (SRO). A sample was taken from the 1570s and 1680s corresponding to that taken by Rachel Garrard in her study of inventory evidence (Garrard 1982), so that the transcripts could be cross-checked against her records. For further details on this research, as well as a discussion of the problems and pitfalls of the use of inventory evidence, see Johnson (nd: 114–16). Fundamentally, the problems raised by the interpretation of inventory evidence, such as those raised in Chapter 5, may be related to the conflict between the way we see space in the surviving house and the way the house was "thought" by the person who made up the inventory. One example already mentioned is the problem of a "tail" of service rooms which may or may not form part of the structure of the house.

I am very grateful to Ms Garrard for her generous willingness to make available her unpublished data.

2. This study owes much in terms of theoretical background to that of Bourdieu on the Kabyle house (1960: 133–53) and substantive inspiration to St George's study of the Puritan farmstead in New England (St George 1986).

CHAPTER 9
STATUS, CLASS AND RELATIONS BETWEEN HOUSES

If the household was a little commonwealth, so the parish was a little community; both were modelled in terms of political thought on the state. Households and their architectural frames therefore need to be examined in a wider sense. We need to ask how contemporary larger and smaller houses differed from one another and what this may tell us about the relations between their inhabitants.

Just as households changed in the early modern period, so did wider communities. Fletcher and Stevenson (1985: 1–41) have discussed what they see as two powerful social forces shaping change in 17th-century rural society. One force was that of class polarization. In "objective" economic terms polarization was seen in the growth of material inequality, landscape change and the rise of farming for profit. In a social and ideological sense it was seen in terms of the withdrawal of upper and middling social groups from the body of shared values and cultural forms representing those values. These values and forms are termed "popular culture". In withdrawing they embraced the second force, that of cultural centralization, through adoption of national, "polite" as opposed to regional, "traditional" or "vernacular" forms of culture and material life. Fletcher & Stevenson see this polarization as being played out partly through the medium of everyday activity: they quote examples of upper- and middle-class withdrawal from Sunday sports, the decline of church ales and other festivities, and so on.

One medium through which such polarization should be manifested is obviously that of architecture. To do this we have to consider first what is meant by the distinction between traditional and polite architecture. Principles of "polite" architecture can be expressed in opposition to traditional principles: polite houses are out of the ordinary, exceptional, national or international in taste and style and large in size. They are expressions of often overt sentiments, explicitly drawn up architectural rules forming grammars such as those of the classical orders, and their meanings form part of an explicit, written discourse.

At a national scale, these characteristics cannot be assumed to be constant between the 15th and 17th centuries. Polite building before 1550 was not generally characterized by explicit formulation of the principles underlying the layout and detail of larger buildings (Airs 1975: 21). The series of changes in terms of the rise of recognized architects and formally composed buildings in the later 16th century at this level are usually seen as part of the impact of the Renaissance, which involved not just the influence of "classical" models in ground plan and decorative detail but also the rise of written discourse on the meanings of architectural features and overall design, the classical antecedent for this being the writings of Vitruvius (Girouard 1983: 6). Such changes were also related to a constellation of new social values legitimating the gentry and aristocracy. These values revolved around knowledge of and power over the landscape. This is most explicitly seen in the production and possession of maps, often portraying a great estate with the landowner's arms displayed prominently (Helgerson 1986, Harley 1988). It is also seen architecturally in the developing need for a great house to have a view over its park and estate, preferably combined with a formal garden, after the 15th century (Stone & Stone 1984: 330–9).

This is not to argue that larger buildings lacked overt or covert social meanings before the later 16th century. In fact a series of architectural features of the earlier 16th century can be seen to refer to a system of "medieval" or "feudal" values: we see the continued use of moats and ornamental crenellations at a time when their military value had long passed, and an explosion in concern with heraldry and its use as architectural decoration (Johnson 1992). The use of these items was clearly not functional and must be interpreted in symbolic terms, even if that symbolism was not clearly or overtly articulated by their medieval builders and users. They were articulated, moreover, within a body of space that had clear social referents: the courtyard. From the later 14th century onwards courtyard houses were often deliberately planned affairs (Thompson 1988). The whole was inward-looking, irregular, often with a relative lack of concern for outward composition or symmetry: the courtyard formed a central focal point for the activities of the household, while the differing statuses of the groups making up the household were emphasized through their varying positions round the court, and signified through architectural detail such as porches, bay windows, relative height, and choice of building material.

This pattern was exemplified by the form of Hengrave Hall, in the parish of Hengrave, built by Sir Thomas Kytson of the Merchant Adventurers

Company in 1525–40; it was built to a courtyard plan, although with novel centralizing elements (Howard 1985: 215; Johnson 1991). Although it does not possess a moat, its gatehouse is crenellated and the gate surmounted by heraldry. Again, the now destroyed Ickworth Manor, 8 km south of Hengrave Hall, probably mid-16th century in date, had a series of wings within a courtyard with brick tower porches and corner turrets (Filmer-Sankey 1986).

It could be added that while this argument stands for the early 16th century when considered in isolation, the use of such symbols to represent a power long gone in reality can be extended back into the 15th and 14th centuries, Coulson's interpretations of religious and domestic crenellation, for example, fitting into such a viewpoint although written from an art-historical rather than social perspective (Coulson 1979, 1982). The central point to be made here is that while late medieval buildings were not the subject of an explicit written discourse, they did carry quite sophisticated systems of social meaning related to their position at the top of the social scale and were not simply a direct reflection of social structure. The implications of these arguments are that we should not expect to see a straightforward, progressive or gradual shift between 15th- and 17th-century polite architecture in terms of our previous definition of "polite": in other words, of its ability to carry overt symbolic meanings or of the structure of the design as a discursively conscious unity. Rather, a more sophisticated interpretation must stress a more subtle shift between the use of practical and discursive consciousness in design of polite architecture. This shift is manifested by the rise of written discourse in the form of architectural treatises and the appearance of recognized architects (Girouard 1983: 6–11).

It follows that the line between polite and traditional architecture is not easy or unshifting: its nature and breadth will change from period to period. We must therefore look at larger vernacular and supra-vernacular houses in western Suffolk and examine their form in relation to houses above and below them in the social scale, in an attempt to explore the nature and breadth of this line.

In terms of internal layout, there is little that is remarkable about larger open houses. Three have a three-cell plan (Fig. 9.1); in only one (Layers Breck, a "Wealden") is there positive evidence of a screens passage or spere truss. Frogs Hall is of three-bay, two-cell form. Both Layers and Mill House have long service wings jettied at the front and extending to the rear with a smoke bay at the rear gable end and indications of service hatches or doors in the side wall. These hatches may be related to the baking of bread and its distribution, but this is conjectural and it is unclear whether this coincidence has any significance.

What does distinguish larger open houses from their smaller contemporaries

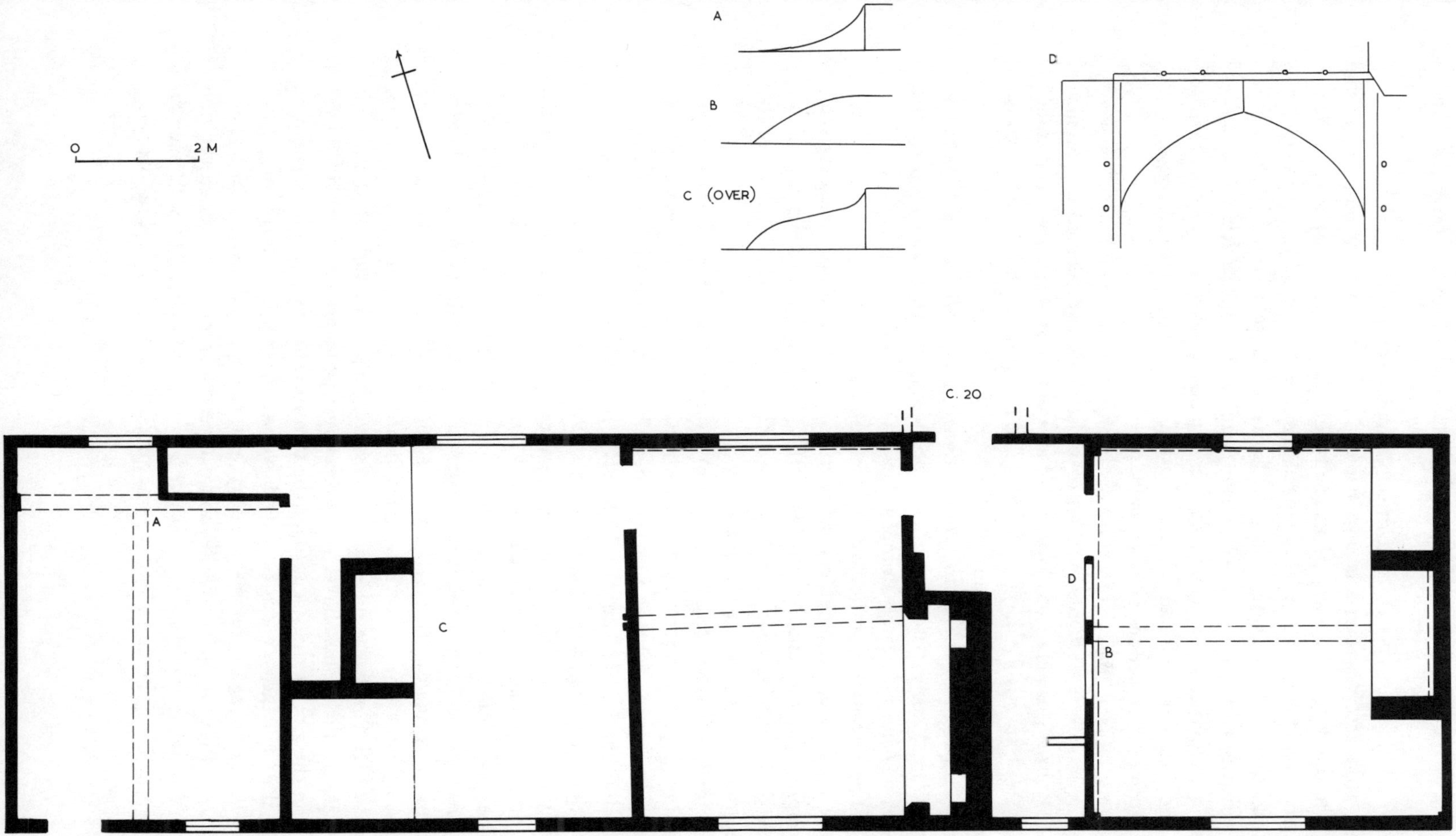

Figure 9.1 Mortimers, Preston St Mary: an open-hall house of complex development. This was formerly the seat of the manor of Mortimers (Bury SRO 326/49– 51; E1/29/3; 449/4/19). The open-hall house was a large version of the usual plan. Blocked service doors, and a pair of wide tension-braces over them. Destroyed partition between cross-passage and hall. At the upper end of the hall, pegs indicate space to S for the door. Roof has a large central crown-post of octagonal section with finely moulded cap. Insertion of stack and ceiling in 16th century against the back of the cross-passage. The mortices for a door to S of stack at this point survive. The house "turned around" and the service end extended to W in the 17th century.

is their relatively early date, their fine appearance and their larger dimensions. Their early date was discussed in Chapter 3, but the relevant point here is that the building can be seen as a socially and economically separate though related phenomenon to the rebuilding at the middling social level of the later 15th century. All such houses have halls that are impressively high, and the open trusses that survive are of ornate form. Layers in particular has close studding, mortises for a porch and a crown-post roof with side arch-braces and moulded corbels (Plate 3a). The third distinguishing factor can be seen in the much greater size of the open halls.

So larger open houses are clearly distinguishable in appearance. However, they are less distinguishable in terms of a distinctive competence and circulation pattern. Frogs Hall and Mortimers are built on standard two- and three-cell plans respectively. Layers and Mill House have extended service wings running back but this feature is also seen, albeit in smaller form, at the Cottage adjacent to the Fenn, Monks Eleigh, and Tudor House, Hitcham. Lower Farm, Risby, has a similar extended wing with possible solar over; the size of this house is large although there are no clues as to its status. The central point here is that despite variations in size and style, the basic layout of the open house did not change with social status; it may be suggested, therefore, that the social meanings attached to that layout did not do so either. Larger and smaller open houses were larger and smaller versions of the same thing, physically and symbolically.

Larger transitional houses show more variety than open houses, as do transitional houses in general. As with open houses, however, there is little in basic plan form as opposed to size or decoration to distinguish these houses. Church Farm, Brettenham, and Wolfe Hall, Barrow, are basic two-cell houses, Church Farm being a rebuild retaining a 15th-century crosswing. These two houses are of medium size although with close studding and fine details. Hawkedon Hall and Thurston End Hall are more complex in form.

The early 16th-century Hawkedon Hall (Fig. 9.2) has a basic three-cell plan with rear service wing. The framing, particularly the hall ceiling, is of massive scantling and fine carpentry. There were opposed doorways at the lower end of the hall; the former service arrangement is obscured but may have been submedieval. Large rear side-wall stacks serve the parlour and hall, both with fireplaces in the rooms above, with access over probably being provided by a stair on the side of the stack. Over the two full storeys is a fine crown-post roof, although this was not displayed over an open hall. In terms of ground plan, in particular the ornate three-bay hall, the opposed doors and the peripheral position of the stack, this house appears conservative; but in the fine suite of rooms served by fireplaces over, and the hall chamber with wide divergent braces at its upper end, its interpretation is unusual and problematic.

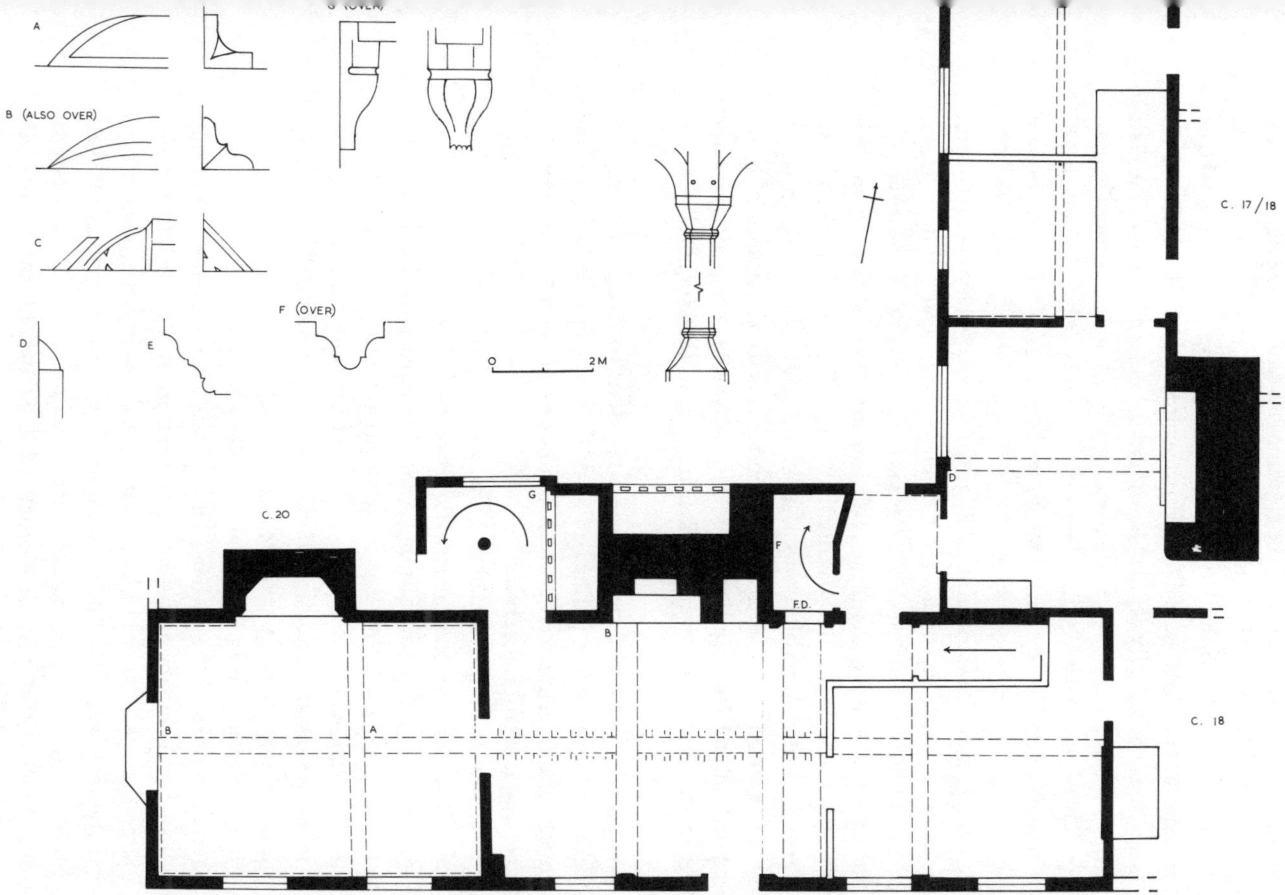

Figure 9.2 Hawkedon Hall, Hawkedon: a large and complex house. The early to mid-16th-century main range has high, impressive ceilings. Probable opposed doors at the lower end of the three-bay hall. Side-wall stack in the parlour has a lintel with foliage designs; that in the hall has a huge lintel resting on two brick arches and supporting a large post. The chambers over the main range are equally lofty and ornamented, with posts and plates of massive scantling. There are two formerly arch-braced trusses over the hall; this room also has wide tension-braces in its W wall. Space in pegs for fireplace over hall. Over this, a roof with two fine crown-posts over the hall but with the collar-purlin extending only 30 cm. beyond the parlour and service partitions; this has not been altered. The location of the stairs is not clear; there may have been a small stair wing, now destroyed, beside the hall stack. The wing to W is of uncertain date; it is fully ceiled, with poor, plain framing of good scantling and a coupled-rafter roof. Large external stack off the side wall. Various additions also to the main range: a newel stair wing to E of hall stack, and wing to W of stack, both 17th century. 17/18th-century extension

Hawkedon Hall is paralleled in several respects by Thurston End Hall (Fig. 9.3), less than 2 km to the south. The core of this house is again of three cells plus crosswing with two full storeys; the framing has brick nogging for infill. Again, there is a three-bay hall with fine ceiling and rear side-wall stack, although there is no indication that the suite of rooms over were of the importance seen at Hawkedon Hall. A third example is Wells Hall, Brent Eleigh, a large house externally similar to the main range at Hawkedon Hall with two large external stacks to the rear side-wall probably serving the hall and parlour. This house sits within a large moat that was brick-lined in the 16th century and behind a fine 16th-century wall with gate with ornamental crenellations.

Both Hawkedon and Thurston End Hall are distinguished by their size and pretensions. Yet in both cases the ground plans were again simply larger versions of the layout of buildings of lesser size. The two plans, however, do indicate the potential within the craft tradition for moving away from this system towards a house form that was qualitatively different. Hawkedon Hall in particular had a fine suite of rooms that could have functioned independently from the ground floor. With all the houses, as with the houses of lesser status discussed in earlier chapters, the ceiling-over of the hall gave the possibility of new patterns of circulation distinctive to that social class emerging.

If we now turn to the closed period, the alterations to two houses suggest a fundamental shift towards a pattern of very different circulation patterns between houses of different social groups. Thurston End was "turned round" and extended: the transitional service end was converted into a parlour end, with a large parlour cell being added and the former service cell remodelled. This service cell had a fine stair inserted and possible study behind. There were also various external modifications. These included two fine gable ends and a large porch dated 1607 with carved detail in polite rather than traditional style. These alterations transform the layout of the building. No examples are known from the socially middling level of an intermediate cell giving extra physical and social distance between parlour and hall.

Monks Hall, Glemsford (Fig. 9.4), was a small open-hall house, with probable extensive alterations in the 16th century. It was again extended and transformed in 1614 by Abraham and Christine Kerington. The resulting house assumed a large but traditional H-plan, with the hall again being heated by a stack against the rear wall. Here it is the facade that is in very different style to the traditional, with massed gables and ornate windows. This is a common design among halls of this period: Cordell Hall, Stansfield, is of this type although with less secure dating, and Chequers Lane, Glemsford, only a mile away and dated 1614, is so similar in design that a common builder or, more

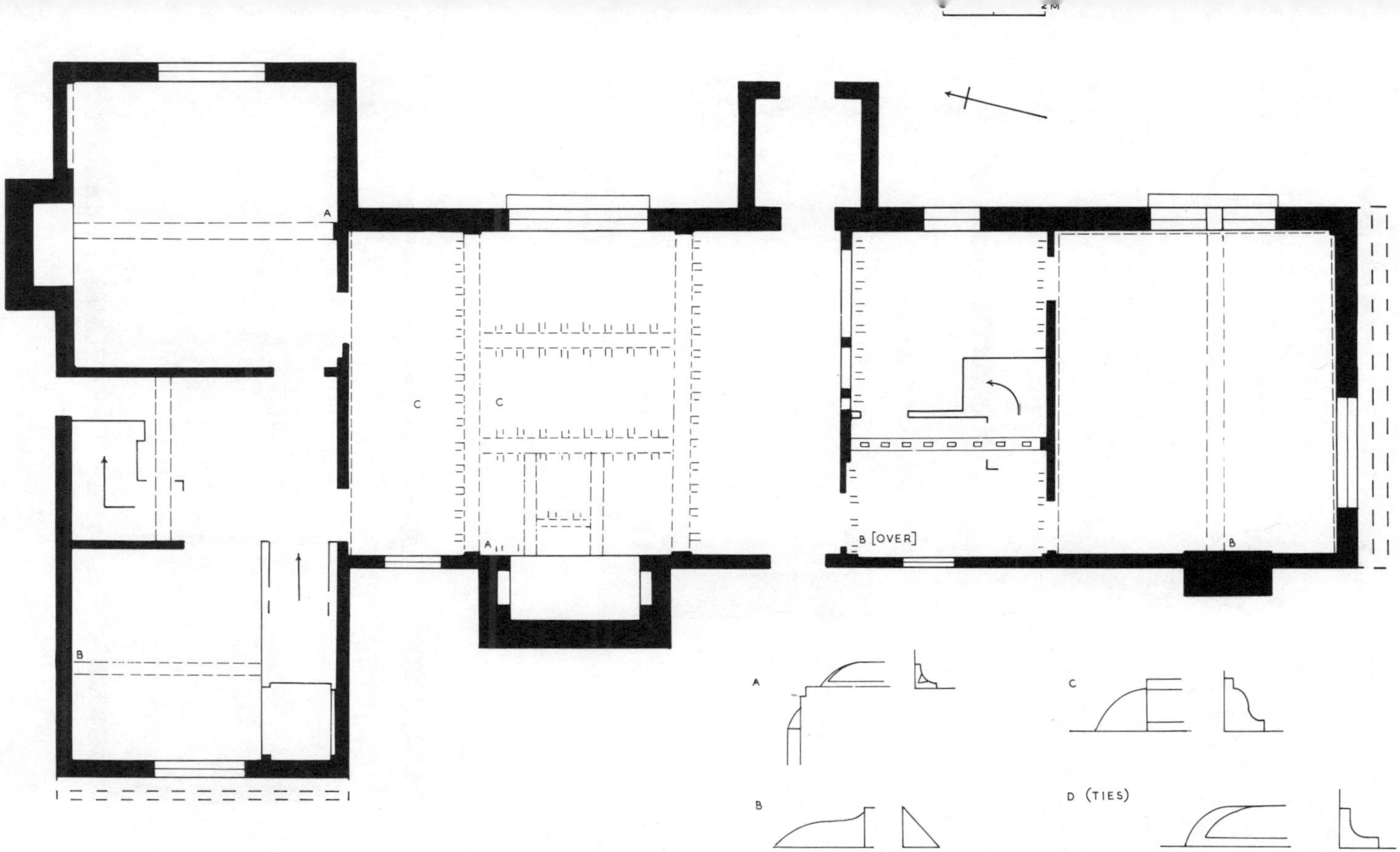

Figure 9.3 Thurston End Hall, Hawkedon: a gentry house with crosswing, altered and extended in 1607. The first phase is of a two-cell main range and projecting crosswing. The three-bay hall has a fine, high ceiling, opposed doors at the lower end, and a side-wall stack with crenellated moulding and two shafts. The service area is masked by later alterations. External stack to parlour. Clasped-purlin roof. Wing stair frame bears the inscription "Pray for well being of Master Doctor Pellis". Its date is uncertain. This phase was altered by the addition of a porch and parlour at the E end, as well as the insertion of a range of mullioned-and-transomed windows to the front. The porch has the date 1607, oak-leaf moulding and open-work carving; above this, two moulded bressumers and six-light mullioned-and-transomed windows. Parlour had decoration similar to the porch. The stack has a 17th century surround but the top is rebuilt. The gabled end has a doubled jetty with moulded bressumers and carved brackets. The former service cell was remodelled as a stair cell with 17th-century panelling. The rear of the crosswing was given a jettied end also. A large quadrangle of 16th century and later farm buildings to SE of the house. The cellar was added in the 18th century.

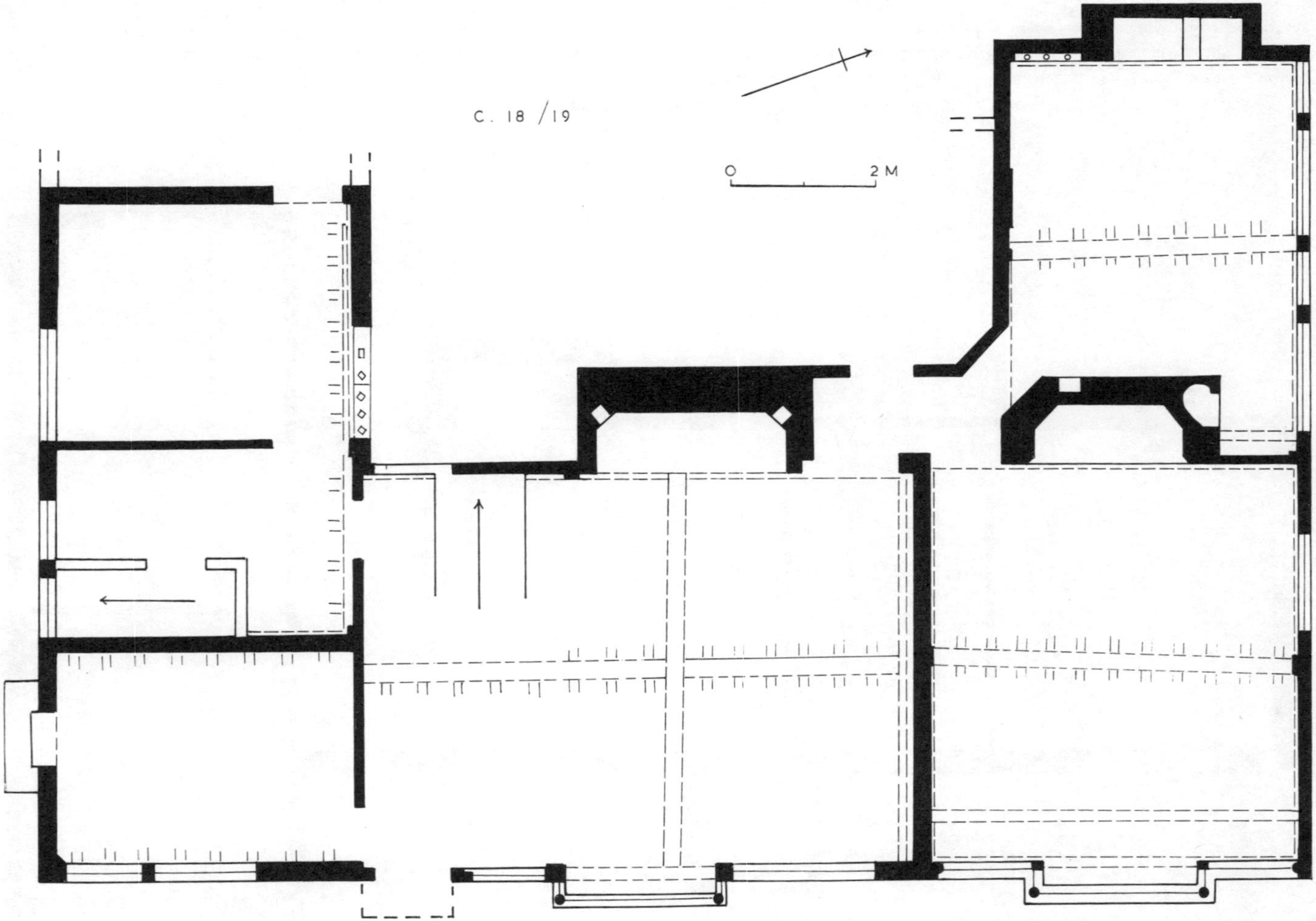
C. 18 /19
0
2 M

likely, competitive emulation may be supposed. Different building materials were also used to signify gentry or higher status. Stanstead Hall, Stanstead, is the only house in the random sample that is not timber-framed: it is of brick and *c.* 1600 in date.

A shift can therefore be detected again of closure, this time closure of the links given by a common use of building material and craft tradition between social groups at the parish or community level. Open houses were of different status, but shared a common spatial, technical and decorative pattern that referred to common structural principles running up and down the social ladder. This common pattern was partially dissolved with the architectural changes of the transitional and closed period. Again, this shift corresponds to a shift between a community based on concepts of status, in which ties are established and maintained through common patterns of paternalism and deference both within and between households, and in which these patterns may be expressed and enforced by common principles structuring architectural settings, and one based on class, in which different social groups may be marked out by different patterns and rhythms of life.

This shift can also be seen in the number of rooms within houses and the rising numbers and new forms of goods to be found in those rooms. This may be seen in the evidence of the inventories. It is difficult to make up a quantifiable index of social status (as defined by occupation) against which to plot house size, so this has only been attempted in terms of the total moveable wealth recorded in the inventory (Fig. 9.5). The earlier sample of inventories clearly show some relationship between house size, measured in

---

Figure 9.4 (opposite) Monks Hall, Glemsford: a large house of complex development. The N wing is probably the oldest element; it has four bays. The two bays to the rear may be part of a 15th century two-cell open-hall house with storeyed part to E and hall to W. Roof over inaccessible and probably rebuilt; now tiled, but with rope for thatching. The S wing appears older than the hall. It had a clasped-purlin roof with wind-braces over which the hall roof has been built. The spine beam of the hall ceiling is inserted into its frame. The hall was built or rebuilt in 1614, with a fine front facade similar to that at Chequers Lane, Glemsford, dated 1618. This is a symmetrical range of three sets of mullioned-and-transomed windows and jetties. The central ten-light window has a projecting gable dormer over; on the tie is the inscription AK*1614*CK. Abraham Kerington died in 1618 leaving a widow Christine Kerington (Bury SRO, Glemsford parish register). The 1614 hall has a large rear side-wall stack with fireplaces at both levels, former opposed doorways, and a stair wing on the W side of the stack. At this time a ceiling carried on inserted rails and posts was placed in the W cell of the wing to N, probably replacing an earlier ceiling. Also at this point the wing was partially rebuilt and two windows inserted into the wing to N. A 16/17th-century design has been painted over a blocked diamond-mullioned window in this wing. Elsewhere, a series of doors have been made out of re-used later 17th-century panelling.

room number and wealth, but this is a very loose one. Two reasons are possible for this. First, a loose correlation may be observed between wealth in terms of moveable goods and status as physically expressed in size of house. Secondly, we may assert that wealth and/or status was still being reflected in size rather than number of rooms; that is, that a high-status house still had the basic layout of its smaller neighbours, being distinguished by relative scale and finery of its fittings.

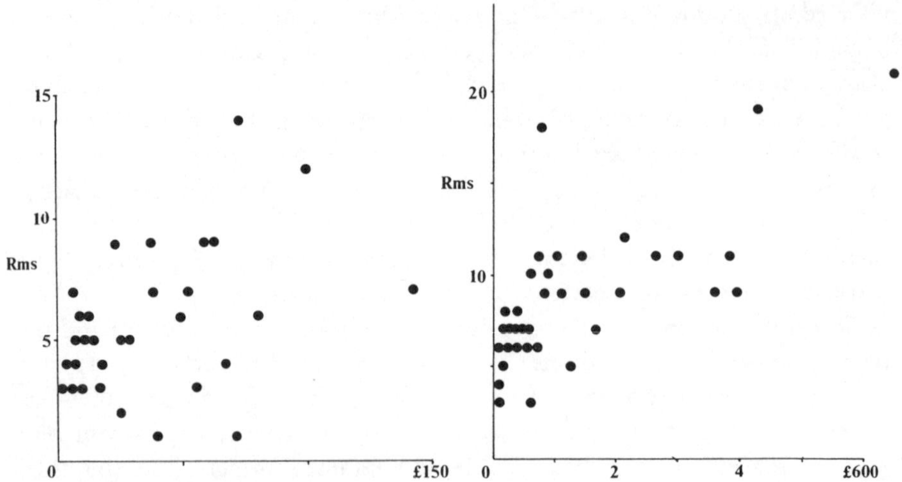

Figure 9.5 Moveable wealth and number of rooms in inventories. Left, early sample; right, late sample

Both these propositions may be true to an extent and this makes interesting the much clearer relation between wealth and room numbers for the later sample of inventories. It implies, first, that social status is much more clearly defined by this time by wealth as reflected in moveable goods; and, secondly, that wealth is now quite clearly reflected by numbers rather than sizes of rooms.

The goods listed in the inventories indicate much wider differences between households for the later sample in other ways. Specific inventories from occupations at upper social levels reveal quantities and specific types of objects not found at levels below that of the gentry. For example, several gentry halls have clocks, absent in the 1570s. These appear to be sensitive status indicators. Books are less sensitive indicators, since they occur in the homes of persons of differing status.

The moveable goods owned by S. Beachcroft, clerk, epitomize the new forms and numbers of objects marking higher social status, while the layout of his house as indicated by the inventory epitomizes the divergence in layout in the closed period. He demonstrated his wealth and status in the parlour not only with six leather-backed chairs, two wrought chairs and stools, but also by having "brass heads" on the otherwise purely functional cobirons, curtains and curtain rods (the only mention of window curtains in the whole sample of inventories), five pictures, a map and a "broken base viol". The variation between this room and less prestigious parlours is very great, although not easily quantifiable: it is certainly more than variation between rooms found in the earlier 16th-century inventories. Beachcroft's "hall" was a heated room with a clock, maps, pictures, two cases of knives, seating and tables, while a room that looks far more like a normal hall is termed the "fire room". There were five chambers above, with garrets over. These all had beds; the parlour chamber had a bed with silk quilt, seven silk cloths, window curtains and hangings. The garrets over performed the storage functions found in the chambers over in middling houses, containing white and grey peas and 155 small cheeses. It seems clear, therefore, that during this period the form of gentry and larger houses in general was beginning to diverge from the craft tradition of the middling classes, in terms of appearance, construction, layout and social values expressed by the house. This divergence is clearly manifested by the middle of the 17th century, but again its deeper causes can be traced back to the transitional period.

It would be both narrow and elitist, however, to see these changing relations solely in terms of the vernacular/polite distinction or, in other words, between the houses of higher and middling social groups. Polarization was a process affecting all levels of society and can be seen at the lower end of the social scale as well. The most obvious example of this is in the growth of numbers of tied cottages.

The growth of tied cottages in terms of numbers surviving today was dated in Chapter 6 to the mid- to late 17th century. However, this is at least partly due to differential survival rates. Their origins can be traced back further: the well known statute of Elizabeth I notes "the erecting and building of great numbers of cottages, which are daily more and more increased in many parts of this land" (Hamilton 1878: 27). It is unlikely that wood-pasture Suffolk at least was one of the areas of great cottage-building at this early date, however. The few early, small houses known from this area need be of no lower than husbandman status.

These early, small houses require some discussion. Only a few fragments of The House near Manor Farm, Monks Eleigh, survive; it appears to be a two-cell, open-hall dwelling with inserted single-fireplace stack (Plate 6a). This structure is important since it shows that houses of this size and status do exist, although traces of their early date may be masked. Smaller houses have also been found in Essex from a much earlier date (Hewitt 1974). The only other open house of comparable size is the Aisled House, Depden Green, although this has lost a cell at one end. Smaller 16th-century houses include No. 32 Pages Lane, Higham, The Lodge, Coney Weston, and Majors Farm, Chedburgh, although the latter two were rapidly extended to the form and size of a three-cell middling house (Fig. 9.6).

So smaller pre-1600 houses do survive, although their form is again not exceptional and these cannot really be considered as a separate class of building. This is not the case for the apparent boom in this type of housing from the mid-17th century onwards. While some of this boom is no doubt due to differential survival, such a rapid rise is at least partly "real". Some houses, Holm Cottage, Barningham and Cottage next to Bell House, Pakenham, for example, clearly fall into the smaller to middling range, but others were purpose-built as ranges of cottages.

Ferncroft, Glemsford, is a classic example of a late 17th-century dwelling in terms of poor scantling and framing technique (Fig. 9.7). It may well have been used as two cottages, and was certainly divided in this way in the 19th century; but there is no provision for separate access to the upper storey and this is unlikely. Other contemporary dwellings were clearly purpose-built as ranges of cottages. Corner Cottage, Stanton, and No. 7 The Green, Fornham (Plate 6b), are both ranges of three or four cottages of this type; Long Gardens, Acton, is another probable example. The Old Post Office, Cavendish (Fig. 9.8), is more doubtful since although now divided into two properties it may be a modified three-cell lobby-entry house (however, it is more probable that this is an original range of two cottages). Certainly, later sets of cottages were built to a deceptive "three-cell lobby-entry" plan just as larger houses could be two such three-cell lobby-entry plans on an L-shape (Cedars, Hopton).

Brook House, Hitcham, Elm Cottage, Lidgate, and Honeymoon Cottage, Brent Eleigh (Fig. 9.9) are very small, two-room dwellings that may be husbandmen's houses but are more likely to be tied cottages. As with larger houses, all these dwellings show distinct divergence from earlier forms of smaller house and from their middling contemporaries. This is true both in terms of technical system (see Ch. 7) and in terms of plan.

In addition to the rise of the purpose-built cottage, many houses were built as single houses but were divided into two or more dwellings by the mid- to late 17th century. There are several sources of evidence for such division. Inserted partitions are not likely to be visible archaeologically since they were as easily removed again leaving no trace in the present house. Where they survive they have often been dated as 18th-century in any case. One probable example is Corner Thatch, Honington (Fig. 9.10), where a late 17th-century

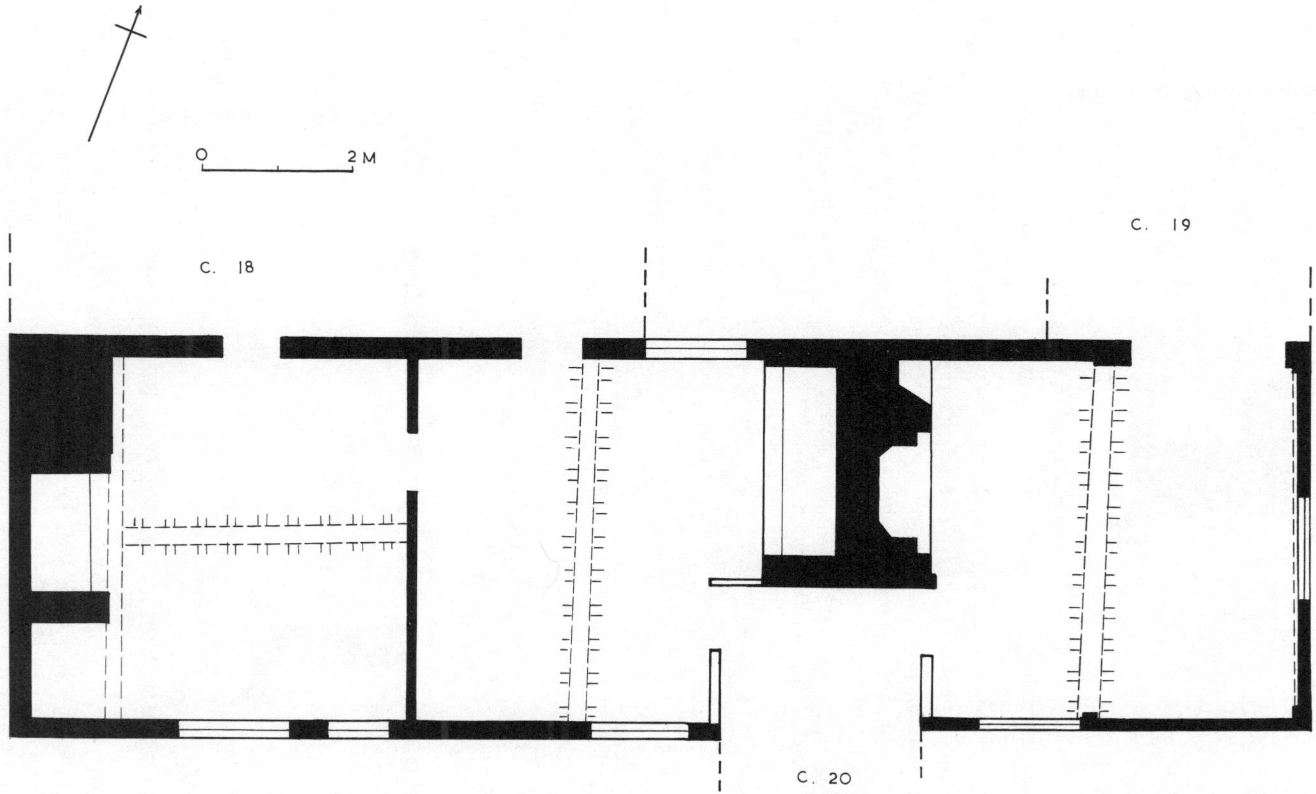

Figure 9.6 Majors Farm, Chedburgh: a 16th-century two- or three-cell house with internal gable end chimney. The stack has a blocked arch for a bread oven. The arrangement of the house E of the hall is unclear since it is obscured by the later alterations; the wall-plates extend as far as the E side of the stack. Converted to a three-cell lobby-entry house in the later 16/17th century with the addition of axial stack with back-to-back fireplaces and a two-bay parlour. The walls were heightened to two full storeys and the roof rebuilt. The fireplace to E has been rebuilt; that to W has a heavy lintel with a series of crude cross motifs added. The new hall ceiling is carried on inserted posts and is similar to that in the parlour. The lobby entry has been destroyed by the 20th-century porch but there is space for a stair at this point. There is also space for a stair in the cell to W. The roof is of clasped-purlin type. Later 17/18th-century panelling in the room to W. According to the occupants there was formerly a well in this room and a cellar under the hall, both now blocked.

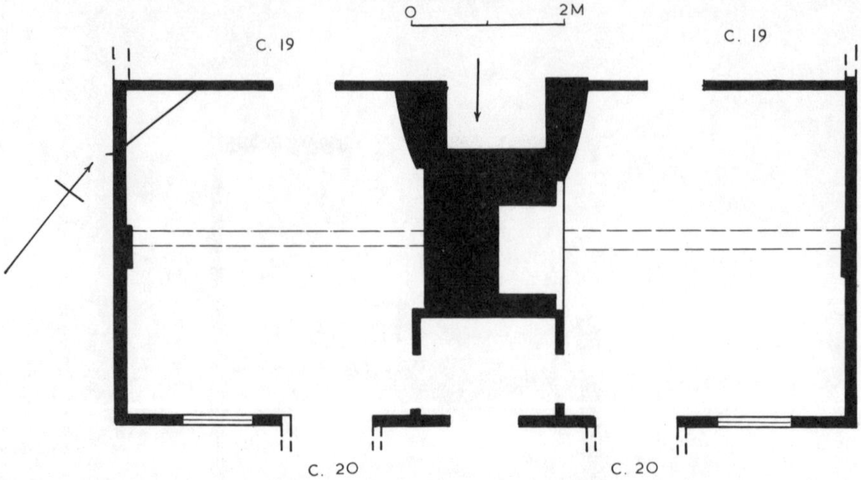

Figure 9.7 Ferncroft, Glemsford: a late 17th-century symmetrical two-cell lobby-entry house. Framing of narrow scantling with spine beams carried on lintels between posts. Much framing re-used. Divergent passing-braces; scarfs in the wall-plate and sill of unusual form. Gabled, thatched clasped-purlin roof. To N of stack is a small area of smoke-blackening, suggesting a probable former curing chamber. Divided in two and a rear outshut added in the 18/19th century.

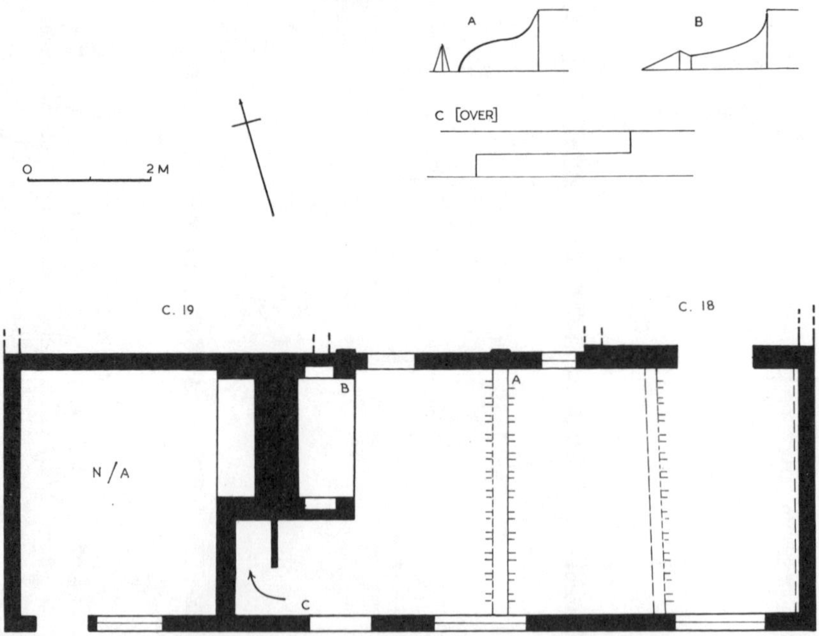

Figure 9.8 Old Post Office, Cavendish: a pair of mid- to late 17th-century cottages with 18th-century wing. Large stack with arched recesses and back-to-back fireplaces. Absence of lobby entry; this is unlikely, therefore, to be one house in its first phase. To E of the stack, three bays with no trace of former division. The cross-beams rest on lintels between posts; joists narrow and unchamfered. Clasped-purlin roof; eyebrow dormer in the cell to W.

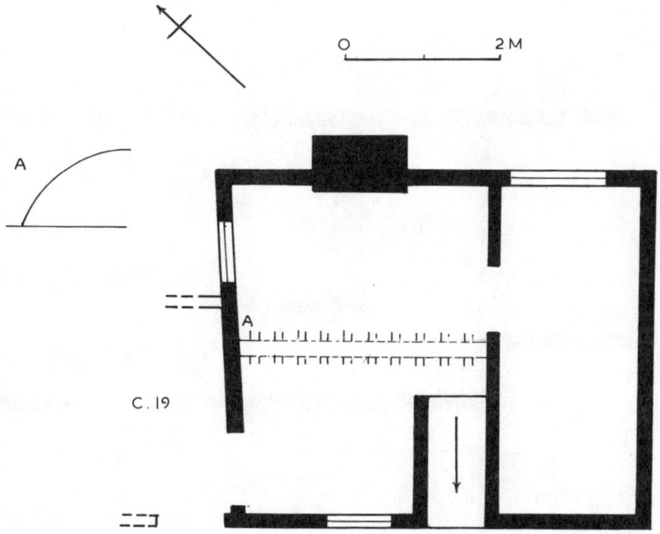

Figure 9.9 Honeymoon Cottage, Brent Eleigh: a small one-cell cottage with first phase outshut along one side and external stack off another. Side-purlin roof, of catslide form over outshut. Former front door in NW end of SW wall. The shell of a backhouse to SW, now attached by later extensions.

wing may mark the conversion of the formerly open house into two two-cell cottages, both with axial stacks. In other examples no physical partition dividing the house need have been made (see below). This practice therefore shows up more clearly in the evidence provided by wills, probate inventories and Hearth Tax returns. Miscellaneous documentary sources may also contain such evidence: in one case such a partition may be inferred from the account of a drinker in an alehouse being thrown through so flimsy a partition that he ended up next door (Clark 1983: 114).

It is not unusual in wills to find some form of specification for the division of the house. The most usual arrangement appears to have been the division down the hall/parlour axis, with the widow or other person being given entry and rights to the hall and hall fireplace. The will of R. Sancty of Wickhambrook, for example, stated that "Bridget Sadler shall dwell in the chamber where I lie as long as she lives, with free access through my hall house and liberty to make a fire in the chimney of the hall house". J. Raneham of Brettenham gave his son Lawrence his house in Bildeston "on condition that he allows my daughter Margaret Osborne widow to have the only habitation of the east end of this tenement. The house is to be divided at the backside of the chimney with the chamber over the east end and the entry now there."

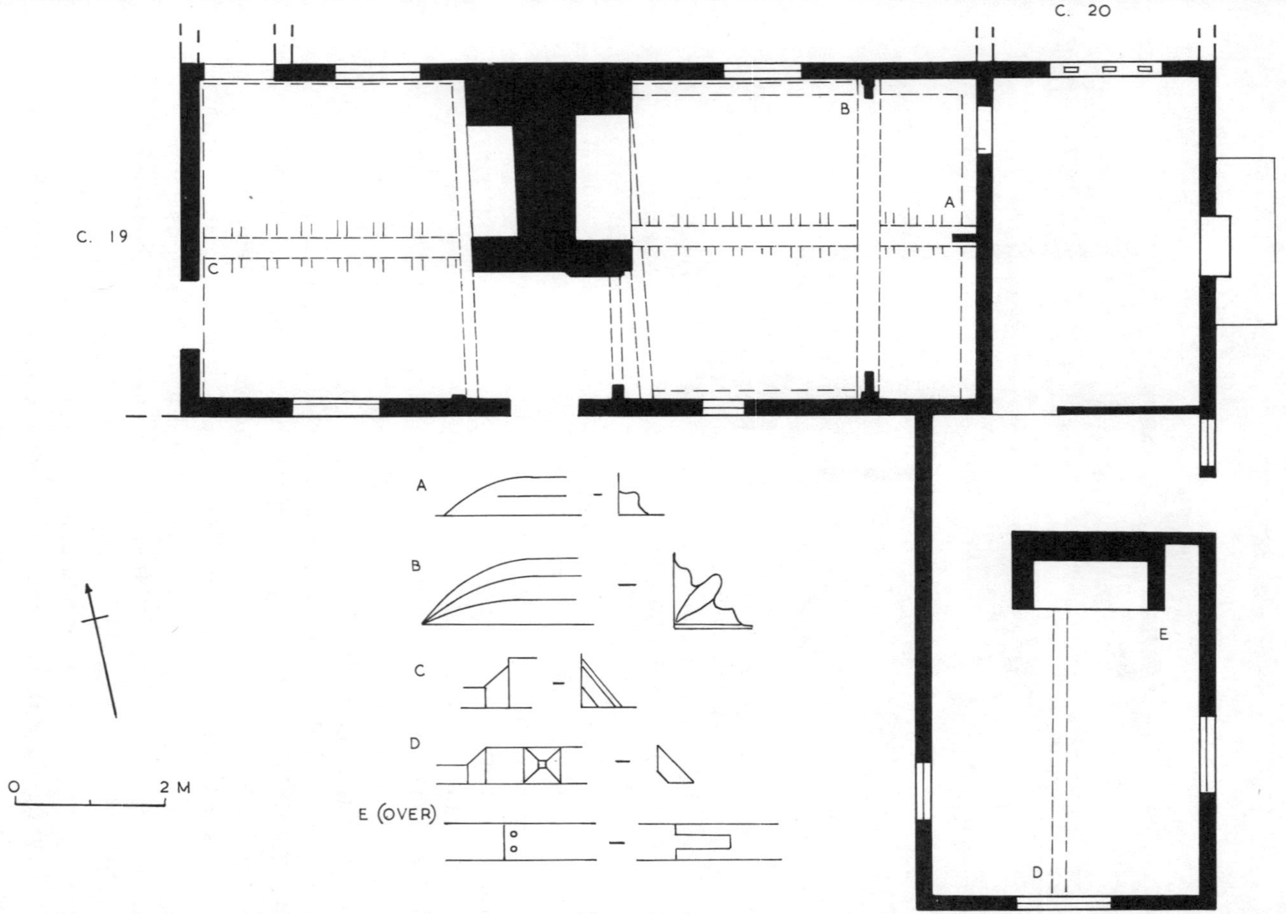

Figure 9.10 Corner Thatch and Heathfield Lodge, Honington: a probable open-hall house ceiled early and with 17th-century crosswing. The arrangement of the open-hall house is uncertain; probably opposed doors at the E end of the hall. There are Roman numerals in the N cross-rail of the cell to E. There is a pair of blocked diamond-mullioned windows over the hall. The roof is inaccessible above collar level; probably of coupled-rafter type or rebuilt in probable clasped-purlin form. The hall ceiling is inserted over the former cross-rails. It has carved vine-leaf and grape ornament of the early to mid-16th century. The stack is of at least two phases, with three attached hexagonal shafts. The conversion to a lobby entry plan is also of uncertain date. The wing to W is mid-/later 17th century and probably dates from the conversion into three cottages. The house is indicated on a map of 1667 (Bury SRO HA513/28/8).

Again, where the house was of lobby-entry form with stair leading off the lobby no partitions need have been inserted at all, as seems to have been the case for the house of J. Howe of Great Welnetham: "My wife is quietly to possess the parlour and parlour chamber in my house for life" (Evans 1986: 150, 323, 347). Where the arrangement was for a widow or other such relative, it would have been limited to the life-span of the person.

A more permanent arrangement may be indicated by the presence in inventories of "lodging rooms". There are only a few of these listed, but this may well be because the room may not be mentioned at all, the possessions within it not belonging to the deceased. One inventory (E. Campian) lists two chambers over lodging rooms with no mention of the rooms beneath, and many of the inventories that are not made out on a room-by-room basis may refer either to single-room dwellings or lodging rooms within shared houses. Finally, many of the Hearth Tax Returns of 1674 probably describe shared houses (Dymond & Martin 1988: 78).

Shared houses are partly the result of pressure on limited housing stock during the population rise of the 17th century. However, this is again only part of a full understanding of the phenomenon. Treating a housing stock in this utilitarian way requires the divorce of the meanings of the house from its structure as discussed in Chapter 7, in that the structure, inseparable in the open period from the values of the household unit, is subdivided to take two or more such units. Subdivision into separate household units also required the provision of several hearths in the same house.

The central conclusion to be drawn from this discussion is that if housing within the sample area is considered as a totality, as a total stock of housing from Hengrave Hall down to shared houses and to the cottages of Fornham and Stanton, we move through time from a conception of domestic architecture which is *quantitatively* different to one that is *qualitatively* different. To clarify, open houses are larger and smaller versions of the same basic layout whereas closed houses have very different forms. This difference has been explored in terms of layout, technical system and decoration, all of which diverge qualitatively. This is most obviously manifested by the mid-17th century but what happens at that point can be seen, again, as a logical unfolding of developments set in train in the transitional period.

The implications for definitions of "polite", "traditional" and "cottage" architecture are that these terms are highly problematic and certainly not a fixed classification regardless of context. In the open period it is difficult to draw a line between polite and traditional architectural competences because that line is not a clear one theoretically or practically. This is only to be expected if houses in the open period express a system of values relating different social groups according to a conception of status. Societies articulated by these means rely on common structural principles, such as those of patriarchy and deference, running up and down the social ladder: the tenant farmer is lord to his household but has in turn a feudal landlord, and so on up the scale. In addition, a community based on face-to-face relationships will rely on expression of those relationships on an everyday level. Open houses, therefore, have a common form because they are expressing a common system of values relating to a common social structure. The meanings of space within the peasant house are congruent with the meanings of space within the manorial seat so that everybody "knows their place" – in both a physical and social sense – within the two social situations.

This suggested interpretation allows the apparent conservatism of many 16th-century gentry and aristocratic houses to be understood more deeply. While the structure outlined above was beginning to be actively modified by other groups in the community, it was logical for those at the top of the older social structure to attempt to retain those social forms and material referents that buttressed and composed that dominant position. The results of this process were the feudal references in polite architecture generally and the conservative plans of larger transitional houses in the sample specifically.

As relations of status broke down or were modified, so this was mediated and expressed through the form of the houses. At polite level this meant a disengagement from the craft tradition in terms of both layout and technical system, most obviously in the use of different building materials. With this divergence came the opportunity to construct an overt written discourse on the meanings of architecture, since these meanings were no longer embedded in what was taken for granted in everyday social relations. At lower social levels changing relations were enforced through the growth of tied cottages and expressed through the form and impoverished technical system of those cottages and through the dissolution of the house/household link seen in shared houses. The implications for the demarcation of polite and traditional architecture are that this whole split is an ethnocentric one: it derives from observing a divide in 18th- and 19th-century architecture and pushing it back to the point at which traditional buildings no longer survive, before which point any discussion of such a divide in such terms is rendered meaningless.[1] Restricted studies of either "traditional" or "polite" architecture are therefore locked into a perspective that obscures the changing social forms which can be associated with this divide, and thus define out of existence the ultimate causes of the changes under study.

In terms of substantive implications for the concept of class polarization the evidence is more complex. The evidence of polite and traditional architecture, on this analysis, supports Lawrence Stone's contention that the early modern period is not so much one of the rise and fall of classes but rather of the changing nature and quality of relations between those classes (Brenner 1989).

To explore this question further, the evidence of qualitative shifts in social meanings developing in the 16th and 17th centuries must be related to the evidence for "profiles" of housing given by the Hearth Tax Returns for 1674[2] (Table 9.1). There is a rough average of 11–40 houses per parish with a lengthy "tail" consisting of the larger villages, such as those along the Bury–Diss road (Ixworth, Stanton, Pakenham, Thelnetham), the Stour Valley (Cavendish and Glemsford) and market centres (Bildeston). When plotted out (Fig. 2.4), we see a marked lack of density of housing on the lighter soils to the north of Bury, while the "low" areas to the south of Bury are largely due to small parish size in these areas rather than low housing density as such. Overall the concentration in the area of richer soils, wood-pasture landscape, mixed farming and the cloth industry is as expected.

The distribution of larger houses, measured in terms of numbers of hearths, is indicated in Figure 9.11. This map offers a way into the question of a typology of parish structure. It is clear that, particularly in the cases of those houses with 20 hearths or over, there is a preponderance in the north and west. These were previously impoverished areas of poor soil and low population (Dymond & Virgoe 1986: 74) into which large landowners moved, or which they controlled from the start, and subsequently dominated the parish politically. Parishes with a large house are certainly smaller communities. The average number of houses for parishes containing a 20-hearth-plus house is 23.3; for parishes without a 20-hearth-plus house it is 33.3 (Johnson nd: 263-5).

As we saw in Chapter 2, this north/south division corresponded with that perceived by contemporary commentators. Richard Blome, for example, stated that "High Suffolk or the Woodland is chiefly the seat of the Yeomanry, few being there either very rich or very poor . . . in . . . the fielding by Bury . . . the Gentry are commonly seated" (quoted in Dymond & Martin 1988: 86). The Hearth Tax Returns indicate a major difference in terms of social structure as well as soil type and economy between those areas enclosed by agreement in the 15th and 16th centuries and those not enclosed until much later.

Thus the separation of vernacular and polite architecture, and in more detail variation between larger and smaller houses, was accompanied by variations in community structure. If an equation between larger houses in the Hearth Tax Returns and the upper gentry and aristocracy is allowed, these social groups concentrated in the areas north of Bury where estates could be built up or in the larger communities in the Stour Valley. Between these regions, the lack of larger houses indicates communities dominated by lesser gentry and yeoman farmers with little differentiation in housing. We therefore need to look more closely at landscape type, parish structure and the distribution of power in local areas. These themes will be explored in Chapter 10.

Table 9.1 Summary of Hearth Tax returns, 1674.

	Shared (2 hearths)				Shared (3)			Shared (4)		Single entries															
Parish	2	3	4	5+	3	4	5+	4	5	1	2	3	4	5	6	7	8	9	10	11	12	13	14	15+	Exempt
Acton	10									7	6	11	2	1	2	1								1(21)	
Alpheton	1	1								1	4	3	2	1			1								1
Ampton	2										1	2												1(21)	1
Bardwell	9									8	9	6	7	3			1	1					2	1(18)	14
Barnham	10	2		2(7,6)		2				1	11	5	3	2	1	1									
Barningham	6	2	1							4	5	4	5	3	1	2								1(33)	6
Barrow	6	1	7		7					1	1	2	2	2		3								1(20)	8
Bildeston		1	1		19	12	1(5)			4	17	11	11	3	4	1	2		1				1	1(15)	40
Boxted	4	2								3	1	2	4	2		1	1							1(22)	
Bradfield Combust	2	1			1						2	3	2	1	1		1	1							3
Bradfield St Clare	3	3		1(5)		1					1	2	2	1	1	1									4
Bradfield St G'ge	4	3	5		4	1					1	8	7	1		1									8
Brent Eleigh	4									2	3	4	2						1	1					
Brettenham	1	1								3	12	2	2	2								1			1
Brockley	5		2		3							3	2		1	1									5
Cavendish	13	3		1(5)						75	8	16	9	6	2			2		1					
Chedburgh	1	1								2	1	1	1												
Chelsworth	5			2(7,5)		6					2	8	3	3	2	1	1								11
Chevington	8	1	4							1		13	3	2	3	1			1						7
Cockfield	4	18	4		13					1	10	8	12	5	1	2	2								28
Coney Weston	4				1					1	1	7	3	1	1										1
Culford	2									1	2	3	1	2										1(29)	1
Denham			1					2			1	3	2	1					1						2
Denston			3	3(5,5,8)		6			1(5)				1			1								1(18)	6
Depden	2	2						2			1	3	4			1	1		1			1			2
Euston					1							1	3				1							1(42)	9
Fakenham Magna	1	1								6	4	1	1		1					2				1(34)	6
Flempton	1		3		1	1						2	1	1											1
Fornham All Saints	2		4							1		6	3	5		1		2							
Fornham St G'vieve	2	1				2				1	2	3	3	1			1								5
Fornham St Martin	1				1	1					3	5	2	1		3									3
Glemsford	67	16	2	1(6)						6	11	13	15	8	3	4	3								81
Great Barton	3	1	6		2	1					1	6	2	1	3	1	2							1(15)	6
Great Saxham		1	4		3			1				1	3	2					1					1(18)	4
Great Livermere	2	3	1		1	2					3	3	2	2		1				1				1(17)	4
Great Waldingfield	8	9	1	2(8,5)	3					1	6	8	2	5	5	1	1								1
Great Welnetham	5	2	2								1	8	2					1	1						4
Hargrave	1	1	6		2							8	2		1										2
Hartest	3	6	1		1					5	19	9	10	5		1	1								
Hawkedon		2	2					1		2	2	3	1		3	2		1	1						4
Hawstead	2	2	1		5						4	8		3	2									2(35,17)	6
Hengrave										1	1	1	2	1										1(51)	
Hepworth		2	2		2	1	1(6)	3	1		7	6	4	3	1										6
Hitcham	20									21	16	11	7	1	3										22

Table 9.1 continued

Parish	Shared (2 hearths) 2	3	4	5+	Shared (3) 3	4	5+	Shared (4) 4	5	Single entries 1	2	3	4	5	6	7	8	9	10	11	12	13	14	15+	Exempt
Honington	1	2								1	6	2		2	1		2								5
Hopton	13	3	1	1(6)	1						15	3	5	1											13
Horringer	3	1	5		6	3				2		6	7	2	2	3	1		1		1			1(15)	11
Ickworth	1	1	1		1						1	3		1										1(18)	1
Ingham	1	1	1							1	2	3	1	2		1									2
Ixworth	23	11	2							2	11	8	7	4	1	1				2				1(16)	32
Ixworth Thorpe	2									2	5	2	2			1									
Kettlebaston	1									2	3	3	2	1	1			1							1
Knettishall		3								1	4		1	1	1										4
Lackford	4	1	1		1										3			1	1						2
Lawshall	12	13	5	3(6,6,5)						2	6	12	6	1								1			2
Little Livermere	4									1	2	2	1					1							2
Little Saxham	1		2	1(5)	1	1						1	1											1(31)	
Little Waldingfield	12	3	1	1(5)	3					3	3	3	4	3	2	1	1	1						1(16)	4
Little Welnetham	1	1	3		2							1	4			1									3
Market Weston	4									10	8	5	3	1	1		2				1				10
Milden	2	3								3	3	1	1	2			1	1							1
Monks Eleigh	12	2	1	2(5,5)						6	7	10	4	2	2	3	1	1							16
Nowton	5		2									4	3	2				1							3
Pakenham	3	5	5	1(6)	1	5	2(5)			1	6	7	5	3	2		1			1				3(23,17,16)	8
Poslingford	4	4	2							2	6	5	2	3	1	1								1(15)	11
Preston St Mary	2	1			1					3	3	9	1			1	2								2
Rede	4	1	1	1(6)	1					1	2		3			1									4
Risby	1		1		2						5	1	2	2	1			1							3
Rougham	6	4	3		5					1	2	5	1	1	3	1	2	2	1	2				1(24)	10
Rushbrooke	1	2	2		1	1						1	1					1						1(33)	3
Sapiston	1	4	1		2					2		2	1	1		1	1								2
Shimpling	7	7	2		4						10	5	2	1	2	1		1							2
Somerton		2								2	2	4	3	1	1										1
Stanningfield	1	3			5	1				1	2	6	2			1					1				6
Stansfield	4		3	1(5)						4	8	2	4	2	1	1									7
Stanstead	10	7		2(6,5)						2	5	9	3	1	1										12
Stanton	7	3	5			17				1	11	9	6	5	3	2		1							22
Thelnetham	22	2	3	1(5)	1					2	6	5	4	2	3			1							10
Thorpe Morieux				1(5)	2	1	1(5)			3	6	9	1	2	1					1					4
Timworth	2	2				2				3	3	4	2	1	2										6
Troston	2	1								6	6	5	2	1			1							1(15)	5
Wattisham	1									7	9	6	1	2						1					2
Westley					1					3	1		2	1	2										3
West Stow	4									2	7	4	1	1										1(17)	6
Whepstead	2	2	6		8	2						5	12	3		2			1						9
Wickhambrook*	7	5	5		1	1		5	4		3	5	10	6	4		2							1(19)	16
Wordwell	1											2			2										2
Total	418	189	127	29	120	70	6	14	5	241	371	412	280	145	85	55	36	22	12	12	3	3	3	31	581

Note: *Wickhambrook also has two five-names, five hearth entries, two six-name entries, one six-name entry and one seven-name ten-hearth entry not listed.

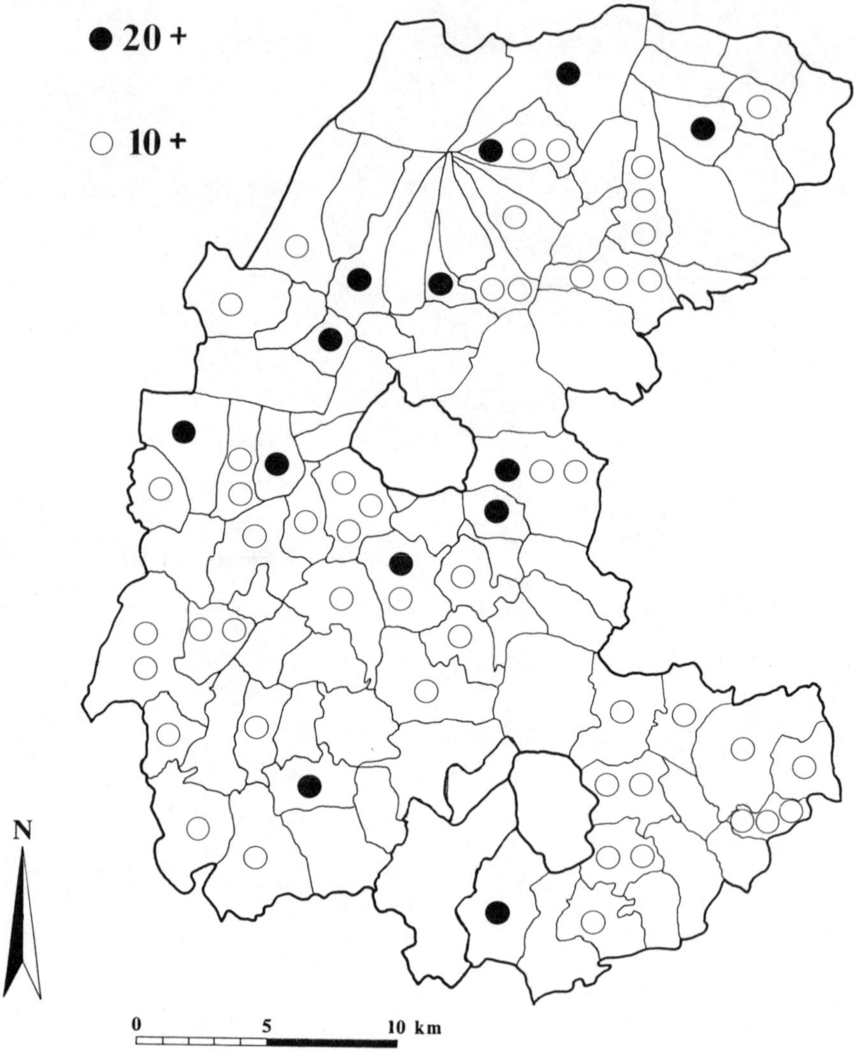

Figure 9.11 Distribution of larger houses in the sample area, 1674; numbers refer to hearths.

Notes

1. It could be countered that the great cathedrals of the 12th and 13th centuries expressed a semi-overt international language, as Panofsky (1957) has elegantly argued; but to deal with this question adequately would require an extension of the argument into the realms of domestic versus ritual architecture, which is beyond the scope of this discussion.

2. The Hearth Tax Returns for 1674 were published in 1905 and spot checks against the original suggest the transcription is accurate (Dymond & Martin 1988: 78). For a full discussion of the problems and potential of this source of evidence, see Johnson (nd: 150–51).

CHAPTER 10
A PROCESS OF ENCLOSURE

So far I have looked at changes in traditional architecture. I have related these changes to other classes of evidence acting as contextual information. I have done this by looking at contemporary changes in traditional aesthetics, household goods and technical systems, changes in the farmstead as a whole, and changes in polite and gentry architecture.

Little has been said, however, of why these changes came about. The most immediate "social" reason given by commentators working on parallel architectural changes in other regions of England is that of the rise of privacy. This is certainly manifested in the heightened degree of segregation found in the buildings but is not sufficient as a complete understanding of the process of closure on three counts. First, as we have seen, the open house was not an unsegregated building nor did it lack elements of privacy (Ch. 4). Secondly, it is easy to "unpack" the notion of privacy: clearly, a need for privacy must arise from the degree to which the society in question views the individual as an autonomous being with separate, distinct needs and desires. The form in which the concept of the individual is manifested will vary from culture to culture and consequently the need for privacy will vary (Ch. 7). Thirdly, the relationship of the individual with the social world will be related to his or her relationship with the "natural" world: the cultural perception of the latter is invariably modelled on the former as it certainly was in 16th- and 17th-century England (Ch. 8). To understand change, therefore, we need to situate the need for privacy within contemporary perceptions of the individual and of the external world.

This chapter will address the question "why?". I shall argue, through a further extension of context, that houses must be related to fields. Both are culturally created and derived patterns of space whose meanings relate to the same community, the same social totality. Both played their part in the same configuration of the rhythms of rural life. I will continue by arguing that in order to understand this relationship, one of both similarity and inversion, a contextual account of changing ethics, world-view and perception of self and others during this period must be given.

Closure of houses, enclosure of fields

Classically, arable fields in medieval England were laid out in "open" form. That is, large fields were subdivided into narrow strips owned by individual peasants, the whole being governed by a complex legal system of ownership and use rights. From the 15th century onwards, these fields were broken up or enclosed at varying paces and in widely differing ways in different regions of England. In western Suffolk two forms of enclosure occurred, roughly corresponding to the divide in soil type. In the northern, "sheep/corn" area enclosure was late, in the late 18th and 19th centuries, and by parliamentary act or, in a few cases, by wholesale reorganization imposed by the great landowners (Dymond 1988: 100). The area remained largely one of open fields before 1700.

The southern, wood-pasture area is more problematic. Here much of the field patterning has its origins in the Roman period or later prehistory (Williamson & Bellamy 1986: 19) and there does not appear to have been a wholesale reorganization of the landscape at any point. Instead strip fields were often laid out within the older boundaries, and the ensuing enclosure was piecemeal (Tawney 1912: 147–58). It is, therefore, much more difficult to chart since by definition it is rarely mentioned in documentary records.

It is also necessary to draw a clear distinction between the violent, extreme forms of enclosure during this period, particularly in the Midlands, and the form of enclosure seen in wood-pasture Suffolk. In the former area the landlord was often able to force tenants off the land, and usually did so as a prelude to a switch from arable to sheep farming in response to market forces: "Down corn, up horn." In particular, it involved the destruction of common property rights. More arguably, it represented a class victory for the great landowner over the poorer tenant. In the wood-pasture areas enclosure was usually "by agreement", within pre-existing field boundaries although not necessarily involving the mutual consent of those concerned as the term might imply, and with no such destruction of common rights. Arguably, it could be carried through by landowners and tenants below gentry level.

This distinction was clearly seen by contemporaries: their definition of enclosure is not the one adopted here. For example, the comment of John Hales makes this clear. Hales was a leading anti-enclosure government official, and wrote in his instructions to enclosure commissions:

> But first, to declare unto you what is meant by the word "inclosures". It is not taken where a man doth enclose and hedge in his own proper

> ground where no man hath commons. For such inclosure is very beneficial to the commonwealth . . . but it is meant thereby, where any man hath taken away and enclosed any other mens commons, or hath pulled down houses of husbandry [depopulation], and converted the lands from tillage to pasture. This is the meaning of this word, and so we pray you to remember it. (Tawney & Power 1924: 41)

This distinction between two forms of enclosed landscape is also seen clearly on the boundary of the sheep/corn and wood-pasture areas (Fig. 10.1).

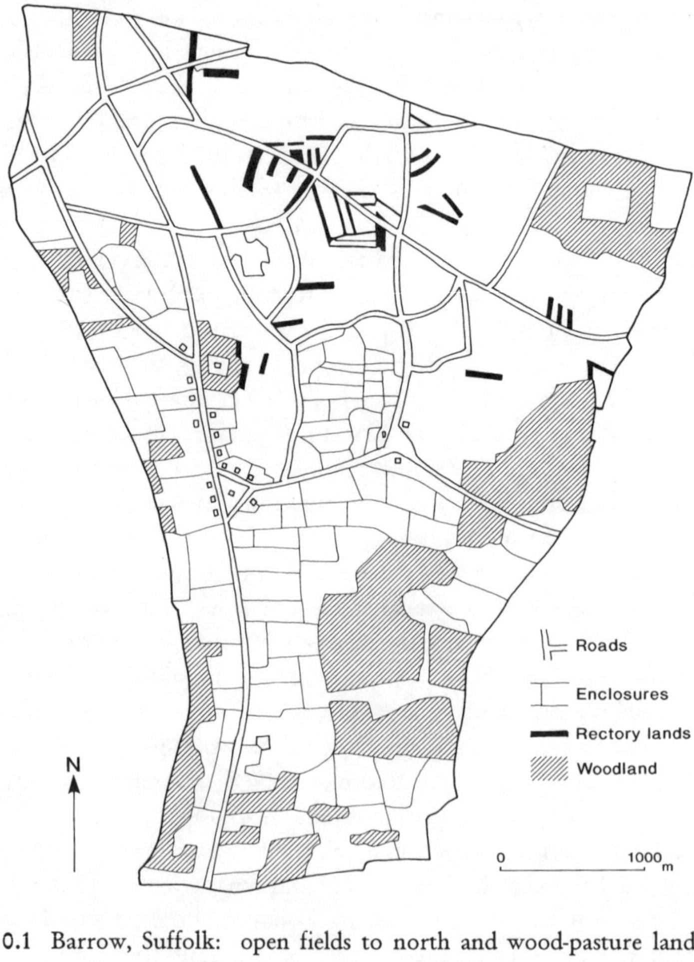

Figure 10.1 Barrow, Suffolk: open fields to north and wood-pasture landscape to south.

The suggestion that enclosure was simply a response to demographic, climatic and market changes is simplistic. These factors were undoubtedly important, particularly in the Midlands and areas of the North, but even in these areas the landlords' ability to evict was dependent on the strength of the village community. Others have pointed out that the system of strip fields was not so "irrational" as it appears: it was appropriate to a certain form of feudal community sharing capital equipment (Dahlman 1980: 93–145). Enclosed fields increase overall yield, are more appropriate to a system governed by market forces and more amenable to the accumulation of private wealth, the individual tenant being freed from the restrictions of the peasant community (Wolf 1966, Williamson & Bellamy 1985: 28).

The central point here is that enclosure was not simply an economic phenomenon, but was intimately bound up with changing social relations in the countryside, as I have argued is the case with houses. We can now narrow our focus by considering the chronology of the form of enclosure found in the wood-pasture areas. This is difficult to assess, but most of this area was probably enclosed by the early 17th century. It is certainly pre-1700.[1] If this is so, there is a close relationship between houses and fields in wood-pasture Suffolk in a temporal sense. The majority of 15th- and 16th-century houses stand within the wood-pasture region of the sample area, while proportionally there is a concentration of 17th-century houses in the northern, sheep-corn area (Fig. 10.2). The 18th- and 19th-century reorganization of the sheep/corn landscape, through its destruction of older farmhouses, might account for the lower overall numbers of pre-1700 houses in this area but not for the relative preponderance of 17th-century houses here. Thus, in the wood-pasture areas, both housing and enclosure are early. In the sheep/corn areas, both housing and enclosure are late.

This close temporal relationship is paralleled by a close relationship in form: I suggest that enclosure in fields and in houses is formally similar, both in terms of parallels between open and enclosed houses and fields and in terms of development through time. Hence the architectural classification adopted in earlier chapters, of open and closed houses. This period sees a "process of enclosure", as I would like to term it, in landscape, in architecture, and in social, economic and cultural life. This is a process particular to the area being discussed but which has parallels with other times and places (e.g. Pred's 1985 study of communities in Sweden).

This formal similarity can be pursued through five parallels. First, open fields are large bounded units "framing" the township in the wider landscape: in other words, the social relations that bind the township together are mapped out onto the landscape, in that open-field systems appear undivided within field boundaries but are in fact split up in terms of ownership and rights within those units, and subject to "customary" limits over that ownership and rights. Secondly, open fields have a "stable" appearance; but in many cases the literature suggests that beneath the stability of medieval forms of

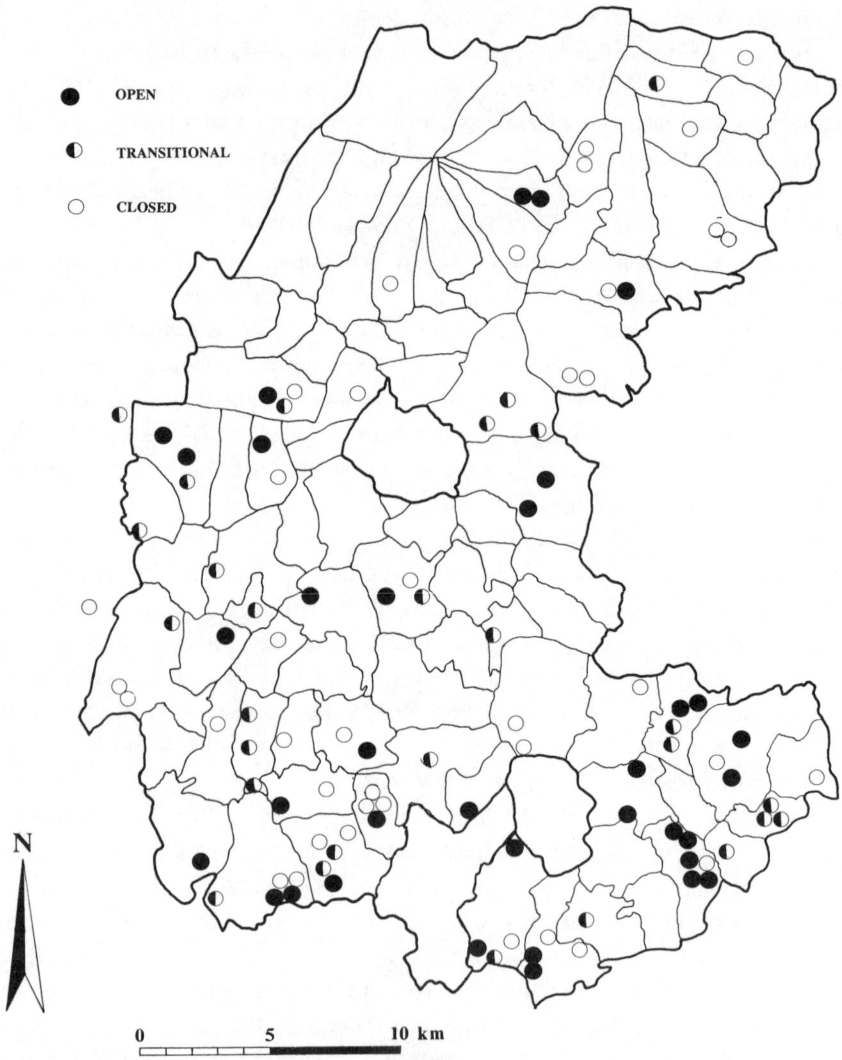

Figure 10.2 Distribution of houses in the sample area (Brent Eleigh excluded).

tenure a great deal of property transfer and other fluidity took place (Macfarlane 1978: 102–130). Thirdly, enclosure of fields is a move from a complex mapping of social relations on the ground to a masking of social relations behind the uniform appearance of the fields. The layout of an enclosed field offers no clue as to its ownership or control. Fourthly, the enclosure of open fields can be seen superficially as a "rational" process, resulting in economically more efficient units seen from the perspective of the individual. Fifthly, however, enclosure is also and more fundamentally a medium and expression of changing social and legal relations on the parish scale. These changing relations may be the unintended consequence of "rational" action. They may also be part and parcel of the change.

An examination of open-hall houses shows that they share these points in common. They are, first, large bounded units "framing" the household unit in the township or parish landscape. It has already been demonstrated that their layout maps out the framework of household relations through their domination by the open hall, a room that appears open to the roof and across all sides, but which is in fact split up into upper and lower ends, centre and margins, front and back. These splits correspond to "customary" social divisions within the household. Again, therefore, there is the tension between stress on the whole versus division into parts. Secondly, in many cases these divisions appear static although membership is fluid (thus where a woman can take the rôle of patriarch at the upper end of the hall; or where other bodies take on that rôle, such as colleges or stewards). Thirdly, closure of houses meant a move from direct mapping of social relations through architectural features to a partial masking of those features through a uniformity within units of space and through masking of the timber frame. Fourthly, the "enclosure" of such houses can be seen as a "rational" process; the ceiling-over of the hall and insertion of the stack made the house warmer, easier to move around in and provided more floor space. Fifthly, however, it was also and more fundamentally a medium and expression of changing social relations on the household scale. These changing relations may well be an unintended consequence. They may also be part and parcel of that change.

Thus, just as the social world was organized and articulated by the layout of house and farmstead, so the natural world was organized by the fields; and these two areas merged into one another and were modelled on each other. It is crucial to stress that this set of parallels works both on a synchronic level and on a diachronic, dynamic one.

At the same time, however, as fields and houses were undergoing a process of enclosure, churches appeared to be moving in the opposite direction. Many of the churches in the wood-pasture area were rebuilt in the later 15th century, particularly in and around Lavenham and Long Melford. These were built according to the traditional pattern of the medieval church, with the space divided up between nave and chancel by the rood screen. Private chantry and guild chapels in the body of the church within their own partitions added to this heavily segregated use of space, and the whole was intimately tied to the structure of social relations. Graves has explored the way parish churches in East Anglia mapped out social and symbolic space through both the architecture and the movement of the priest (Graves 1989).

The Edwardian Reformation involved removal of these divisions in whatever form, whether by shifting the congregation formerly behind the screen into the chancel or by partial or total destruction of the rood screen (Platt 1981: 162–6; Addleshaw & Etchells 1948: 20–26). At Brent Eleigh the church was gutted and the wall paintings plastered over (Fitch 1986: 3–4); the newly built church at Lavenham was stripped of its divisions and chantry and guild chapels (Dymond & Betterton 1982). The nature and extent of the divisions between nave, altar and chancels continued to be a matter of concern, with many of the people of Suffolk pressing for their removal. The Laudian reforms of the early 17th century, intent on restoring some of these divisions, were strenuously resisted in many parishes. The Proceedings of the Suffolk Committee for Scandalous Ministers record many routine complaints from lay folk that their ministers complied too readily with the Laudian practice of surrounding the altar with rails (Holmes 1970).

The visible manifestations of the processes of enclosure and closure are thus closely related, and must be seen as part of a larger matrix of social, cultural and economic changes in late medieval and early modern England. Further, they are related – albeit in a complex way involving symbolic inversion – to changes in the architectural patterning of parish churches. If the phenomenon we are trying to understand is thus a very large one, the possibility of laying out a complete, satisfactory understanding of the causes of the process of closure within this final chapter are limited. Such an understanding would involve a single unitary model or explanation whose nature would do violence to the particular, contextual nature of the changes under discussion. As Tilley (1991) has argued, such a model would impose an illusory finality on the text rather than any real understanding. Rather, therefore, an attempt at listing a set of causes will be more limited. I will attempt to make a link hitherto little explored in material terms or at a social level below that of the gentry. This is a link between the process of closure and the change from a medieval to an early modern world-view. This will necessarily neglect other sides of a many-sided causal chain or, more accurately, one thread in a tangle of causal networks.

Puritanism and the middling household

It is now necessary to be more specific about the social groupings involved in the process of closure. In Chapter 9, it was assumed that the bulk of the housing stock was "middling": that it corresponded to the social levels of the lesser gentry, yeomen, and some of the more prosperous husbandmen.[2] This identification is important since it allows changes in ethic and world-view at a finer resolution than that of society as a whole. In particular, an avenue into some of the explicit ideas going hand in hand with closure may be made through an exploration of one ideology of the period, that of Protestantism and its more extreme form, Puritanism. Puritanism has long been seen, albeit controversially, as an ideology of many of the lower gentry, yeomen and textile workers in early modern England by both contemporaries and historians (Hill 1966: 23), and the cloth-producing areas in Suffolk in particular certainly formed the core of the Eastern Association in the English Revolution (Everitt 1960). Underdown (1985b: 40–43) has argued that these social groups were attracted to radical religious belief and Puritanism in particular in certain social situations. He bases this conclusion on an analysis of the West Country of England, drawing a distinction between the "chalk" and "cheese" communities of that area that closely parallels that between sheep/corn and wood-pasture regions in Suffolk. His suggestion that religious radicals flourished in "cheese country" adds support to the concentration of Puritanism, and the dominance of social groups below the upper gentry in general, in the wood-pasture area of Suffolk, a concentration confirmed by mapping the relative influence of Puritan and non-Puritan gentry in the wood-pasture areas, particularly around Lavenham, during the Civil War; conversely the dominance of Royalist gentry in the sheep-corn areas (Dymond & Martin 1988: 84). Whatever the reaction to the Reformation in other areas, Macculloch has found little opposition in the county to the Edwardian reforms and political dominance of Suffolk by Puritanism by 1589 (Macculloch 1986: 218).

Protestantism in general was thus an increasingly powerful force in the area. In any case, many of the stresses within Puritan belief, for example on the individual, may be taken as extreme examples of wider intellectual and ideological shifts going on at that time. It is therefore legitimate to look to the content of Puritan belief for some understanding of the social meanings carried by these houses and their landscape context. Some of these links have already been examined in Chapter 8. The issues of the relationship of Puritanism to political events of the 17th century and its long-term influence on the origins of capitalism are highly contentious (see Walzer 1966, Hill 1966, Lake 1987, and many others); I am making no assumptions about these aspects of a complex debate within cultural history.

Definitions of Puritans and Puritan belief are problematic, and this is not the place for an extended discussion of this topic. What is important is to make clear the heightened sense of self manifested in Protestantism in general and Puritanism in particular. The Protestant system of belief as a whole centred on the removal of priest as intermediary between "Man" and God and the introduction of a "this-worldly" rather than "other-worldly" system of belief. Central to Puritanism was a sharp distinction drawn between the "inner man" and "outward man". The man who got on with his neighbours but who failed to monitor his inner self was doomed to Hell; only by a constant vigilance and self-monitoring could one enter Heaven (Morgan 1944: 1). If Puritans and Protestants in general had a heightened sense of self then Puritanism was also an attack on traditional values of neighbourliness. A Puritan was "such an one as loves God with all his soul but hates his neighbour with all his heart" (quoted in Hill 1966: 24). Along with more general trends in belief and morality, it went hand in hand with the social and economic polarization discussed in Chapter 9.

Christopher Hill has accurately identified a stress within Protestant belief on the notion of discipline and, further, on discipline attained through active enforcement on the part of the male householder. This discipline was to be extended over the person himself, the members of his household, and over nature and natural products as a whole. Enclosure of the landscape in wood-pasture areas, where Puritan denunciation of the destruction of property rights was absent, can thus be seen as an attempt to impose a heightened sense of order on nature and natural products. Control over nature was logically extended to include control over society: "a hedge in the field is as necessary in its kind as government in the church or commonwealth", argued John Lee in *A vindication of regulated enclosure* (cited in Hill 1966: 491).

Within the household, children were often seen as natural beings who had to be tamed. McCracken (1983: 310) has suggested that in the 16th century this taming was symbolically reinforced by children's association with food preparation and presentation. "Does not every father teach his son, every master his servant?" one Puritan asked. "Parents and masters of families are in God's stead to their children and servants . . . every chief householder hath . . . the charge of the souls of his family" another continued. "Every master of a household must be commanded to instruct, or cause to be instructed, his children, servants and family in the principles of the Christian religion." In an ideal Puritan community, those failing would be penalized in court (Hill 1966: 450–54).

Servants were seen as in need of imposition of labour discipline. Those who lived "under good families or good tutors . . . are as wolves tied up"; they "naturally have an averseness to and hatred of all that is good", just as children have (Hill 1966: 475). Hence part of the Puritan stress on Sabbatarianism: in traditional communities, Sunday was "the servant's revelling day, which is spent in bull-baitings, bear-baitings, bowls, dicing, carding, drunkenness and whoredom, inasmuch as men could not keep their servants from lying out of their houses the same Sabbath day at night". Attendance at church was therefore compulsory: "We be enjoined to it . . . we have law to enforce them [servants] to come to be instructed by a book." Rather than playing games, Sunday should be spent in "hearing the word of God read and taught, in private and public prayers, [good works] . . . and godly conversation" (Hill 1966: 171, 175, 475). So the Puritan master controlled his servants by systematizing time (prohibiting saints' days and marking regular Sundays) and tying this in with spatial discipline (servants to be kept indoors and made to go to church).

At the same time the stress on rationality and discipline was manifested in a very different way within the church. The link between secular and church activity was clearly made by Puritans in the sense of strengthening the idea of the father as God's representative: "Domestic and family worship is a necessary duty, and as far as it is possible, even moral and natural." "First reform your own families, and then you will be the fitter to reform the family of God. Let the master reform his servant, the father his child, the husband his wife." Opponents saw this link also: "It was never merry world since there was so many Puritans and such running to sermons as there is now", said one; "It was never merry world since there was so much preaching; for now all hospitality and good fellowship was lain abed", commented another. Given the "absence of other media . . . sermons were for the majority of Englishmen their main source of political information and political ideas". The church was thus a political battleground: the livery of the priest was seen as part of a pattern of feudal deference while the conflict over the Laudian reforms has already been mentioned (Hill 1966: 15, 32, 44, 69, 444–5).

Finally, the same analogy was used to justify male domination over women, who were seen as "strange and inconstant" and "a lamentable weak creature" (note that this term is quoted from a man who has just given in to his wife; Wrightson 1982: 96). Wives were to be catechized just as servants were. Eve did not fall simply because she was evil, but because Adam had failed to give her proper moral instruction (Hill 1966: 458).

So the turning inward of the Puritan soul meant a greater sense of the individual and of personal privacy, but also a much greater imposition of work discipline and personal surveillance on the subordinate members of the household. I am arguing here that there is a tension within this form of Protestantism between the individual standing alone before God and stress on the household and parish as commonwealth. This was resolved through two strategies. First, the ambiguous use of the term "Man" to imply both male householders only on the one hand and all souls, whether male or female or master or servant, on the other; also to designate the elect versus the whole community. This ambiguous use will have been clear from the quotations given above. The second strategy was greater stress on both personal and community discipline and order. Hence the greater division and order in secular life but the breakdown of divisions between "Man", however defined, and God in the church. Of course, many of these tensions underlay the whole conception of patriarchy in late medieval and early modern society, whatever the overt religious affiliation of the specific household (Amussen 1988: 34–66); what is particularly striking in Puritan belief is the continual stress on discipline and monitoring of personal behaviour at all levels, the stress on the distinction between inner and outward self and the peculiarly reforming nature of the belief system (Walzer 1966).

Responses to Puritanism and the resulting clash of interests at the household and parish level were resolved as part of the underlying process of closure. The upper orders of society saw the strategy of Sabbatarianism only too well: "because under this pretence [of observing the Sabbath] they kept the people to sermons, expositions, repetitions and such-like exercises, which were the most useful tools they could employ in their design" (Hill 1966: 208). In the long term, the Sabbath became part of the weekly round, imposing social discipline (time made regular and church attendance remaining compulsory) without its religious core: a long-term picture brought out elegantly by Rhys Isaac in the context of the parish structure of 18th-century Virginia, modelled on that of England (Isaac 1983).

The lower orders were similarly aware of the social agenda underlying godliness: "Give over thy stinking family duties", one wrote during the brief break in censorship of the English Revolution, "for under them all lies snapping, snarling, biting, besides covetousness, horrid hypocrisy, envy, malice, evil-surmising" (Hill 1966: 480). Records abound of ridicule of Puritans through the traditional festivities they tried to abolish (Wrightson 1982: 176–83) and through insistence on ties of neighbourliness and community. Macfarlane (1970) and Thomas (1971: 561) have argued that the response of socially middling households to the latter strategy was that of accusation of witchcraft; we have seen (Ch. 7) how the planting of witch-bottles under the hearth was a common practice at this time.

Puritanism was thus an extreme example of the general process affecting the conception of self, the social and external and natural world as seen by male householders in the 16th and 17th centuries. These trends are manifested also in other, milder forms of Protestantism and in the changing contemporary view at all social levels above those of the labouring classes of the religious, social and natural world over the long term (Thomas 1971, 1983).

Hill notes the links between Protestantism, what he sees as emergent middle-class life, and changes in housing at the direct, physical level: "middle-class talent and industry were creating homes of unprecedented comfort and privacy, thanks to glass windows, coal fires, upstairs bedrooms, chairs replacing benches. Middle-class houses became places to which friends could be invited, to sing, to play, to discuss" (Hill 1966: 488). Direct linkages between closed plans, Puritan communities and regional variations in settlement have been clearly seen in the "test case" of New England (Ch. 6; see also Ch. 11). It has been argued that in addition to these overt, material links, changing ethic and world-view are related to housing change in more subtle ways. These can now be summarized.

The growing sense of discipline was related to the process of closure in a series of ways. Discipline over the self meant a sharper drawing of physical, material and symbolic boundaries between the self and the external, social and natural world. This is the most obvious way in which changing attitudes led to a process of closure and its manifestation in increasing segregation and the concept of privacy. In a more subtle sense, it led to the drawing of boundaries between house and farmstead, and between the yeoman farmer and successive degrees of the social and natural world around him, seen in Chapter 8. A sharper sense of self-identity leads also to a sharper sense of class and gender interest as distinct from that of the household and community, and thus contributed to the breakdown of status-based relations seen to govern the layout of open houses in Chapter 4. It led also to a separation of masters' and servants' worlds and a divide between men's and women's worlds. Finally, when separated from its religious husk in the long term it implied a weakening of any conception of the house as organic and moral unit, a conception seen to underlie the open technical system in Chapter 7.

The extension of discipline by the master over the household had implications for the development of class relations, particularly when associated with a work ethic. The linkage of discipline with observation appears superficially to contradict the process of closure and of segregation: segregation militates against discipline and observation. But at a deeper level discipline and observation depend on spatial and social separation between observer and observed of a different nature than that provided by a purely status-based community. Discipline over the household not only implies a changing nature of segregation, but also suggests the clearer functional differentiation between rooms discussed for the later inventories in Chapter 8.

Finally, the extension of discipline over the natural world held implications for the changing technical system. Chapter 7 explored how the frame of the house was always evidence of the remorseless imposition of cultural onto natural forms, and demonstrated how the process of closure involved a more "rational", exploitative view of timber framing and house construction. Enclosure of the wild, natural landscape was also quite explicitly seen as moral and necessary (Thomas 1983: 254).

The process of closure can therefore be defined as the material form in which changing attitudes towards the self, the family and household, and the wider social and natural world were played out. These changing attitudes drove many male householders, by a process of elective affinity, towards one overt manifestation of these underlying changes: Protestantism and Puritanism, involving a heightened sense of self and an ethic of discipline. It also loosened the ties of the village community and created a climate in which individuals of varying sentiments and social classes were able to enclose open fields in whatever form. Enclosure of houses and of fields was not caused by Puritanism: both are manifestations of a deeper social and cultural shift, ripples betraying stronger and more complex economic, social and cultural currents beneath the surface of history.

The link made between changing world-view and the process of closure can be widened further. Over the very long term several crucial shifts can be seen. The first is what those shifts signify: the transition from a community based on face-to-face relations of authority and deference, within which individuals fill certain expected rôles, towards a social structure based on changing networks of relations between individuals in which the values of community are less important: a shift between *Gemeinschaft* and *Gesellschaft* already explored in Chapters 4 and 7–9. The second is how they signify this shift: by moving from a close binding of the social, technical and moral aspects of the house or action to a looser binding, again partly explored in Chapter 7. The third is the way they are used in social action: from framing that action within a customary, accepted scheme or reference, towards a richer, more varied material environment but one which has symbolic value, cultural meaning, more freely reassigned to it (Miller 1987).

I suggest, therefore, that one of the reasons these shifts took place was as part of the changing social structure of early modern Suffolk and England, a structure that was moving away from a medieval, feudal pattern towards an early modern, capitalist one. The implication of this analysis is that the changing design and use of material objects such as houses and the goods within them played a crucial rôle in the unfolding of this process at an everyday level.

Notes

1. The arguments of Wordie (1983: 503-5) on a national level may be disputed in their particulars but his general argument that 45 per cent of the English landscape was enclosed by 1550 and 81 per cent by 1700 would imply that most if not all of this area of early enclosure was enclosed by that date (if not much earlier); whether one accepts Wordie's figures or not, his conclusion is also that of Astill & Grant (1988: 81) and Kerridge (1969). Other areas of the wood-pasture region were enclosed by the later 16th century: Evans suggests this is the case for the Waveney Valley a few kilometres

to the north-east of the sample area (Evans 1984: 304); Thomas Tusser, writing in 1571 from his observations on the Suffolk/Essex border, assumes that the entirety of the wood-pasture landscape is "several" or enclosed (Hartley 1931: 179); the southern half of the parish of Barrow, sitting on the champion/wood-pasture divide, was enclosed by 1597 (Postgate 1973: 289-90). The only areas left unenclosed by *c.* 1700 were the greens, which were probably the focus of too many legally upheld common rights to enclose at this point, but which were in any case being steadily encroached upon (Dymond & Martin 1988: 48).

2. This is confirmed by two sources. The sample of probate inventories taken reveals a preponderance of these classes, and the numbers of rooms given and types of room patterning revealed by the inventories correspond to that of the surviving sample. The occupations given in the inventories are overwhelmingly that of gentry, yeomen or more prosperous husbandmen, plus those involved in the cloth industry and "widows" (Appendix 1). The second source of evidence is that of the Hearth Tax Returns. All but the very smallest houses surveyed had more than one hearth by the later 17th century; they therefore fall above the mass of one-hearth houses occupied by the labouring poor, and possibly even the lower groups of husbandmen, and are recorded in numbers in the returns (Table 9.1).

The term "middling" has, throughout this study, been applied to houses rather than to social groups. The pitfalls of using this term in indiscriminately lumping together status groups between the levels of upper gentry and labourer in the late medieval and early modern periods are acknowledged. The necessarily coarser resolution of the social status of houses in the absence of documentary evidence makes it legitimate to use the term in that context.

CHAPTER 11
CONCLUSION: OLD HOUSES, MODERN MEANINGS

The central conclusion to be drawn from the preceding pages is that domestic architecture in western Suffolk underwent a fundamental transformation between the 15th and 17th centuries. This transformation manifested itself in aspects of the layout, technical system and decoration of houses. Purely economic and typological explanations were found to be inadequate. Instead, cultural change was postulated to be at the core of the underlying changes in domestic space.

However, several qualifications need to be made to this thesis. First, elements of continuity were seen in other areas of the evidence such as the technical system underlying timber framing as well as a conflicting pattern involving elements of a reverse transformation in terms of ritual space. A blithe ascription of a very complex pattern to any single factor, or to a vague set of factors under the heading of "social change", was felt to be limited (as has been stated for the specific phenomenon of enclosure; Yelling 1977: 2). A final example of such elements of continuity is the lack of a nuclear/isolated shift in location of houses (Johnson nd: 266–8). The process of closure might lead one to expect a dispersal of houses out of the physical and social constraints of the village community through time; but this does not happen. Albeit crudely measured through distance from church, house location did not change significantly between 1400 and 1700; a smaller distance for closed houses is probably due to the larger numbers of later 17th-century cottages built near the church. Late medieval houses were often built on isolated, older sites, demonstrably so in the case of moated sites; thus in wood-pasture areas, the closed layout of the landscape lay latent within the open, as with the plan and technical system of the house.

Secondly, it was necessary to look at specific cultural and ideational influences in order to understand the root causes of this transformation, and to grasp the links between housing and wider landscape changes. This was done in a general sense in Chapter 8, taking care to link the system of ideas being discussed with the activities and material correlates of the closed house and household. It was done more specifically in terms of Protestant belief and the way this was manifested in a changing ethic and world-view in Chapter 10.

Thirdly, the "process of closure" was mapped out as a very long-term process at an underlying, cultural level. It is important to remember that it was nevertheless historically particular and dependent on a series of conjunctures at the level of the medium term. Closure was both structured and structuring through the medium of everyday activity. Amussen (1988: 180–9) argues, for example, that the stress on personal and household discipline in early 17th century England occurred at a specific moment when the stability of society and state was under threat. It consequently served to maintain social and political order at a very basic level. When that threat receded in the later 17th century, the direct moral and political linkage made between "every man's house" and the social order in general declined in resonance. It could be added that the establishment of an order and conception of discipline conducive to further capitalistic development was therefore established at the regional, community and household level in England in the 17th century. In contrast such an establishment of discipline and its associated values had to be accomplished by the national state in 18th- and 19th-century France (Foucault 1979).

One final implication of this study needs to be followed through. I have drawn a contrast between open and closed houses, centring on a transformation occurring in the 16th century. This contrast is a necessary one to establish but is nevertheless simplistic. If we remember the discussion of open houses, the majority of these were built as part of the same process of closure. As noted above, open houses were built on sites away from the physical centre of the community; they constituted a rebuilding at the level of society below that of the gentry (Ch. 4); and they can be seen as part of a general wave of rebuilding spanning both open and transitional housing from the later 15th to later 16th centuries. So the building of open houses in the later 15th and their transformation in the 16th century are closely related processes, both in terms of chronology and in terms of the social groups involved. Yet open and closed houses apparently differ in the symbolic meanings they carry.

This is a paradox that can only be resolved in the abstract. I begin with Christopher Hill's observation that just as Tawney said that the apparent growth of 16th-century poverty was in fact due to the growth of 16th-century documentation of such problems, and therefore their greater prominence in the historical record, so the apparent late 16th- and 17th-century rise in the kinds of sentiment explored in Chapter 10 is partly due to a rise in its level of documentation (Hill 1966: 451). In perceiving archaeologically that the process of closure is actually emergent in the early 16th century (if not before), we may be exploring the rise of a sentiment that only surfaces in the documents a little later.

Systems of values in the minds of men and women, as I have repeatedly stressed, arise out of and are moulded through practical as well as discursive consciousness. They are formed from the expression and renegotiation of the meanings of everyday activity at the household and community level. It should not surprise us, therefore, to see one form of expression of everyday activity, ordinary houses, showing signs of the process of closure before this process "surfaces" into discursive consciousness and writing. We may, by stretching this proposition a little, go a step further. The implicit, everyday meanings of material culture need not correspond to the overt world-view of its creators and users. As Marx pointed out, as social groups come into being they do so both "in themselves" and "for themselves": the process of becoming a class for itself is an active one and can and must take place through everyday activity. Marx was commenting on what he saw as the rise and fall of social classes: the problem here, as Stone (1965), Searle (1988: 132) and Brenner (1989) have pointed out, is rather to grasp the changing quality of social relations between groups and at the same time the changing nature of their mentality, their world-view.

So those building permanent, traditional, middling houses in the 15th century expressed their rise in what they saw as traditional forms: bequests to the Church, and a form of house plan referring to the traditional values of the medieval community. Hilton has noted the lack of overt ideological challenges to the existing order at this time, despite underlying social shifts (1985: 246–52). As social relations in the countryside changed in nature, changes in accompanying systems of values were expressed and worked through first by modifying and rejecting the open-hall plan, then up through practical to discursive levels of consciousness in the explosion of religious and cultural radicalism at the local level seen in the later 16th and early 17th centuries.

This "bottom-up" view of changes in mentality is difficult to prove; indeed, it is difficult to bring traditional forms of evidence to bear upon it. But it would explain the open form of late 15th-century housing in terms of historical antecedent and allow for its swift transformation after *c.* 1500. It could also be related to parallel developments in the Perpendicular style of late Gothic architecture, which Pevsner explicitly links to the rise of what he sees as the middle-class temperament (Pevsner 1956: 113). It is unlikely to be popular with some traditional historians, given its implication that their documentary analyses of overt sentiments will by definition rarely approach the underlying structures of *mentalité* below the surface of past sentiment and society; but the current level of popularity in academic circles of an historical argument is rarely a secure indication of its cogency.

A contextual analysis

This study can be termed a contextual one: it has been found necessary, through the logic of the research, to look for contextual evidence to accompany the account of changing domestic space, to relate parallel and conflicting patterns in different classes of evidence. It was also necessary to account for these changes in a way particular to the time and place considered, in other words the specific conjuncture of antecedent forms of landscape, certain social and economic conditions, and the ideology of Protestantism. Finally, it has been necessary to attempt to understand the "inside" of the transformation, to understand what the process of closure meant in the minds of men and women long dead rather than simply to observe and correlate its external manifestations. In these respects, this study may be seen as a case study of the sort of contextual archaeology advocated by Hodder (1986: 118–45). It is worth noting that it did not start out by being so. Originally a fairly orthodox structuralist stance was taken, leaning heavily on the example of Glassie (1975). This was abandoned by degrees as such a framework was seen to be less and less able to deal with the problems raised in Chapter 10.

It is, therefore, rhetorically appropriate that one of the substantive conclusions of the research bears heavily on one of the historical cases cited by Hodder of contextual understanding, the ascription by Weber of the origins of capitalism to changes in mentality in general and the Protestant work ethic in particular (Hodder 1986: 81–4; Weber 1930). As we have seen, that particular debate has moved a long way since the time of Weber and Tawney, but a heavily modified form of such an argument was presented as one possible strong understanding of changes in material life in western Suffolk. The substantive implications of this research are in this sense quite clear. Architectural evidence points to a decisive shift in social structure in Suffolk during the period in question. This shift gathered weight in the 17th century but its origins must be traced back deep into the later 15th and 16th century. This shift should not be seen in terms of the rise and fall of classes, but rather as a change in the nature and quality of social relationships, as Brenner has recently commented in terms of landlord/tenant relations (Brenner 1989: 297–300). It involved changes in gender, class, and status relations as well as landscape changes; these changes were manifested and played out in everyday life and may thus be traced back through domestic architecture. Such changes can be seen in terms of the origins of capitalism. Here, however, in an attempt to get away from the underlying assumptions of much Marxist research, and also to make the link between housing and landscape change very clear, such change has been termed a process of closure.

The choice of stress on cultural factors as being particularly bound up with these wider changes is partly a polemical or rhetorical one. Like Weber's argument, it is merely describing one side of a many-sided causal chain, the other sides of which are such factors as demography, economics, social relations, and so on. It arises theoretically out of a dissatisfaction with other forms of monocausal explanations, particularly those of evolutionary theory and crude Marxism, and the resultant backlash into a backward, reactionary historical particularism by many recent scholars. I do not accept the objection that no one ultimate driving force is specified, since there is no *a priori* reason to believe in the existence of one ultimate driving force in history. I accept Tilley's point that there is no final explanation or set of causes to be offered for any object of study in the human sciences in any case (Tilley 1991: 172). Nevertheless there are particular long-term forces and enduring structures that interact with the short and medium term, and with the event, and some of these have been sketched out in this study.

Some of these long-term forces leave traces today. While the craft tradition governing traditional architecture does not survive in 20th-century England, the traditional buildings themselves still carry social meanings. Old houses are still lived in, altered or "conserved"; they still embody values that are important to us today.

The arguments of any book dealing with traditional houses are therefore advanced within a field of discourse that has always been culturally charged. There is the historical tradition of Ruskin, quoted in Chapter 1, of Victorian and later uses of elements of the vernacular; the Oxford Movement of the 19th century linked this, together with the use of Gothic, with a developed view of the rural past which stressed the values of community rent asunder, in their view, by industrialization. For such a group the images of traditional houses were part of a conservative reaction to industrialization and economic liberalism. This was a strand taken up also by the early socialist movements, most notably William Morris and the Arts and Crafts Movement, but also earlier than this by Thomas Paine and other writers stressing the rights of the free-born Englishman (Thompson 1963: 77–101). This strand continues in the work of the explicitly conservative architect Quinlan Terry, who ironically stresses the craft tradition in implicitly Marxist terms in bemoaning the alienation of worker from object in modern architecture.

At the same time the urban middle classes have appropriated the meanings of traditional houses for their own dwellings through the use of "Stockbroker

Tudor" and related styles (Miller 1984). Again, the stress is on tradition, although here it has become the preserve of the middle classes as opposed to the modernism of institutional and working-class housing. A further complexity is added by the counterpoint of the Georgian tradition and the centrality of the non-traditional "stately home" to the rise of the heritage industry (Hewison 1987). Images of traditional houses have played little explicit part in this, sandwiched between the great houses on the one hand and the recreated working-class communities of the North of England on the other.

Old houses do not, then, present a simple set of historical and cultural meanings. Rather, they owe their continuing power to their carrying of diverse and often apparently contradictory social messages. They have become part of a wider field upon which each group can mobilize its view of the world and the historical past. And these social messages are not ones at odds with "reality", with the meanings involved with the construction and use of the houses from the 15th to 17th centuries. Just as now their meanings are tied up with the diverse and often contradictory sentiments of middle-class life, so their meanings were then caught up in that web. Just as symbols now acquire their power from being derived from the past, so 16th-century symbols derived their power from referring to a medieval past. Old houses are part of a continually reinvented tradition, an endless process of appropriation of the past for the present.

Writing about houses thus becomes more than a detached academic exercise in search of objective truth. It becomes an attempt to understand the world around us today and the historical traditions and discontinuities that have shaped that world. It becomes a meditation on modernity. I started this book by stating, quite transparently, that it was about old houses. It is also, when all is said and done, about modern meanings.

APPENDIX ONE
LIST OF HOUSES

What follows is a list of all houses examined or whose records were consulted in the course of this research. Full gazetteer entries, plans and other details of these houses may be found in Johnson nd, 187–223.

Balsdon Hall Farm, Acton	TL874459 R
Clarkes Farm, Acton	TL880440 R
Long Gardens, Acton	TL893449 R
The Old Cottage, Acton	TL874459 J
Mill House, Alpheton	TL882510 J
Holm Cottage, Barningham	TL969768 R
Frogs Hall, Barrow	TL756642 J
No. 34 and the Town Estate Room, Barrow	TL763636 R
Wolfe Hall, Barrow	TL771622 R
Bildeston Post Office, Bildeston	TL993494 J
Crown Hotel, Bildeston	TL993495 J
No. 22 (Newbury Farm), Bildeston	TL994491 R
Nos. 47 and 49–53, Chapel St, Bildeston	TL992496 R
Fishers, Boxted	TL808504 J
Nos. Three and Four The Street, Boxted	TL827513 R
Truckett's Hall, Boxted	TL811500 J
Block Farm, Bradfield Combust	TL892566 R
Bradfield House Rest, Bradfield Combust	TL893575 J
Bridge Cottage, Brent Eleigh	TL943480 J
Colliers, Brent Eleigh	TL945495 J
Corner Farm, Brent Eleigh	TL943478 J
Corrie Farm, Brent Eleigh	TL937481 J
Highbank, Brent Eleigh	TL944477 J
Honeymoon Cottage, Brent Eleigh	TL944478 J
Hill Farm, Brent Eleigh	TL933478 J
Old Cottage, Brent Eleigh	TL943477 J
Street Farm, High Street, Brent Eleigh	TL945476 J
Swan Cottage, Brent Eleigh	TL944477 J
Tudor Cottage, Brent Eleigh	TL944477 J
Vaideys Farm, Brent Eleigh	TL934470 J
Wells Hall, Brent Eleigh	TL946474 J
Church Farm, Brettenham	TL968541 J
House at 960536, Brettenham	TL960536 J
Pond Farm, Brettenham	TL954534 J
Poplars Farm, Brettenham	TL974451 R

Chinnerys, Cavendish	TL795465 R
House at 796458, Cavendish	TL796458 J
The Old Post Office and PO Cottage, Cavendish	TL807466 R
Spring View and Waver View, Cavendish	TL806465 R
Virginia House, Cavendish	TL805464 R
Majors Farm, Chedburgh	TL781580 R
Riverside Cottage, Chelsworth	TL978481 J
The Old Rectory, Chevington	TL785596 R
Abbey Farm, Cockfield	TL900543 R
House at 907534, Cockfield	TL907534 J
The Lodge, Coney Weston	TL957782 R
Denham Priory, Denham	TL752611 R
Aisled House, Depden Green, Depden	? J
No. Seven The Green, Fornham All Saints	TL837675 R
Ferncroft, Glemsford	TL824494 R
Hall Farm, Glemsford	TL829490 R
No. 31 Egremont Street, Glemsford	TL829475 J
No. 42 Egremont St (Greyhound Cottage), Glemsford	TL828473 R
Monks Hall, Glemsford	TL834488 R
Great Barton Lodge, Great Barton	TL884665 J
The Old House, Great Barton	TL885674 R
Shrub End, Great Barton	TL900652 R
Church Farm, Great Waldingfield	TL912439 J
Garrison Cottage, Garrison Lane, Gt Waldingfield	TL904434 R
Malting Barn, Great Waldingfield	TL904433 R
Powers Farm, Great Waldingfield	TL922437 R
Cawstons Farm, Hartest	TL841519 R
Cooks Farm, Hartest	TL839529 R
Tan Office Farm, Hartest	TL833532 R
Hawkedon Hall, Hawkedon	TL797528 R
Langleys Newhouse, Hawkedon	TL804539 R
Thurston End Hall, Hawkedon	TL795518 J
Bryers Farm, Hawstead	TL856581 R
Mill Post Farm, Hawstead	TL853577 R
Shepherd's Cottage, Hawstead	TL863587 R
No. 30, Pages Lane, Higham	TL744656 J
Brook Cottage, Hitcham	TL983513 J
Bush Farm, Hitcham	TL989525 R
The Old House, Hitcham	TL985510 R
Tudor House, Hitcham	TL989523 R
Corner Thatch and Heathfield Lodge, Honington	TL915475 R
No. One, Troston Road, Honington	TL912746 R
The Cedars, Hopton	TL996796 R
Dairy Cottages, Ingham	TL852694 J
Dover House, Ixworth	TL933705 J
Nos. 52–54–56 High Street, Ixworth	TL933705 J
Elm Cottage, Lidgate	TL725577 J
Honeyhill Farm, Little Saxham	TL801646 R

Lodge Farm, Little Saxham	TL799635 R
Wood Hall, Little Waldingfield	TL925456 J
Moat Farm, Milden	TL960467 R
Brereton and Rosslynne, Monks Eleigh	TL966474 R
Cottage adjoining the Fenn, Monks Eleigh	TL963473 J
Hawkins Farm, Monks Eleigh	TL956485 R
Hobarts, Back Lane, Monks Eleigh	TL963474 J
House near Manor Farm, Monks Eleigh	TL961480 J
House S of Swan Inn, Monks Eleigh	TL967476 J
Swan Inn, Monks Eleigh	TL967476 R
Bridge House, Pakenham	TL926674 R
Cottage next to Bell House, Pakenham	TL928673 R
Seldom In, Poslingford	TL770485 R
Chestnuts, Whelp Street, Preston St Mary	TL947497 R
Mortimers Farm, Preston St Mary	TL944512 R
Rushbrooke Farm, Preston St Mary	TL948515 R
House at 806553, Rede	TL806553 J
Lower Farm, Risby	TL796665 R
Quays Farm, Risby	TL802664 R
St Giles' Cottage/Church House, Risby	TL802663 J
Cottage next to Oak Farm, Rougham	TL910618 R
Eastlow Hill Farm, Rougham	TL905615 R
Layers Breck Farm, Rougham	TL903631 J
Drift House and Drift Cottage, Sapiston	TL912758 J
Grange Farm, Sapiston	TL920944 R
Triangles, Sapiston	TL920755 R
Clockhouse Farm, Shimpling	TL862513 R
Church Cottage, Somerton	TL811531 R
Little Saxes Farm, Stanningfield	TL874560 R
Cordell Hall, Stansfield	TL785541 R
Ivy House, Stansfield	TL784520 R
Woodcote, Stansfield	TL773515 R
House at 849479, Stanstead	TL849479 J
Oaklands, Stanstead	TL844492 J
Sparrows, Stanstead	TL841487 R
Stanstead Hall, Stanstead	TL843493 R
Corner Cottage, Dawn Cottage and Rosley, Stanton	TL966736 R
Gable End, Stanton	TL966736 R
House at 943520, Thorpe Morieux	TL943520 J
Street Farm, Troston	TL897723 R
Wattisham Hall, Wattisham	TM010513 R
Ark Farm, Whepstead	TL817588 J
Vincents Farm, Whepstead	TL830589 R
Cottage adjoining the White House, Wickhambrook	TL755545 J
Black Horse Farm, Wickhambrook	TL769572 R
House at 745551, Wickhambrook	TL745551 J

APPENDIX TWO
LIST OF PROBATE INVENTORIES

The following is a list of those probate inventories examined in connection with this research. The abbreviation SRO refers to the Suffolk Records Office, Bury St Edmunds, and that of NRO to the Norfolk Record Office, Norwich. The former office holds those inventories registered with the Archdeaconry of Sudbury; the latter, those whose wills were proved at Norwich. Full details can be found in Johnson nd, 184–6. I am very grateful to Rachel Garrard for her generous permission to consult her unpublished material.

Early sample

Name	*Date*	*Parish*	*Reference*
William Baker	30.04.1576	Bildeston	SRO500/3/1/39
Richard Collinson	??.??.1576	Stradishall	SRO500/3/174/91
Thomas Cooksage	31.05.1576	Hopton	SRO500/3/1112
John Corder	09.05.1576	Lawshall	SRO500/3/1117
Thomas Crowch	02.01.1576	Ixworth	SRO500/3/118
Lawrence Deathe	??.??.1576	Shimpling	SRO500/3/149
John Desborow	25.07.1576	Wickhambrook	SRO500/3/170
Henry Foster	03.11.1588	Hengrave	NRO4/152
Thomas Frank	17.??.1576	Great Barton	SRO500/3/1119
John Fraunces	09.12.1576	Sapiston	SRO500/3/140
Richard Frost	02.09.1575	Brockley	SRO500/3/180
Margery Fuller	31.05.1576	Ixworth	SRO500/3/111
Robert Game	08.11.1576	Shimpling	SRO500/3/147
Roger Gayfford	26.02.1575	Hopton	SRO500/3/148
John Gowre	06.10.1584	Preston S Mary	NRO 2/45
John Grymes	02.01.1576	Edwardstone	SRO500/3/156
Jeannes Hall	30.05.1576	Fornham AS	SRO500/3/188
Thomas Hayward	05.04.1576	Glemsford	SRO500/3/153
George Hoowe	13.10.1576	Gt Welnetham	SRO500/3/130
Richard Hudson	18.11.1576	Wickhambrook	SRO500/3/144
John Leesse	08.??.1576	Lackford	SRO500/3/9
Walter Lorde	??.??.1576	Wickhambrook	SRO500/3/171
John Ludbroke	01.09.1576	Cockfield	SRO500/3/118
Edward Manwood	??.??.1576	Gt Cornard	SRO500/3/120
John Mauldon	05.11.1576	Bildeston	SRO500/3/131
John Morlye	15.02.1576	Gt Barton	SRO500/3/1120

Name	*Date*	*Parish*	*Reference*
Henry Munford	01.02.1576	Milden	SRO500/3/121
Andrew Myles	27.01.1576	Bildeston	SRO500/3/145
John Norfolk	??.08.1588	Lt Waldngfield	NRO4/56
Robert Osmonde	??.??.1588	Bildeston	NRO4/160
Walter Nunne	13.11.1576	Whepstead	SRO500/3/142
John Parman	10.05.1576	Wickhambrook	SRO500/3/1107
Richard Payne	20.11.1576	Boxted	SRO500/3/146
Richard Pecok	25.05.1576	Pakenham	SRO500/3/1114
William Peeck	28.10.1576	Fornham SGen	SRO500/3/154
Thomas Plowers	24.01.1576	Welnetham	SRO500/3/116
Elyn Pratt	15.04.1574	Redgrave	SRO500/3/184
Richard Rastall	21.01.1575	Fornham SGen	SRO500/3/1115
Arthur Selfe	24.02.1588	Denham	NRO4/156
George Smith	20.06.1576	Wickhambrook	SRO500/3/1
William Stockinge	??.??.1576	?	SRO500/3/164
Robert Usher	21.08.1576	?	SRO500/3/172
Alice Webe	09.01.1576	Preston S Mary	SRO500/3/117
John Whiters	09.09.1576	Cavendish	SRO500/3/160

Late sample

Name	*Date*	*Parish*	*Reference*
Samuel Beachcroft	17.07.1686	Semer	SRO500/3/22104
John Boggas	07.01.1685	Fornham S Gen	SRO500/3/223
John Booler	18.09.1686	Barnham	SRO500/3/2284
Henry Bradford	08.11.1686	Cowlinge	SRO500/3/22117
Roger Brett	09.02.1686	Bardwell	SRO500/3/22139
Elizabeth Bridge	03.06.1686	Glemsford	SRO500/3/2297
Thomas Brincklie	31.03.1688	Redgrave	NRO65/36
Edward Campian	21.08.1686	Edwardstone	SRO500/3/2266
John Challes	12.06.1686	Barrow	SRO500/3/2273
John Chilver	18.05.1685	Denham	NRO63/130
John Cole	07.10.1686	Wattisham	SRO500/3/2294
John Colling	20.09.1686	Poslinford	SRO500/3/2299
Catherine Coston	01.05.1685	Fornham S Gen	SRO500/3/2250
John Debenham	21.??.1686	Cockfield	SRO500/3/2285
William Flack	01.12.1686	Stansfield	SRO500/3/22115
Frances French	07.04.1686	Wickhambrook	SRO500/3/2232
Nathaniel Frost	12.05.1686	Denston	SRO50/3/2213
William Frysan	29.12.1686	Stanstead	SRO500/3/22134
Anne Gardner	17.04.1686	Glemsford	SRO500/3/2252
George Gardner	23.06.1686	Stanstead	SRO500/3/2238
William Grant	14.02.1689	Hitcham	NRO65/78
Elizabeth Grouse	20.05.1686	Cowlinge	SRO500/3/22106
Henry Hill	12.16.1686	West Stow	SRO500/3/22121

Name	*Date*	*Parish*	*Reference*
Thomas Holmes	??.01.1688	Nedging	NRO65/17
John How	24.07.1685	Bradfld S Clare	SRO500/3/22155
John How elder	08.10.1686	Glemsford	SRO500/3/22102
John Johnson	08.11.1686	Shimpling	SRO500/3/22110
Margaret Jowers	05.07.1686	Bildeston	SRO500/3/2246
John Kerington	02.04.1686	Bdfld Combust	SRO500/3/2253
John Kingbury	16.04.1686	Gt Cornard	SRO500/3/2281
Benjamin Knockes	28.05.1686	Thorpe Morieux	SRO300/3/22152
Robert Lettelproud	03.07.1686	Bardwell	SRO500/3/2262
Henry Liley	08.05.1685	Ixworth	SRO500/3/22160
Margaret Metcalfe	22.02.1685	Poslingford	SRO500/3/2251
John Mynnes	21.01.1695	Chelsworth	SRO500/3/226
William Muskett	21.09.1686	Coney Weston	SRO500/3/2288
James Nelsegood	04.05.1686	Hopton	SRO500/3/2263
John Nickell	23.11.1685	Rougham	SRO500/3/22157
Ralph Nobes	23.03.1685	Glemsford	SRO500/3/2215
Robert Park	06.01.1686	Cornard	SRO550/3/2291
John Parkin	01.06.1686	Mkt Weston	SRO500/3/2211
Abraham Payne	08.05.1686	Glemsford	SRO500/3/2224
Dorcas Plampin	16.12.1686	Shimpling	SRO500/3/22120
Robert Plampin	31.05.1689	Gt Cornard	NRO65/67
Edmund Pleasans	05.06.1686	Risby	SRO50/3/2270
Robert Poulter	29.11.1686	Lidgate	SRO500/3/22119
Benjamin Robinson	08.01.1686	Rede	SRO500/3/22130
Ann Rout	07.12.1686	Newton	SRO500/3/22118
Robert Scultrike	30.05.1686	Sapiston	SRO500/3/2244
Ambrose Smith	02.08.1686	Boxted	SRO500/3/2275
Benjamin Smyth	10.04.1688	Bildeston	NRO65/10
John Sparrow	20.03.1686	Chevington	SRO500/3/2232
Daniel Steden	28.04.1685	Lt Cornard	SRO500/3/2217
Thomas Stewart	21.03.1686	Brockley	SRO500/03/22149
John Sturgeon	17.05.1686	Hawstead	SRO500/3/2226
Hilary Tillney	04.07.1684	Denham	NRO63/95B
Adam Wright	23.12.1686	Stanstead	SRO500/3/22127

GLOSSARY

Architectural definitions have in the main been taken from Mercer (1975: 229–32): definitions of inventory terms from Steer (1969: 12–27) and Jennings (1981); definitions of historical terms from Wrightson (1982: 17–39). See also Figure 3.1.

anchor-beam A beam functioning like a tie, but at cross-rail rather than wall-plate level.
andirons Supports for spits; also cobirons.
arch.
four-centered: of four arcs;
segmented: one arc struck from below the springing line;
depressed: of three arcs.
axial At right-angles to the main axis of the structure.

baluster Support to a hand-rail on a stair.
bargeboards Timbers laid along the sloping sides of a gable end, frequently decorated.
batter Slope, of a wall or the side of a stack.
bay The division between two trusses of cross-frames.
boulster A piece of bed furniture.
box-frame Where the frame apart from the roof consists of upright and horizontal members.
brace A diagonal timber supporting the frame.
arch-brace: between post and plate above
passing-brace: of considerable length, cutting rather than being halved into studs between
serpentine: of one or more ogee curves
stud: tension brace where the lower end is pegged into the nearest stud rather than the plate
tension-brace: between post and plate below
wind: in the roof, between principals and side purlins.
bressumer Plate resting on or in front of the joists to form a jetty and supporting the posts over.
bullimong A mixture of various kinds of grain sown together for feeding cattle.

cambered Of a beam whose centre is higher than the ends.
canopy Curving hood over the upper end of an open hall.
cell Unit of a house, usually corresponding to bay and room divisions.
chamber A room, though sometimes used to designate its first-floor counterpart; thus the "hall chamber" is the room over the hall.
chamfer The planing away of the corner of the profile of a timber.
chest Used for storage of linen, often an heirloom.

clay-lump A technique of construction using unfired dried clay bricks.
cobirons *See* andirons.
collar Beam coupling a pair of rafters above the wall-plate.
corbel A projecting stone or timber which supports a weight.
couple A pair of rafters, in Suffolk usually halved together at the apex.
crenel The upright part of a castle battlement between two embrasures, also used in decorative contexts.
cross-frame *See* truss.
cross-rail A main plate between sill-beam and wall-plate, often receiving ceiling joists.
cross-beam A beam supprting common rafters laid across the building.
crown-post A post resting on a tie supporting a collar purlin and collar, often braced to these.
cruck A pair of curved timbers joined together at the top.
cupboard Either a table upon which items were placed, or similar to a sideboard; often readily moveable.
curtains Usually round the bed.

dais Raised platform at the upper end of a hall.
desk Originally a portable box fitted with locks.
dormer Window above the eaves line, either with its own gable or of eyebrow (surmounted by a curve in the thatch) form.
double-pile Plan two rooms deep.
dragon-post A diagonal post or bracket at the corner of two jettied walls.

facing-in The placing of timbers so that the "fair face" or internal face of the timber, with the heads of the pegs, is facing the upper end of the hall.
firehood A timber and plaster hood over a hearth, to channel the smoke upwards.
fireplace Area under the lintel of a stack for the placing of a hearth.

gable The inverted V-shape made by the roof at an end wall, and the wall within it.
gentry A class of "substantial landowners and agents of government".

half-hipped Of a roof, gabled in the lower part and hipped in the upper.
halved Of two timbers, when cut back to half their depth to join one another.
hipped Of a roof, built with a slope at the ends as well as at the sides.
husbandmen A class of small farmers, below that of yeomen.
hutch Usually smaller than a chest, used for storage of clothes.

jack Device to make the spit revolve automatically, or a large leather container.
jetty Projection of an upper storey over that below.
jetty plate The cross-rail below the joists supporting the bressumer.
joint.
lap-joint: junction of two timbers at different angles, usually halved.
scarf-joint: junction of two end-on timbers.
straight-joint: unbonded between two parts of a structure, often indicating two builds.
jowl Enlarged head of a vertical post.

keyed Of a timber, notched to provide a hold for plaster covering.

lintel Horizontal timber over an opening or fireplace.
livery cupboard Small cupboard with shelf on top, either on legs or hanging on wall. The name derives from the "liveries" of wine, bread and beer which would be taken to the bedroom on retiring for the night.

men's chamber "A survival of the older order when farm workers lodged and boarded with their master."
mortice Socket in a piece of wood, to receive a tenon.
moulding The carved profile of a timber.
Roll-moulded: involving convex and concave profiles.
Ovolo-moulded: involving convex profiles.
mullion An upright dividing a window into lights.

newel stair A spiral stair with the steps framed into the central post.
nogging Brick infill in a timber frame.

outshut Extension to a building under a lean-to roof.
over On the floor above.

pargeting Moulded patterning in plaster, either patterned or figurative.
pillow beer A piece of bed furniture.
plank-and-muntin Of screens, made of thin planks grooved into narrow, thicker planks.
plate Any horizontal timber.
post Any vertical timber forming part of the main frame.
pothook Hook and chain attached to bar in chimney; also known as trammel in early modern East Anglia.
principals Rafters over the main posts, often larger than common rafters though rarely so in Suffolk.
purlin A horizontal timber between the wall-plates and apex of the roof to provide longitudinal support; a collar purlin is central, supporting the collars.

rail A horizontal timber.
reel For winding yarn.
rendering Plaster covering.
roof
butt-purlin: where the purlins are discontinuous between bays, being tenoned into the principals;
catslide: the main slope descending without interruption over an outshut;
clasped-purlin: with side purlins clasped between collars and principals;
coupled-rafter: each pair of rafters connected by a collar;
hipped: with a sloping rather than gabled end;
mansard or gambrel: with the pitch of two angles, the steeper one below;
queen-post: with a pair of timbers standing on the tie, supporting side-purlins.

scantling Dimensions of a timber.
sill The lower member of a window frame, or the rail at the foot of the frame.
skillet Shallow bowl or frying-pan with three legs; also used in Suffolk to refer to a

skimmer for removing cream.
soffit The underside of a timber or arch.
solar Withdrawing room, traditionally over the parlour.
spandrel The space between an arch and its enclosing rectangle.
spere A truss at the lower end of an open hall with a partition at the sides but not in the middle; the open space was probably filled with a moveable screen.
spit Bar or series of bars attached to joint of meat to turn it over the fire, often mechanically.
spine-beam A beam supporting common rafters laid along the centre of the building.
stack Abbreviation of "chimney-stack".
stop The end to a chamfer.
stud Common vertical timbers between the posts, closely or widely spaced (hence "close studding").
substantivism The view that non-Western societies do not operate under rules of "rational" economic logic; rather, that economic life is "embedded" in social and cultural life.

tenon Diminished end of a timber to fit in a mortice.
tenure Form of landholding, of various forms and degrees of security. Freehold and copyhold by inheritance were reasonably secure forms.
tie or tie-beam The horizontal timber of a truss at wall-plate level connecting the tops of the posts.
trammel *See* pothook.
transom An intermediate bar across a window.
truss A pair of posts and principals and the frame connecting, such that the timber frame is made up of a series of trusses.

underbuilt Having a later wall added beneath a jetty.

wall-plate A rail running along the top of the wall.
waney Of a timber: with its curved edge left on, usually due to poor scantling.
wealden A form of three-cell open-hall house with both parlour and service ends jettied to the front. The wall-plate over the jetties continues over the front of the unjettied hall thus forming an overhang.
window
dormer: window on the slope of the roof with a roof of its own;
eyebrow dormer: where the window roof is covered by a curve in the thatch.

yeomen A socially middling class of tenant farmers of reasonable security and wealth.

REFERENCES

Addleshaw, G. W. O. & F. Etchells 1948. *The architectural setting of Anglican worship*. London: Faber and Faber.

Addy, S. O. 1898. *The evolution of the English house*. London: Allen & Unwin.

Airs, M. 1975. *The making of the English country house, 1500–1640*. London: Architectural Press.

Alcock, N. W. & M. Laithwaite 1973. Medieval houses in Devon and their modernisation. *Medieval Archaeology* **17**, 100–125.

Amussen, S. D. 1988. *An ordered society: gender and class in early modern England*. Oxford: Blackwell.

Anderson, M. 1980. *Approaches to the history of the western family, 1500–1914*. London: Macmillan.

Aries, P. 1962. *Centuries of childhood*. London: Cape.

Astill, G. & A. Grant (eds) 1988. *The countryside of medieval England*. Cambridge: Cambridge University Press.

Aston, T. H. (ed.) 1987. *Landlords, peasants and politics in medieval England*. Cambridge: Cambridge University Press.

Aston, T. H. & C. H. E. Philpin 1985. *The Brenner debate: agrarian class structure and economic development in pre-industrial Europe*. Cambridge: Cambridge University Press.

Bailey, F. (ed.) 1971. *Gifts and poison*. Oxford: Blackwell.

Baker, A. R. H. & R. A. Butlin (eds) 1973. *Studies of field systems in the British Isles*. Cambridge: Cambridge University Press.

Barley, M. W. 1967. Rural housing in England. In Thirsk (ed.), 696–766.

Barley, M. W. 1979. The double-pile house. *Archaeological Journal* **136**, 153–64.

Barley, M. W. 1985. Rural building in England. In Thirsk (ed.), 590–682.

Beaudry, M. C. (ed.) 1988. *Documentary archaeology in the New World*. Cambridge: Cambridge University Press.

Binford, L. R. 1964. Archaeology as anthropology. *American Antiquity* **28**, 217–25.

Bourdieu, P. 1977. *Outline of a theory of practice*. Cambridge: Cambridge University Press.

Boyer, P. & S. Nissenbaum 1974. *Salem possessed: the social origins of witchcraft*. Cambridge: Harvard University Press.

Braudel, F. 1973. *Capitalism and material life 1400–1800*. London: Weidenfeld & Nicholson.

Brown, F. E. 1986. Continuity and change in the urban house: developments in domestic space organisation in 17th century London. *Comparative Studies in Society and History* **28**, 558–590.

Brunskill, R. W. 1978. Distributions of building materials and some plan types in the domestic architecture of England and Wales. *Transactions of the Ancient Monuments Society of England and Wales* **23** (new series), 41–66.

Brunskill, R. W. 1981. *Traditional buildings of Britain*. London: Gollancz.

Bucaille, R. & L. Levi-Strauss 1980. *L'architecture rurale Française: corpus des genres, des types et des varientes: Bourgogne*. Paris: Payot.

Carrick, M. 1985. Wall paintings in Feering and Kelvedon. *Historic Buildings in Essex* **2**, 5–8.

Carrithers, M. , S. Collins & S. Lukes (eds) 1985. *The category of the person: anthropology, philosophy, history*. Cambridge: Cambridge University Press.

Charles, L. & L. Duffin (eds) 1985. *Women and work in pre-industrial England*. London: Croom Helm.

Chomsky, N. 1957. *Syntactic structures*. Mouton: The Hague.

Chomsky, N. 1965. *Aspects of the theory of syntax*. Cambridge: MIT Press.

Clark, P. 1983. *The English alehouse: a social history, 1200–1830*. Harlow: Longman.

Clarke, H. 1984. *The archaeology of medieval England*. London: British Museum.

Colman, S. 1967. Two small medieval houses: Walnut Tree Cottage, Wattisfield, and Friars Hall, Rattlesden. *Proceedings of the Suffolk Institute of Archaeology and History* **31**, 64–71.

Colman, S. 1968. The West Suffolk inventories for 1665: some clues to house types. *Suffolk Review* **3**, 190–96.

Colman, S. 1973. The Hearth Tax Returns for the Hundred of Blackbourne, 1662. *Proceedings of the Suffolk Institute of Archaeology and History* **32**, 168–93.

Colman, S. 1974. A late aisled hall in Suffolk. *Vernacular Architecture* **4**, 14–18.

Colman, S. 1979. Post-medieval houses in Suffolk. *Proceedings of the Suffolk Institute of Archaeology and History* **34**, 181–90.

Cosgrove, D. & S. Daniels (eds) 1988. *The iconography of landscape: essays on the symbolic representation, design and use of past environments*. Cambridge: Cambridge University Press.

Coulson, C. 1979. Structural symbolism in medieval castle architecture. *Journal of the British Archaeological Association* **88**, 73–90.

Coulson, C. 1982. Hierarchism in conventual crenellation: an essay in the sociology and metaphysics of medieval fortification. *Medieval Archaeology* **26**, 69–100.

Cullum, J. 1813. *The history and antiquities of Hawstead and Hardwick, in the county of Suffolk*, 2nd edn. London: Nichols & Bentley.

Cummings, A. L. 1979. *The framed houses of Massachusetts Bay, 1625–1675*. London: Harvard University Press.

Cunningham, C. E. 1964. Order in the Atoni house. *Bijdragen Tot de Taal-, Land-en Volkenkunde* **120**, 34–68.

Currie, C. 1988. Time and chance: modelling the attrition of old houses. *Vernacular Architecture* **19**, 1–9.

Dalton, H. (ed.) 1971. *Primitive, archaic and modern economies: essays of Karl Polanyi.*

New York: Natural History Press.

Dahlman, C. J. 1980. *Common fields and enclosure in England 1450–1850*. London, Macmillan.

Darby, H. C. (ed.) 1973. *A new historical geography of England*. Cambridge: Cambridge University Press.

Deetz, J. 1967. *Invitation to archaeology*. New York: The Natural History Press.

Deetz, J. 1977. *In small things forgotten*. New York: Anchor Press.

Dickens, P. 1980. Social science and design theory. *Environment and Planning B* **7**, 353–60.

Dobrolowski, K. 1971. Peasant traditional culture. In *Peasants and peasant societies*, T. Shanin (ed.), 277–98. Harmondsworth, England: Penguin.

Drury, P. J. 1984. An unusual late-medieval timber-framed building at Harwich, Essex. *Vernacular Architecture* **15**, 34–8.

Dyer, C. C. 1986. English peasant houses in the later middle ages. *Medieval Archaeology* **30**, 19–45.

Dymond, D. P. & A. Betterton 1982. *Lavenham: 700 years of textile making*. Wood bridge: Boydell.

Dymond, D. P. & E. Martin (eds) 1988. *An historical atlas of Suffolk*. Ipswich: Suffolk County Council.

Dymond, D. P. & P. Northeast 1985. *A history of Suffolk*. Chichester: Pillimore.

Dymond, D. P. & R. Virgoe 1986. The reduced population and wealth of early 15th century Suffolk. *Proceedings of the Suffolk Institute of Archaeology and History* **35**, 73–100.

Easton, T. 1986. The internal decorative treatment of brick in 16th and 17th century Suffolk. *Post-Medieval Archaeology* **20**, 1–19.

Eden, P. 1968. Smaller post-medieval houses in eastern England. See Munby (1968), 71–93.

Evans, N. (ed.) 1987. *Wills of the Archdeaconry of Sudbury 1630–1635*. Suffolk Records Society 29.

Everitt, A. (ed.) 1960. *Suffolk and the Great Rebeliion, 1640–1660*. Suffolk Records Society 3.

Evans, N. 1984. Farming and land-holding in wood-pasture East Anglia 1550–1650. *Proceedings of the Suffolk Institute of Archaeology and History* **35**, 303–315.

Ewart Evans, G. 1966. *The pattern under the plough: aspects of the folk-life of East Anglia*. London: Faber and Faber.

Fildes, V. (ed.) 1990. *Women as mothers in pre-industrial England*. London: Routledge.

Filmer-Sankey, W. 1986. The excavations on the site of Ickworth Manor. *Proceed ings of the Suffolk Institute of Archaeology and History* **36**, 65–72.

Fitch, J. 1986. *Brent Eleigh church: A history and guide*. Brent Eleigh: no publisher stated.

Flannery, K. (ed.) 1976. *The early Mesoamerican village*. London: Academic Press.

Fletcher, A. & J. Stephenson (eds) 1985. *Order and disorder in Early Modern England*. Cambridge: Cambridge University Press.

Fox, Sir Cyril & Lord Raglan 1951. *Monmouthshire houses: a study of building techniques and smaller house-plans in the 15th to 17th Centuries*. Cardiff: National Museum of Wales.

Foucault, M. 1979. *Discipline and punish: the birth of the prison*. Harmondsworth, England: Penguin.

Fraser, A. 1984. *The weaker vessel*. London: Weidenfeld & Nicholson.

Gage, J. 1838. *The history and antiquities of Suffolk: Thingoe hundred*. London: Samuel Bentley.

Garrard, R. 1982. English probate inventories and their use in studying the significance of the domestic interior, 1570–1700. *Afdeling Agrarische Bijdragen* **28**, 55–77.

Giddens, A. 1978. *Central problems in social theory: action, structure and contradiction in social analysis*. London: Macmillan.

Giddens, A. 1985. Time, space and regionalisation. In *Social relations and spatial structures*, D. Gregory & J. Urry (eds), 265–295. London: Methuen.

Giles, C. 1985. *Rural houses of West Yorkshire, 1400–1830*. London: Her Majesty's Stationery Office.

Girouard, M. 1978. *Life in the English country house: a social and architectural history*. London: Yale University Press.

Girouard, M. 1983. *Robert Smythson and the Elizabethan country house*. London: Yale University Press.

Glassie, H. 1975. *Folk housing in middle Virginia: a structural analysis of historic artifacts*. Knoxville: University of Tennessee Press.

Glassie, H. 1982. *Passing the time: folklore and history of an Ulster community*. Dublin: O'Brien.

Goodridge, J. F. (ed.) 1959. *Piers the ploughman*. Harmondsworth, England: Penguin.

Graves, C. P. 1989. Social space in the English parish church. *Economy and Society* **18**(3), 297–322.

Greaves, R. L. 1981. *Society and religion in Elizabethan England*. Minneapolis: University of Minnesota Press.

Hamilton, A. H. A. 1878. *Quarter sessions from Elizabeth to Anne*. London: Low.

Harley, J. B. 1988. Maps, knowledge and power. In *The iconography of landscape: essays on the symbolic representation, design and use of past environments*, D. Cosgrove & B. Daniels (eds), 277–312. Cambridge: Cambridge University Press.

Harris, R. 1978. *Discovering timber-framed buildings*. Aylesbury: Shire.

Harris, R. 1989. The grammar of carpentry. *Vernacular Architecture* 20, 1–8.

Harrison, B. & B. Hutton 1984. *Vernacular houses in North Yorkshire and Cleveland*. Edinburgh: Donald.

Harvey, N. 1984. *A history of farm buildings in England and Wales*, 2nd edn. London: David & Charles.

Hartley, D. (ed.) 1931. *Thomas Tusser: his good points of husbandry*. London: Country Life.

Helgerson, R. 1986. The land speaks: cartography, chorography and subversion in Renaissance England. *Representations* **16**, 50–85.

Hervey, F. (ed.) 1902. *Suffolk in the 17th century: the breviary of Suffolk by Robert Reyce, 1618*. London: Murray.

Hervey, S. H. A. 1905. *Suffolk in 1674*. Suffolk Green Books 11.

Hervey, S. H. A. 1909. *Suffolk in 1568: being the return of a subsidy granted in 1566*. Suffolk Green Books 12.

Hervey, S. H. A. 1910. *Suffolk in 1564: being the return of a subsidy granted in 1523*. Suffolk Green Books 10.

Hewison, R. 1987. *The heritage industry: Britain in a climate of decline*. London: Methuen.

Hewitt, C. A. 1969. *The development of carpentry, 1200–1700: an Essex study*. London: David & Charles.

Hewitt, C. A. 1973. The development of the post-medieval house. *Post-Medieval Archaeology* **7**, 60–78.

Hewitt, C. A. 1974. The smaller medieval house in Essex. *Archaeological Journal* **7**, 60–78.

Hewitt: C. 1980. *English historic carpentry*. London: Philimore.

Hill, C. 1966. *Society and Puritanism in pre-revolutionary England*. London: Heineman.

Hillier, W. & J. Hanson 1984. *The social logic of space*. Cambridge: Cambridge University Press.

Hilton, R. H. 1975. *The English peasantry in the later Middle Ages*. Oxford: Clarendon Press.

Hilton, R. H. 1985. *Class conflict and the crisis of feudalism: essays in medieval social history*. London: Hambledon.

Hinton, D. (ed.) 1983. *25 years of medieval archaeology*. Department of Archaeology & Prehistory, University of Sheffield.

Hodder, I. (ed.) 1987. *Archaeology as long-term history*. Cambridge: Cambridge University Press.

Hodder, I. 1991. *Reading the past*, 2nd edn. Cambridge: Cambridge University Press.

Hodges, R. 1982. *Dark age economics*. London: Duckworth.

Hodges, R. 1988. *Primitive and peasant markets*. Oxford: Blackwells.

Holmes, C. (ed.) 1970. *The Suffolk committees for scandalous ministers, 1644–46*. Suffolk Records Society 13.

Hoskins, W. G. 1953. The rebuilding of rural England, 1570–1640. *Past and Present* **4**, 44–59.

Hoskins, W. G. 1964. Harvest fluctuations and English economic history, 1480–1619. *Agricultural History Review* **12**, 28–46.

Hoskins, W. G. 1968. Harvest fluctuations and English economic history, 1620–1759. *Agricultural History Review* **16**, 15–31.

Howard, M. 1985. *The early Tudor country house: architecture and politics 1490–1550*. London: George Philip.

Howell, M. C. 1986. *Women, production and patriarchy in late medieval cities*. London: University of Chicago Press.

Hubka, K. 1986. Just folks designing: vernacular designers and the generation of form. In *Common places: readings in American vernacular architecture*, Upton & Vlach (eds), 426–32. London: University of Georgia Press.

Humphrey, C. 1974. Inside a Mongolian tent. *New Society* **31**, 45–8.

Hunt, L. (ed.) 1989. *The new cultural history*. London: University of California Press.

Ingold, T. 1990. Society, nature and the concept of technology. *Archaeological Review from Cambridge* **9**(1), 5–17.

Innocent, C. 1916. *The development of English building construction*. Cambridge: Cambridge University Press.

Isaac, R. 1983. *The Transformation of Virginia; 1760–1820*. Chapel Hill: University of North Carolina Press.

James, M. 1986. *Society, politics and culture: studies in early modern England*. Cambridge: Cambridge University Press.

Jennings, S. 1981. *Eighteen centuries of pottery from Norwich*. East Anglian Archaeology 3.

Johnson, I. 1981. Hill Farm, Laxfield: a late 17th century house. *Proceedings of the Suffolk Institute of Archaeology and History* **35**, 53–9.

Johnson, M. H. 1989. Conceptions of agency in archaeological interpretation. *Journal of Anthropological Archaeology* **8**, 189–211.

Johnson, M. H. 1992. Meanings of polite architecture in 16th century England. In *The meanings of consumption: ongoing research in historical archaeology*, B. Little & P. Shackel (eds), 46–56. Washington, Society for Historical Archaeology.

Johnson, M. H. nd. *A contextual study of traditional houses in western Suffolk*, AD *1400–1700*. Doctoral dissertation, University of Cambridge.

Jope, E. M. 1973. The transmission of new ideas: archaeological evidence for implant and dispersal. *World Archaeology* **4**, 368–73.

Kent, S. (ed.) 1989. *Domestic architecture and the use of space*. Cambridge: Cambridge University Press.

Kerridge, E. 1969. *Agrarian problems in the 16th century and after*. London: Allen & Unwin.

Kussmaul, A. 1981. *Servants in husbandry in early modern England*. Cambridge: Cambridge University Press.

Laslett, P. 1965. *The world we have lost*. London: Methuen.

Lake, P. G. 1987. Calvinism and the English Church 1570–1635. *Past and Present* **114**, 32–76.

Lawrence, R. J. 1983. Interpretation in vernacular architecture. *Vernacular Architecture* **14**, 19–28.

Le Roy Ladurie, E. 1985. Reply to Brenner. See Aston & Philpin (1985), 101–6.

Lemonnier, P. 1986. The study of material culture today: towards an anthropology of technical systems. *Journal of Anthropological Archaeology* **5**(2), 147–86.

Leone, M. 1984. Interpreting ideology in historical archaeology: the William Paca Garden in Annapolis, Maryland. In *Ideology, power and prehistory*, D. Miller & C. Tilley (eds), 25–36. Cambridge: Cambridge University Press.

Leone, M. & P. Potter 1988. *The recovery of meaning in historical archaeology*. Washington: Smithsonian Institution.

Levi-Strauss, C. 1970. *The raw and the cooked*. London: Cape.

Lloyd, C. 1986. *Explanation in social history*. London, Routledge.

McCann, J. 1984. No. Two Church Path, Wendens Ambo, Essex. *Historic Buildings in Essex* **1**, 11–16.

McCann, J. 1985. The introduction of the lambs' tongue stop. *Historic Buildings in Essex* 2, 2–4.

McCracken, G. 1983. The exchange of children in Tudor England: an anthropological phenomenon in historical context. *Journal of Family History* **8**, 303–313.

McIntosh, M. K. 1984. Servants and the household unit in an Elizabethan English community. *Journal of Family History* **9**(1), 3–23.

Macculloch, D. (ed.) 1976. *A Chorography of Suffolk*. Ipswich: Suffolk Records Society.

Macculloch, D. 1986 *Suffolk and the Tudors: politics and religion in an English county, 1500–1600*. Oxford: Oxford University Press.

Macfarlane, A. 1978. *The origins of English individualism*. Oxford: Blackwell.

McClellan, D. (ed.) 1977. *Karl Marx: selected writings*. Oxford: Oxford University Press.

McGuire, R. H. & M. B. Schiffer 1983. A theory of architectural design. *Journal of Anthropological Archaeology* **2**, 277–303.

Machin, R. 1977. The Great Rebuilding: a reassessment. *Past and Present* **77**, 33–56.

Machin, R. 1978. *The houses of Yetminster*. University of Bristol, Department of Extra-Mural Studies.

Marx, K. 1977a. The 18th Brumaire of Louis Bonaparte. In *Karl Marx: selected writings*, D. McClellan (ed.), 300–325. Oxford: Oxford University Press.

Mate, M. 1987. Pastoral farming in south-east England in the 15th century. *Economic History Review* **11**(4) (2nd series), 523–36.

Mercer, E. 1975. *English vernacular houses: a study of traditional farmhouses and cottages*. London: Her Majesty's Stationery Office.

Merrifield, R. & N. Smedley 1961. Two witch-bottles from Suffolk. *Proceedings of the Suffolk Institute of Archaeology and History* **28**(1), 97–100.

Mertes, K. 1988. *The English noble household 1250–1600: good governance and politic rule*. Oxford: Blackwell.

Miller, D. 1984. Modernism and suburbia. In *Ideology, power and prehistory*, D. Miller & C. Tilley (eds), 37–49. Cambridge: Cambridge University Press.

Miller, D. 1987. *Material culture and mass consumption*. Oxford: Blackwell.

Moore, H. L. 1985. *Space, text and gender*. Cambridge: Cambridge University Press.

Morgan, E. S. 1944. *The Puritan family: religion and domestic relations in 17th century New England*. New York: Harper & Row.
Munby, L. M. (ed.) 1968. *East Anglian studies*. Cambridge: Heffers.

Neiman, F. D. 1986. Domestic architecture at the Clifts Plantation: the social context of early Virginia building. See Upton & Vlach (1986), 292–314.

Padfield, A. 1985a. Summers Farm, Doddinghurst. *Historic Buildings in Essex* **2**, 9–11.
Padfield, A. 1985b. Lucas Farm, White Roding. *Historic Buildings in Essex* **2**, 12–14.
Page, W. (ed.) 1907. *The Victoria history of the county of Suffolk*. London: Constable.
Panofsky, E. 1957. *Gothic architecture and scholasticism*. London: Thames & Hudson.
Pearson, S. 1985. *Rural houses of the Lancashire Pennines*. London: Her Majesty's Stationery Office.
Pevsner, N. 1956. *The Englishness of English art*. London: The Architectural Press.
Pfaffenberger, B. 1988. Fetishised objects and humanised nature: towards an anthropology of technology. *Man* **23**(2), 236–52.
Platt, C. 1978. *Medieval England: an archaeology and social history from the Conquest to 1600*. London: Routledge & Kegan Paul.
Platt, C. 1981. *The parish churches of medieval England*. London: Secker & Warburg.
Pollock, A. 1983. *Forgotten children: parent–child relations from 1500 to 1900*. Cambridge: Cambridge University Press.
Postgate, M. R. 1973. Field systems of East Anglia. See Baker & Butlin (1973), 281–322.
Pound, J. (ed.) 1986. *The Military Survey of 1522 for Babergh Hundred*. Suffolk Records Society 28.
Pred, A. 1985. The social becomes the spatial, the spatial becomes the social: enclosures, social change and the becoming of places in Skane. See Gregory & Urry (1985), 337–65.
Preziosi, D. 1979. *The semiotics of the built environment*. Bloomington: Indiana University Press.
Prior, M. (ed.) 1985. *Women in English society 1500–1800*. London: Methuen.

Quimby, I. M. G. (ed.) 1984. *The craftsman in early America*. London: Winterthur Publications.

Rackham, O. 1986. *The history of the countryside*. London: Dent.
Raglan, Lord 1957. The house: shelter or temple? *Archaeologia Cambrensis* **106**, 72–89.
Rahtz, P. 1983. The new medieval archaeology. See Hinton (1983).
Rapoport, A. 1982. *The meaning of the built environment*. London: Sage.
Rapoport, A. 1990. Systems of activities and systems of settings. See Kent (1989), 9–18.
Razi, Z. 1987. Family, land and the village community in later medieval England. See Aston (1987), 377–93.
Redstone, V. B. (ed.) 1904. *The Ship-Money Returns for the County of Suffolk, 1639–40*. Ipswich: Harrison.

Roberts, M. 1985. "Words they are women, and deeds they are men": images of work and gender in early modern England. See Charles & Duffin (1985), 122–80. London: Croom Helm.

Ruskin, J. 1880. *The seven lamps of architecture*.

Ryan, P. R. 1986. 15th-century continental brickmasons. *Medieval Archaeology* **30**, 112–113.

St George, R. B. 1986. "Set thine house in order": the domestication of the yeomanry in 17th-century New England. In *Common places: readings in American vernacular architecture*, Upton and Vlach (1986), 336–65. Athens, Ga.: University of Georgia Press.

St George, R. B. (ed.) 1988. *Material life in America 1600–1800*. Boston: Northeastern University Press.

St George, R. B. nd. Maintenance relations and the erotics of property in historical thought. Unpublished manuscript in possession of author.

Salzman, L. F. 1952. *Building in England down to 1540: a documentary history*. Oxford: Oxford University Press.

Saussure, F. de 1983. *Course in general linguistics* [first published 1916]. London: Duckworth.

Scott, D. H. 1984a. The Courthouse, Widdington, Essex. *Historic Buildings in Essex* **1**, 6–10.

Scott, D. H. 1984b. No. 65 High Street, Brentwood, Essex. *Historic Buildings in Essex* **1**, 20–24.

Searle, C. E. 1986. Custom, class conflict and agrarian capitalism: the Cumbrian monetary economy in the 18th century. *Past and Present* **110**, 106–133.

Shanks, M. & C. Tilley 1987. *Social theory and archaeology*. Cambridge: Polity Press.

Smith, J. T. 1970. The evolution of the English peasant house to the late 17th century: the evidence of buildings. *Journal of the British Archaeological Association* **33** (3rd series), 122–47.

Smith, J. T. 1985. Short-lived and mobile houses in late 17th century England. *Vernacular Architecture* **16**, 33–34.

Smith, J. T. 1992. *English houses 1200–1800: the Hertfordshire evidence*. London: Her Majesty's Stationery Office.

Smith, P. 1985. Rural building in Wales. See Thirsk (1985), 686–813.

Smith, P. 1988. *Houses of the Welsh countryside*.

Smith, T. P. 1985. *The medieval brickmaking industry in England 1400–1450*. BAR British Series 138. Oxford: British Archaeological Reports.

Steer, F. (ed.) 1964. *Inventories of mid Essex, 1635–1749*. Chichester, Phillimore.

Stiny, G. 1976. Two exercises in formal composition. *Environment and Planning B* **3**, 187–210.

Stiny, G. 1978. The Palladian grammar. *Environment and Planning B* 5, 5–18.

Stone, G. W. 1988. Artefacts are not enough. In *Documentary archaeology in the New World*, M. C. Beaudry (ed.), 68–77. Cambridge: Cambridge University Press.

Stone, L. 1965. *The crisis of the aristocracy, 1558–1641*. Oxford: Clarendon Press.

Stone, L. 1977. *The family, sex and marriage in England, 1500–1800*. London: Weidenfeld & Nicholson.

Stone, L. & J. C. Stone 1984. *An open elite? England 1540–1880*. Oxford: Oxford University Press.

Tawney, R. H. 1912. *The agrarian problem in the 16th century*. London: Longmans.

Tawney, R. H. 1926. *Religion and the rise of capitalism*. London: Nicholls.

Tawney, R. H. & E. Power 1924. *Tudor economic documents: being select documents illustrating the social and economic history of Tudor England*. London: Longman.

Thirsk, J. (ed.) 1967. *The agrarian history of England and Wales, volume four: 1500–1640*. Cambridge: Cambridge University Press.

Thirsk, J. (ed.) 1985. *The agrarian history of England and Wales, volume five: 1640–1750. Two: agrarian change*. Cambridge: Cambridge University Press.

Thomas, K. 1971. *Religion and the decline of magic: popular beliefs in 16th and 17th century England*. London: Weidenfeld & Nicholson.

Thomas, K. 1983. *Man and the natural world: changing attitudes in England 1500–1800*. London: Allen Lane.

Thompson, E. P. 1963. *The making of the English working class*. London: Gollancz.

Thompson, R. 1984. Adolescent culture in colonial Massachusetts. *Journal of Family History* 9(2), 127–44.

Thompson, M. W. 1988. *The decline of the castle*. Cambridge: Cambridge University Press.

Tilley, C. 1991. *Material culture and text: the art of ambiguity*. London: Routledge.

Tillyard, E. M. W. 1972. *The Elizabethan world picture*. Harmondsworth, England: Penguin.

Underdown, D. 1985a. The taming of the scold. In *Order and disorder in early modern England*, A. Fletcher & J. Stephenson (eds). Cambridge: Cambridge University Press.

Underdown, D. 1985b. *Revel, riot and rebellion: popular politics and culture in England, 1603–1660*. Oxford: Oxford University Press.

Unwin, G. 1907. Industries. In *The Victoria history of the county of Suffolk*, W. Page, (ed.), 247–88. London: Constable.

Upton, D. 1982. Vernacular domestic architecture in 18th century Virginia. *Winterthur Portfolio* 17, 95–119.

Upton, D. & J. M. Vlach (eds) 1986. *Common places: readings in American vernacular architecture*. Athens, Ga.: University of Georgia Press.

Walzer, M. 1966. *The revolution of the saints*. London: Lowe & Brydone.

Warner, P. 1987. *Greens, commons and clayland colonisation: the origins and development of green-side settlement in East Suffolk*. Leicester: Leicester University Press.

Washburn, D. 1983. Towards a theory of structural style in art. In *Structure and cognition in art*, D. Washburn (ed.). Cambridge: Cambridge University Press.

Weber, M. 1930. *The Protestant ethic and the spirit of capitalism*. Translated by Talcott Parsons. New York: Scribner.

Williamson, T. M. 1987. Early co-axial field systems on the East Anglian boulder clays. *Proceedings of the Prehistoric Society* **53**, 419–31.

Williamson, T. M. & L. Bellamy 1986. *Property and landscape: a social history of the English countryside*. London: George Philip.

Wilson, A. 1990. The ceremony of childbirth and its interpretation. In *Women as mothers in pre-industrial England*, V. Fildes (ed.), 68–107. London: Routledge.

Wilson, D. M. 1959. Almgren and chronology: a summary and some comments. *Medieval Archaeology* **3**, 112–9.

Wolf, E. R. 1966. *Peasants*. New Jersey: Prentice-Hall.

Woodward, D. 1985. "Swords into ploughshares": recycling in pre-industrial England. *Economic History Review* **38**, 175–90.

Wordie, J. R. 1983. The chronology of English enclosure, 1500–1914. *Economic History Review* **36**, 483–505.

Wrightson, K. 1982. *English society 1580–1680*. London: Hutchinson.

Yates, E. M. 1982. Vernacular buildings in early maps of the Weald. *Transactions of the Ancient Monuments Society* **26**(ns), 210–26.

Yelling, J. A. 1977. *Common fields and enclosure in England 1450–1850*. London: Macmillan.

Yelling, J. A. 1982. Rationality in the common fields. *Economic History Review* **35**, 409–15.

Yentsch, A. 1988. Archaeology is not enough. See Beaudry (1988), 5–17.

INDEX

Numbers in *italics* refer to illustrations; numbers in **bold** refer to tables.